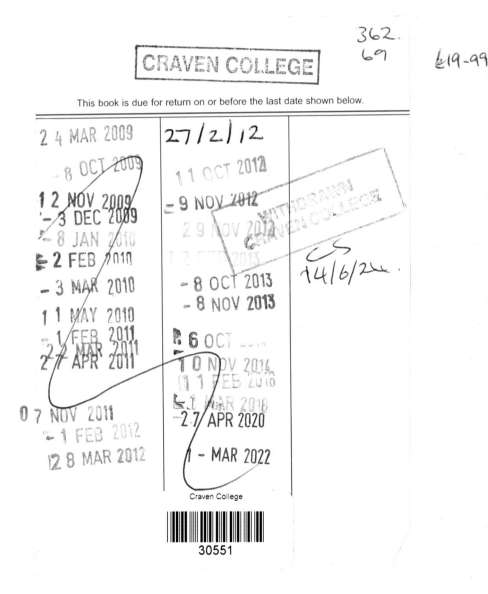

also in the series

Children Taken Seriously
In Theory, Policy and Practice
Edited by Jan Mason and Toby Fattore
Foreword by Mary John
ISBN 978 1 84310 250 2

Children's Rights and Power
Charging Up for a New Century
Mary John
ISBN 978 1 85302 659 1 (Paperback)
ISBN 978 1 85302 658 4 (Hardback)

Children's Rights in Education
*Edited by Stuart Hart, Cynthia Price Cohen, Martha Farrell Erickson
and Målfrid Grude Flekkøy*
ISBN 978 1 85302 977 6

Traveller Children: A Voice for Themselves
Cathy Kiddle
ISBN 978 1 85302 684 3

Educational Citizenship and Independent Learning
Rhys Griffith
ISBN 978 1 85302 611 9

Children as Citizens: Education for Participation
Edited by Cathie Holden and Nick Clough
ISBN 978 1 85302 566 2

**The Participation Rights of the Child: Rights
and Responsibilities in Family and Society**
Målfrid Grude Flekkøy and Natalie Hevener Kaufman
ISBN 978 1 85302 490 0

A Charge Against Society: The Child's Right to Protection
Edited by Mary John
ISBN 978 1 85302 411 5

Children in Our Charge: The Child's Right to Resources
Edited by Mary John
ISBN 978 1 85302 369 9

Children in Charge: The Child's Right to a Fair Hearing
Edited by Mary John
ISBN 978 1 85302 368 2

CHILDREN IN CHARGE 13

Young Children's Rights

Exploring Beliefs, Principles and Practice
Second Edition

Priscilla Alderson

Foreword by Mary John

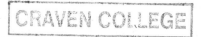

Jessica Kingsley Publishers
London and Philadelphia

The author and publishers are grateful to the proprietors below for their permission to use the following material: Figure 8.1 by Dorothy Judd, from *Give Sorrow words: Working with a Dying Child, Second Edition* (1995) by Dorothy Judd. Copyright © John Wiley and Sons Limited. Reproduced with permission.

First edition published in 2000

This edition published in 2008
by Jessica Kingsley Publishers
116 Pentonville Road
London N1 9JB, UK
and
400 Market Street, Suite 400
Philadelphia, PA 19106, USA

www.jkp.com

Library of Congress Cataloging in Publication Data

Alderson, Priscilla.
Young children's rights : exploring beliefs, principles and practice / Priscilla Alderson. -- 2nd ed.
p. cm. -- (Children in charge series ; 13)
Includes bibliographical references.
ISBN 978-1-84310-599-2 (pb : alk. paper) 1. Children's rights. 2. Children and adults. 3. Interpersonal communication. I. Title.
HQ789.A618 2008
305.230941--dc22

2007038887

British Library Cataloguing in Publication Data

A CIP catalogue record for this book is available from the British Library

ISBN 978 1 84310 599 2

Printed and bound in Great Britain by
Athenaeum Press, Gateshead, Tyne and Wear

To my mother, Dr Dorothy Clift, who since the 1940s
has set her six children an example of respect
for young children.

Acknowledgements

I am very grateful to: Save the Children, and especially Nicky Road, Sue Emerson and colleagues for planning the first edition of this book and commissioning me to write it; Mary John for inviting me to write this book for the 'Children in Charge' series; and all the children and adults whose views and experiences have contributed to this book. I would like to express my gratitude to: my colleagues, especially Berry Mayall, Ginny Morrow, Liz Brooker and Helen Penn; our informative students from around the world at the Institute of Education, University of London, who are working on children's rights, childhood and early childhood; other colleagues who have generously provided too many examples of active young children for me to be able to include all of them in this book; Rob Gayton at Save the Children; and Stephen Jones, Karin Knudsen and Maggie Pettifer at Jessica Kingsley Publishers. I thank Dorothy Judd for giving permission for the child's drawing to be reproduced in Chapter 8, and Professor Michael Freeman for permission to summarise his article 'Why it remains important to take children's rights seriously' (2007) on pages 132–4.

I am responsible for any shortcomings in the text and for the views expressed herein. All royalties from the book will go to Save the Children.

Contents

Foreword

This is a welcome second edition of a book that attracted much attention when it first appeared in the *Children in Charge* series in 2000. Much has happened in the intervening seven years, almost too much to grasp. Children remain a concern of political parties bent on tackling a 'broken' society seen by some, and hyped by the media, as out of control. Childhood appears to have become a lucrative field for the journalist, the neo-libertarian pundit, a focus for commercial exploitation and various other vested interests. A free-for-all was not what was meant by children's rights and participation but to the extent we believe what we read in the papers it has raised questions about when did it all start to go wrong? Rights have had a bad press. It is refreshing in the midst of this to hear once more the calm sane voice of a distinguished practitioner and researcher in the field, Priscilla Alderson.

The *Children in Charge* series in its accumulating volumes has brought together accounts of activities taking place throughout the world in the realisation of the aims of the United Nations Convention on the Rights of the Child, and the publisher had appreciated early how significant work in this area would be. The series was named 'Children in Charge' quite deliberately to emphasise the stance adopted throughout. So far it has looked in detail at elements of the processes by which children claim and exercise their rights and are facilitated in doing so in a variety of contexts. This was explored in an interdisciplinary, multicultural way by the papers in the first three volumes about this relatively new field which sprang from the World Conference held at Exeter University in 1992. This was the first international conference in which young people were crucially involved.

In the initial volumes the implications of the United Nations Convention in practical, theoretical and research terms were teased out, aided by the arguments, participation and inside knowledge of our Young People's

Evaluation Panel. Those volumes (*Children in Charge, Children in Our Charge, A Charge Against Society*) crystallised around the 'three Ps' by which the various articles of the Convention have been traditionally grouped: Provision, Protection and Participation. It has been thought that it is the realisation of the last of these three that has been the most challenging aspect, being addressed warily by many practitioners, researchers and policy-makers alike.

November 1999 marked the tenth anniversary of the signing of the Convention, so tracking the achievements in the first decade was particularly important in raising awareness of the full implications of this legally binding instrument. The appearance in 2000 of *Young Children's Rights: Exploring Beliefs, Principles and Practice*, which Priscilla Alderson was commissioned to write by Save the Children as Volume 10 in the series, was particularly important in describing and evaluating that first decade of progress. There she sought to redress the imbalance in the literature on children's rights which, at that stage, had been sorely limited when the critical gaze fell on very young children. This 'blind spot' in itself was interesting as children were often said, or thought to be, 'not yet' adults and as a consequence marginalised and ignored. Moreover, it seemed that infants and young children were not yet even regarded 'children' and therefore in disciplines and practices that should have been concerned to protect and promote their important place as people and citizens they had again been overlooked. Until this first edition appeared, little material had been provided on the participation of infants and young children and how this might be facilitated and encouraged. We are indeed privileged to have Priscilla Alderson in this important new edition taking up the story from there.

Here she examines the ways in which the personhood of babies and young children has been more generally accepted, and the political strength and impetus for recognition of rights within this age range more appropriately understood. From babyhood children are significant actors and potentially powerful partners in shaping the relationships and societies in which they live. Priscilla Alderson suggests that developments have been so numerous and profound that at times they can only be alluded to briefly and sources of further reading suggested. The issues she raises here are so intriguing I am sure that many readers will follow these suggestions with interest. It is a dynamic growing field so this will serve as a sourcebook. She concentrates in this present edition on broad issues whilst at the same time illustrating her points in the practical arena with examples from work with babies and young children up to eight years of age. What has happened in the intervening years since the first edition she diagnoses as: the increasing political confidence about rights that many adults and children now assume; the quality of communication between adults and babies and young children as an essential focus (which fits the orientation of this series on 'voicing' particularly well); the argument that all rights are limited and that when we talk of children's rights we are not promoting selfish individualism but rather a sophisticated intermeshing of needs, values and rights in the relationship between the child and the social world. She writes about this convincingly and has the rare gift of being able to communicate rigorous research to those who stand to gain most from it.

Priscilla Alderson has researched and published tirelessly in children's rights. It came as fitting recognition that at the London Institute of Education, as part of their Centenary Celebrations, she presented her Inaugural Lecture as Professor of Childhood Studies on 'Institutional rights and rites: a century of childhood'. In this she outlined the ways newer research methods of working with young children have been rediscovering how highly competent, organised and motivated they can be. She challenged traditional views in education of stage development theories on which schools have frequently been based. The challenge of educational institutions in this new millennium she stressed would be to base their work on up-to-date research methods and theories. Included in this would have to be a rethinking of child–adult and learning-and-teaching relationships, and working with children and adults to transform schools and society through promoting everyone's right to respect for their worth and dignity.

The part Priscilla Alderson has played in this transformation over the last few years has been pivotal and substantial. Her research is held in wide regard and is a fine example in the social sciences of three criteria of ethical science as summarised at the British Association's 2007 Festival of Science in that is 'rigorous, respectful and responsible'. This second edition of her book makes a further addition to the literature in the area which is no longer sparse but nevertheless requires skilful positioning and evaluation to understand progress fully. This is a thoughtful critique of the developments by someone well networked in the field.

I began this Foreword mentioning the maelstrom of political and media panics about children and children's rights, rather gloomily expecting that children will be targets of similar attention for the many years this edition will be in print. After reading research which is rigorous, responsible and respectful, such as we have here in this new book, there comes the question what difference will this research make? The 'So what?' question. It is my hope that the beliefs, principles and practices that Priscilla Alderson has taken us through here will raise consciousness of the issues to such an extent that she will have added to the vocabulary of our understanding of the nature of rights. We are indeed proud to have this new book as part of the Children in Charge series and in looking at the extent to which this will influence future policies and provision it would be wise to realise that this is a slow process. The late Barbara Tizard (1990) warned about the importance of identifying the gateways, the gatekeepers and the key by which research findings reach policy-makers and practitioners. A second feature which affects the range of influence of research is the assumptions in the questions asked and the method adopted. Priscilla Alderson's work has led the way in acknowledging infants and young children's rights and sweeping away some of the cobwebs of misapprehension. The belief that the scholar is the servant of power serving as a simple reflection of the needs and desires of her society is confounded here. Priscilla Alderson's challenging critique will have an influence if only by making the policy-maker and practitioner stop, look and listen, and think again.

Mary John
Series Editor

Introduction

Children's rights

> The idea of children's rights, then, may be a beacon guiding the way to the future – but it is also illuminating how many adults neglect their responsibilities towards children and how children are too often the victims of the ugliest and most shameful human activities.
>
> *(Kofi Annan, UN Secretary-General, September 2001)*

This book is mainly about young children's rights in Britain, specifically England. Most of these children may seem quite safe and fortunate when compared to millions of children in Asia, Africa and South America, in war zones or areas of extreme droughts or floods or great poverty. Respect for children's rights can seem more urgent for those children in greatest need. Yet one aim of this book is to show how respect for young children's rights can increase the wellbeing of children, and adults, everywhere. As the main subject is young children in the UK, no claims are made that the subject is young children everywhere (a series of books is needed for that), although some examples come from other countries, when they help us to understand more clearly the state of children in the UK, and of children's rights generally. British children themselves have too many mixed origins and backgrounds, and unknown potentials, to allow many generalisations about them. Yet although the UN Convention on the Rights of the Child (UN 1989) (referred to as the UNCRC) is often respected in local ways, it is based on broad principles which affect all children.

When Save the Children commissioned the first edition of this book, we began by asking: Which rights apply to young children aged up to eight years (we chose that as the usual age group for early years policies and services) and which rights cannot be relevant to them? It soon became clear that all the UNCRC articles are relevant, some particularly so to the youngest children – the rights to a name, an identity, a family, to be registered. Potentially, therefore, this could be an enormous book – see Cynthia Price Cohen's (2005) work of over 4000 pages, and Michael Freeman's (2004) extensive two volumes on *Children's Rights*.

However, our aim in this book was to produce a fairly short, introductory, readable text, mainly for people working with young children and/or studying on courses about them. We hope to help readers to relate the UNCRC to their everyday concerns and to apply ideas suggested in these pages both directly and indirectly as they think of new ways to explore how to relate the UNCRC to the young children they work with and care for. Inevitably, therefore, far more relevant material is omitted from this book than is included. Complex debates are skimmed over. A few brief examples stand in for countless others that could be reviewed. And readers are referred to practical texts on listening to children (for example, Clark and Moss 2005; Lancaster 2004). We hope that readers will often fill in gaps by reflecting on examples from their own experiences and reading.

At the Institute of Education, we suggest to our students that they keep a commonplace book – a private record of their thoughts and memories, notes of readings, press cuttings, reviews, poems, pictures, things that help them to connect their thinking and feeling on theories and practices, personal and political aspects of children's rights – in order to deepen their insights. Readers may like to make a similar record while they read this book.

Another aim in this book was to include examples of children, so to begin with here are Albert, Kevin and Margaret to show how children's rights and responsibilities, and their place in European society, have changed over the past century.

Albert Parr remembered, as an old man, that when he was aged four, in the 1900s in Stavanger, Norway, he enjoyed walking to the station alone for five or ten minutes, buying a ticket, watching the trains and riding over the long bridge to the harbour. He watched the boats, sometimes went into the fisheries museum, passed the park where the band played, or the shops or the fire station, explored the fish market, selected and haggled for the fish, bought them and returned home (Parr 1994).

Kevin aged five and **Alan** aged seven in 1998 were boisterous, rather tough-looking boys who lived in a small rural English town. They walked to school with their mother, the school gate being about 90 seconds walk away within sight of their home. They lived in a busy side-road lined with parked cars, and many drivers regularly exceeded the speed limit. One day, Alan was ill and their mother told Kevin to walk on his own to school while she watched from the front door. After a short way, he ran back crying and very frightened. Like many of his friends, he had never walked alone along the street before.

Margaret and Elizabeth. In 1902, Elizabeth, aged three, had been in hospital for months. A message was sent to her mother at the other side of Derby to fetch Elizabeth. As her mother was at home in labour, she sent Margaret, aged five, with a push-chair to collect her sister. In her 90s, Margaret remembered that the matron asked: 'Where is your mother?', and was annoyed when Margaret replied: 'In bed'. Margaret took Elizabeth, who screamed all the way home. Both her mother and the matron assumed that Margaret was old enough to do this.

'We hear far too much about children's rights' is a frequently made assertion. It is often stated in response to examples of children appearing to be greedy, selfish and irresponsible, demanding anything from holidays in Florida to designer trainers. Yet these luxuries have little to do with children's rights.

The difference between luxuries and rights is illustrated by, for example, media stories during the school holidays of parents having to ferry children around from one expensive treat to the next – swimming pools, sports and music sessions, zoos and theme parks. These outings are very enjoyable but, when asked what they most enjoy, children tend to say 'being with my family', 'time with my friends', 'playing outside', 'messing about at home, or on the beach, or by the river', 'taking my dog for a walk'. These answers are closer to basic human rights: freedom to enjoy and move around the area where they live, to meet their friends and be members of their local community, to enjoy nature, to play actively and creatively rather than be passive consumers.

Many children are denied these simple freedoms because of dangerous traffic and undue fear of strangers, exacerbated by media panics, and when crowded built-up areas have no safe, clean, outdoor spaces to play, and so much of the countryside is fenced-off as private property. As a result, young children usually have to rely on busy adults to escort them. In contrast, in 1971, 80 per cent of seven to eight-year-olds in Britain went to school on their own, and by 1990 only 9 per cent did so (Hillman, Adams and Whiteleg 1990). Whereas children used to play in large groups in the streets in 1900, now they are a much smaller part of the population and they live further apart. If they want to see friends, their parents often have to telephone to arrange a meeting, and drive them there. Many children are virtually imprisoned for long periods in their own homes – a kind of solitary confinement from their peers for only children.

For families without large-enough gardens, the easiest way to enjoy being outside with friends is to go on an outing, to pay for access to pools, or woods, or animals, or space to play sports. Over the past few decades, the closing down of public spaces to children (even school grounds are locked up during the holidays) and the opening up of commercial services to replace the free public ones have made children's ability to exercise basic rights seem like luxuries. Compare British childhoods today with those a few decades ago, such as Laurie Lee's childhood in Gloucestershire (Lee 1959).

It is adults, however, who have made this commercial transformation, including the pressures from advertising. It is therefore illogical and ironic to blame children for this change, and to see their requests for simple rights, such as to meet their friends, as greedy irresponsible demands. A further irony is that children are often asking to do what health promoters exhort people to do, to take more exercise and spend time with friends. Yet when children cannot run about or ride bikes near their homes, their chances to be active have to be turned into special outings arranged by adults. Local planning and other pressures make young children much more dependent on adults than they actually need to be, as later examples will show, so that again it is ironic to blame children for their enforced de-pendence and to call it being lazy or irresponsible. Claims that 'we hear too much about children's rights' raise questions about which rights are being referred to, and are they really rights?

Rights and obligations

One purpose of this book is to see how the UNCRC applies to babies and the youngest of children. Some rights are thought to apply only to adults or to people aged over 16, 12 or 7 years. If they can be shown to apply to babies, then implicitly they apply to all children and adults. The following chapters review how the UNCRC defines and qualifies children's rights, with examples of how these affect children's daily lives. The UNCRC is by far the most widely agreed international treaty, ratified by all 192 governments in the world except for Somalia, which has no government, and the USA, which does not ratify UN treaties. Ratification means that governments undertake to implement the UNCRC in law, policy and practice in its comprehensive 54 articles and to report regularly to the UN Committee on the Rights of the Child on their progress in doing so. A Convention – for example, the Geneva Convention – is the strongest form of international treaty. The 1989 UNCRC's formally agreed standards cover three partly overlapping kinds of rights:

- provision rights (to necessary, not luxury, goods, services and resources)

- protection rights (from neglect, abuse, exploitation and discrimination)

- participation rights, when children are respected as active members of their family, community and society, as contributors from their first years.

Tools for change

The UNCRC and the regular government reports, with the UN Committee's responses (all published on the UNICEF website), can act as tools for change, in reviewing progress in each country (or lack of progress) since the previous report.

The third UK government report to the UN Committee was published in 2007 (DfES/DCSF 2007b). Children's charities also produce alternative reports, which tend to be much more critical and challenging than the government ones (Lansdown and Newell 1994; CRAE 2007).

Limitations on rights

All rights are *limited*. As legal concepts they concern freedoms, entitlements and obligations, which can be deliberately honoured – or withheld. Parents cannot be taken to court, for example, for not loving their child. It would be useless and cruel to prosecute a mother who is too depressed to love her baby. Love and happiness cannot be willed or enforced so they cannot be rights. Yet adults can be prosecuted for obvious neglect or abuse, and children do have the right to be protected from these. The UNCRC sets possible standards, which can be enforced to help adults to give loving care, and the UNCRC's preamble states the importance of every child living 'in an atmosphere of happiness, love and understanding'. The UNCRC enshrines minimum standards, which may rise in future as the world's children come to be more respected.

Some rights are *aspirational*, not yet fully realisable, but only 'to the maximum extent of [each nation's] available resources'(4).[1] Richer nations are expected to help poorer ones to respect children's economic rights (24.4).

Rights are not *absolute* but *conditional*, affected by the 'evolving capacities of the child', the 'responsibilities, rights and duties of parents'(5), 'the primary responsibility of the parents' (18), and the national law. 'The best interests of the child shall be a primary consideration'(3). Children's rights cannot be exercised in ways that would harm the child or other people. In exercising their rights, people must 'respect the rights and reputations of others', as well as 'national security and public order, health and morals' (13).

Rights are *shared*, being about solidarity, equality in social justice and fair distribution, 'our' rights not 'my' rights. The UNCRC is not about selfish individualism. To claim a right acknowledges that everyone has an equal claim to it and so reaffirms the worth and dignity of every person. Children's rights are part of promoting 'social progress and better stan-

---

1   Figures in brackets refer to the relevant article of the 1989 Convention.

dards of life in larger freedom'. The preamble states that the child 'needs special safeguards and care, including appropriate legal protection', and the UNCRC begins 'in recognition of the inherent dignity and of the equal and inalienable rights of all members of the human family [as] the foundation of freedom, justice and peace in the world'.

Rights are about *necessities* not luxuries – clean safe water, freedom to play.

One argument against children's rights is that rights cannot be bestowed. They can only apply to groups, which understand and claim and exercise rights for themselves, as some, though far from all, women, black and disabled people have struggled to do. Yet the provision and protection rights involve *duties*, which adults owe to children, who did not ask to be born and who are inevitably dependent at first. With the participation rights, although young children may not use rights language, they repeatedly say they want adults to listen to them and take heed of their views (Lansdown and Newell 1994; Save the Children 1999).

It is also said that rights go with *obligations and responsibilities*, and that children are irresponsible or pre-responsible. Adults are responsible for ensuring that many children's rights are respected. Yet children often want some participation rights so that they can share more responsibility with adults, as later examples will show.

The UNCRC is about broad *principles*, which can be interpreted and applied in different ways according to local values and traditions. There is therefore at times confusion and *disagreement* about how best to honour children's rights. One example is the debates about child poverty, what it means and how it can be relieved. The UNCRC's 54 articles *combine* all children's rights, which are not seen as separate items but as complementary, and this coherent overall view can inform ways to apply the UNCRC. The UNCRC goes beyond earlier children's rights documents on provision and protection to add participation rights, which can help young children and adults to enjoy more equal and mutually rewarding lives and relationships. Central to participation is the right to form and express views.

Can and should young children be asked to give their views on matters which affect them?

The first edition of this book began to be written in the late 1990s with the tentative questions: Can we listen to the youngest children? Do they have views worth hearing? Can their views possibly influence policy and practice? The second edition has moved from emphasising personal examples towards the political confidence about rights that many children and adults now assume. Involving young children and learning from them is not only possible but it is accepted as essential if their rights and best interests are to be respected. Early drafts began with titles such as *Consulting Young Children* or *Listening to Young Children*. Gradually the adult-centredness of such titles became clearer. They imply active adults taking the lead, setting the agenda and starting the interactions, while children more passively follow and respond – or do not respond.

Children and adults communicating is the main theme of this book, though often in the form of questions about how it is possible or worthwhile, wise or kind, for adults to consult and involve the youngest children. As part of Jessica Kingsley's *Children in Charge* series, this book sets out partly to untangle common perceptions about young children from direct examples of their own words and activities. Another aim is to show how very early young children, and even babies, can share in complex activities.

The UNCRC (UN 1989) Article 12 says that States shall assure 'to the child who is capable of forming his or her own views the right to express those views freely in all matters affecting the child'. The Children Act of England and Wales (DoH 1989) says: 'Have regard in particular to the ascertainable wishes and feelings of the child concerned', and the 2004 Children Act (DfES 2004) refers to consulting children. *Birth to Three Matters* (Sure Start 2002) sees children as 'skilful communicators'. Yet how do these policies help or harm children and adults? To begin with, here are examples of young children expressing their views, taken from growing numbers of reports on this topic. I have kept some of the older examples from the first edition of this book to show that involving children is not just a recent idea.

The Mosaic approach. Using the Mosaic method with Alison Clark (Clark and Moss 2005), children combined talking with taking photographs, making drawings and maps, conferencing, making a magic carpet trip (with slides of other places to inform and draw on children's wider knowledge), conducting and recording tours of the outdoor space in their pre-school groups, and making books of their work, aided by a toy dog. The children indicated which toys, activities, spaces and secret places they most enjoyed. The children's ideas were used to create a sensory garden and much more accessible and interesting outdoor spaces, which they could use all year round.

The Kids' Council in Everton first began by running a disco. All young people in the area of the age of two years and over could be a member, until the minimum age was raised to eight years in 1993. They met monthly and employed a children's worker from 1993. They were concerned about conditions for old people, for whom they ran popular bingo sessions, as well as being concerned about children and teenagers. Half the houses on the estate were empty and vandalised, and the Kids' Council advised the local authority about which houses to restore and about traffic calming methods, as well as sharing in street clean-ups and the local gala. They spent time talking about how to learn from their achievements and mistakes – one of their main aims (Save the Children 1997).

Tackling bullying. At one school, seven-year-olds suggested conducting a survey about bullying. Bullying is so often discussed in terms of *who* bullies *whom*. Instead, they went round the school asking *where* and *when* were people most likely to be bullied. Certain areas of the playground were often cited. As a result of the survey of the children's own knowledge, lunch-time supervisors spread out around the playground and near to these areas, and there was far less bullying (Rowe 1999).

Replanning a housing estate. When a run-down housing estate was being renovated, the adults were consulted but not, at first, the children. Then children aged from three to eight years began to be asked about the new plans, and about what they enjoyed or would like to have on the estate. This started almost by chance; initially the adults were surprised by the children's clear views, and worked step-by-step with the children about how to involve them. 'I've done a lot of work with children in this age group', said the Children Should be Heard project worker, Brian Wood. 'But it was a huge leap from working as someone who was providing a service to recognising that children actually have views on services and issues where they live.'

His first questions did not gain many replies, so he asked the children to show him around the estate as a newcomer, and to take photographs of things that were important to them. Ten children joined in the tour, showing a heap of sand, a stream and a bridge they had made. Eventually the children wrote a report, illustrating it with their drawings, maps, photos, and including details of their survey of other children's views. They discussed the report with senior council officers. A play area had been planned for them beyond the perimeter road. On their advice it was sited instead in the centre of the estate, away from traffic and passing strangers, and where the children could safely arrive and play without needing their parents to be with them (Newson 1995a).

Children's meetings in schools

- Some primary schools encourage children to arrange their own meetings, such as a music or drama group, or meetings for school captains or for peer mediators (Highfield School 1997). The teachers believe it is important to encourage the children to be responsible, and to have time and space to work out their own ideas and activities.

- In contrast, one secondary school senior teacher, speaking of young people aged 11 to 18, said that at her school: 'We would like to do things like that, but the children cannot be allowed to hold meetings without staff present. Someone might flick a paper clip into someone's eye, and it could get into the newspapers. Parents would stop sending their children to this school, and I would have to sack some of the teachers. Everyone would suffer, and we just cannot afford to take this kind of risk. It is all for their own good that we do not let the children have this kind of meeting.'

Joining in

Monika Riihelda (1996) pioneered Storyride, in which adults listen intently to young children's stories, write them down and read them back to the child. Among the reported benefits are the children's and adults' enjoyment and new habits of listening more carefully to one another. One four-year-old told over 700 stories. Asked the age at which she believes children can begin to be consulted, Monika Riihelda replied 'eight months' and gave the following example.

Five Finnish children aged up to five years sat round a table, and each child in turn told a story which the adult wrote down and read back. Finally all the children turned to look at the baby at the end of the row who was watching. He made noises and was clearly pleased when the adult wrote them down and read them back.

Monika added:

But I think the principle is that every human being has stories to be told, if there is somebody who has the interest to listen to them. So it does not depend on the age of the teller, but on the sensitivity of the listener. A newborn baby is looking in your eyes, making silent questions, asking for cooperation, for building a common world. That is

one of the beginnings of the stories. (Monika Riihelda, personal communication, 1998)

The baby had grasped some of the essentials. He wanted to take part with
the others and be listened to, despite not completely understanding. When
adults make major decisions they cannot necessarily understand and
foresee all that is involved. The key questions, when consulting adults or
children, rather than 'Do they either understand or not?' are: 'Do they understand enough? And, if not, could they understand enough if they had
more information, or if they were asked in different ways?'. Children's decisions are often about wanting to take a fuller part and a greater responsibility in activities which they see others doing. Some of the earlier
examples show how children can have unique knowledge about solutions,
which can very much benefit children and adults.

The readers

This book is written for a wide range of people: those who work closely
with young children and care for them, others who spend more time in
management and policy-making, people who want to extend the ways
they already consult children, and those who have not yet consulted them
much. The book is for people from a range of backgrounds: play and education, health and welfare services and other local government and voluntary services. Many ideas for this second edition came from working with
students at the Institute of Education on courses in childhood studies, children's rights and early childhood. I hope that students and their tutors will
find this book a useful resource, as an overview of ideas and also of many
related publications. Parents may find this book useful in their relationships with their own children, and when they want to encourage other
adults, such as teachers or planners, to listen to children. Examples will be
given of children talking – for instance, about play or health care – to make
points about children's general understanding and abilities, which readers
from other disciplines can apply to their work.

Practical ideas

This book is mainly about *ideas* on children and adults communicating and
consulting, for three reasons:

- Powerful hidden ideas and assumptions lead people to want to begin or to block communication. These ideas need to be discussed openly so that their impact is understood, including older and newer ideas about childhood.

- Rather than duplicating the excellent practical books already published, this book describes a few of their working examples and refers readers to them.

- Involving and consulting children means taking a fresh approach to *their* ideas, including how to talk and listen to them. It sometimes involves following their leads, and relying less on methods that other adults may have used.

This book is not like a recipe book – a blueprint for reproducing predictable food. Instead, it is more about creating an understanding which will help adults and children to create their own methods, and perhaps to become more aware of ways they are already communicating. Talking and inventing, watching and listening are the keys, with confidence in one's own ideas and in the ideas of older and younger colleagues, and of the children themselves.

Background to, and outline of, the book

This book draws on two main sources: many published reports of people's experiences and research, their reviews and ideas (references are given for these), and my own material – examples and ideas drawn from the early years centres, playgroups and play schemes, children's homes, schools and hospitals where I have researched, from decades of living with young children, plus anecdotes by and about friends whose real names are not given, to protect their privacy. Some of my own material is not referenced. Direct examples are used to reflect children's daily lives.

This book is not an original research report but a collection of practical ideas and examples and a resource to help people to think about the main questions. Examples are not given to suggest that they are typical but to illustrate a point, and at times to expand notions of what a 'typical child' might be like.

Writing this book has been a slow process because so many new ideas are scattered over so many places. Furthermore, I have found myself writing about what adults *do to* children, and my sentences therefore needed rewriting so that children are also the actors. For example, we tend to talk of children being 'dropped off' and 'picked up' at school (by adults) instead of children themselves 'going' to school. Sometimes, to include children as people and agents feels like writing in a new language. The earlier feminists wrote about having to reshape deep assumptions by re-writing language and grammar: to replace the generic 'he', for example, showing that this word did not apply to everyone, as used to be assumed, but excluded women. 'Women are half the human race', feminists would add. Yet their words repeat patriarchy's mistake of ignoring children and young people, who are half the human race. Men and women are about one-quarter each.

Chapter 1 reviews young children's provision rights within the UNCRC, Chapter 2 the protection rights, and Chapter 3 the participation rights. Chapter 4 considers how young children are seen as real people, human beings now rather than human becomings and future adults, and explores the tensions between protecting children and respecting them. Standard beliefs and deeper feelings about whether young children can or should be consulted are reviewed in Chapter 5. Some confidence and trust on each side are needed, and these are affected by adults' and children's beliefs about childhood abilities. Chapter 6 looks at methods and levels of listening to and working with young children: one is children's level or degree of involvement and participation, and the other is the spaces or arena for involving them from small groups to international policies. Con-tradictions between notions of play and work when consulting children are considered in Chapter 7, which discusses further complications that discourage adults from consulting young children: worries about risk and control, conflict and violence. Relationships and interactions continue to be reviewed in Chapter 8: children and adults working together and sharing some decisions, responsibility for oneself and for others, and re-specting and influencing one another's views and feelings, decisions and behaviour. Finally, the key messages from the evidence and experiences are summarised in Chapter 9. The references are meant to be a resource for readers who like to follow up topics raised in this book.

CHAPTER ONE

Children's Provision Rights

This chapter reviews main provision rights in the United Nations 1989 Convention on the Rights of the Child (UNCRC): standards of care, health care, review when looked after (by the local authority), right to an adequate standard of living, to education and childcare, to cultural life and the arts, and to know about the UNCRC. The chapter also looks at how children can share with adults in providing for their care. The UNCRC involves 'state parties', and so children's rights are mainly reviewed from the viewpoint of government services and their support and respect for children. The UK *Every Child Matters* Policy (HM Treasury *et al.* 2003) is mainly reviewed in Chapter 2, as it emphasises protection as much as provision.

Standards of care and consultation

All services for children 'shall conform with the standards established by competent authorities, particularly in the areas of safety, health, in the number and suitability of their staff as well as competent supervision' (3).[1]

Agreed standards are vital in ensuring reasonable quality of care. Some standards may be vague and unhelpful. For example, the main care and education inspection agency in England, OFSTED (www.ofsted.gov.uk), set standards in September 2001. These state that there must be adequate natural daylight in settings, but they do not say what this means. Nurseries

---

1   Figures in brackets refer to the relevant article in the 1989 Convention.

in basements needing to have the lights on all the time can therefore pass inspections and remain open. So too can centres without outdoor play space, or with only tiny paved yards. In centres with gardens and playgrounds, young children show how eager they are to enjoy these all year round. Even battery hens have legally specified amounts of space, and nurseries tend to fill indoor spaces with furniture, leaving few if any areas for vigorous play. Lack of space and time outside have been associated with poorer mental health and behaviour in children.

It is therefore important to consult children and parents when setting standards. Parents are a vital source of information, for their own views and for helping their child's views to be heard more clearly. In Britain, parents, and not children, are seen as the main 'consumers' of day care and education. Yet parents are usually absent, and so do not know exactly what is going on. They may be afraid to express concerns. They may worry that their child will be unpopular or victimised, or that they will lose the child's place, or that the parents will be blamed for the child's problems, if they make comments. Parents may be misunderstood. Traveller parents, for example, may be seen as uncooperative if they stop their children from sharing in school outings in case they might have to collect the children in an emergency if the police suddenly evict the family from their site (Kiddle 1999). Consulting with parents therefore needs to be seen as a way to increase understanding and trust between staff and families, as well as to work together with children to raise standards and, at times, to resolve problems.

Health care
The child has the right to 'the enjoyment of the highest attainable standard of health and to facilities for treatment of illness and rehabilitation of health', especially 'to diminish infant and child mortality' (24). State parties shall develop primary health care, and provide 'adequate nutritious foods and clean drinking water…appropriate pre- and post-natal health care for mothers…health education [including] basic knowledge of child health and nutrition, the advantages of breast feeding, hygiene, and environmental sanitation and the prevention of accidents…and family planning services' (24).

Babies as health workers. From their first weeks, children share in their own health care. The baby is necessarily the most active partner in breast- or bottle-feeding. With breast-feeding, the baby creates the demand which builds up the supply, and success depends on responding to the baby's requests for frequent feeds at first.

After eating most of the foods they are offered, from 18 to 24 months, many babies begin to refuse unfamiliar food. There may be a useful reason for their caution about one year after weaning, which works well in societies with limited diets and where young children roam quite freely. The children accept all the familiar seasonal foods, and are unlikely to try strange food like poisonous berries (Leidloff 1976).

Recently, school meals have been changing from 'junk' food to healthy food. Children have shown how new diets cannot simply be imposed on them, and that they accept the changes better when they learn about nutrition and help to prepare, cook and even grow some of the food – when they are actively involved.

Even premature babies work hard to organise their bodies. They soothe themselves by sucking their fingers and stroking their cheeks. They wriggle into corners and they like fabric nests, which contain and fold their limbs together, so that they do not have to sprawl, limbs stretched out, when they become tired and upset. They turn away from bright light. In these and other subtle ways, premature babies show the kinds of quiet, shaded settings they prefer, and which benefit all the babies. Although these responses might be seen as more to do with biology and instinct, they have social implications, when nurses and parents work out the most comfortable way for the babies to lie, and the babies are then better able to rest, sleep and gain the energy to grow, feed and resist infections (Goldson 1999). Unfortunately, most intensive care neonatal units are bright noisy places, but a few are 'baby-led' units, taking great care to follow the babies' cues in the unit's design, routines, policies and staff training (Als 1999; Alderson, Hawthorne and Killen 2005a, 2005b).

Old ideas that babies, and even young children, are pre-rational are challenged by the evidence. It is clear that from birth babies have the capacity to respond and relate, to take part in the 'micro-dance' of human communication, nodding in time to speech patterns, making eye contact, and taking turns to vocalise when the other person pauses and is silent (Stern 1977, Brazelton and Nugent 1995). Small babies show emotions of disgust, sadness, joy, fear and interest (Murray and Andrews 2000). Babies make meaning: when six months old, they are startled if they see 'effect' seeming to happen before 'cause' (Siegal 1997).

Sean in the bath. In some neonatal units, babies are bathed quickly whatever their mood or protests. In other units, adults wait until the baby is ready, neither too sleepy nor too upset, but relaxed and alert. Babies are wrapped in a sheet so that they do not startle and shoot out their limbs when put into the water. They are gently and slowly dipped in the bath and when the baby is ready the sheet is unwrapped. Sean was born 15 weeks early and when he was eight weeks old, his mother said: 'He's a very fussy little boy...even when he was in an incubator and he had a tube down his throat...you would soon know if there was something that he didn't like, so he's a good communicator...one minute the hands are out there to say "stop", and the next minute he's crying 'cos he wants to be picked up, so he's very finicky. [During his first bath] he was wrapped up for it but he pretty much decided to degown himself. He enjoyed it. He was amazing, so relaxed, and he cried when I took him out' (Alderson *et al.* 2005a).

Babies as partners. Very soon babies start to share in dressing, by holding their arms flexibly to help to put on sleeves, instead of being like limp or rigid dolls. From about 12 months, they assert their independence, for example, by refusing to wear a coat on a cold or wet day. If they are consulted they soon learn to know when they need to wear a coat, as long as they are not teased or punished when they change their minds. Young children are very keen to feed themselves, initiate games and interactions, and to cooperate and help. During their second year they become active in their own and others' health care, when helping with cooking and cleaning.

A study of mothers' and health visitors' views of 20-month-old children (Mayall 1993) found that the mothers tended to see the children as real people, full members of the family. The health visitors, even those who were mothers, tended to believe out-of-date texts about young children's inabilities and their need to be controlled and stimulated by adults. The professionals tended not to advise consulting children. The mothers went beyond consulting, towards living in a kind of partnership with the children. Mothers and health visitors believed that adults must quite firmly control and protect children but, perhaps subconsciously, they took rather different approaches. The mothers were happier to negotiate and share control. They saw the benefits, for them and for the children, in helping the children to become more active and responsible. The health visitors tended to assume that adults' power should be enforced clearly, through conflict if necessary, rather than through consulting and negotiating.

Babies as carers. A television programme in 1997 showed a single mother who was deaf and blind and the social workers who felt that her baby should live with another family. The film showed the six-month-old smiling, friendly baby watching the spoonful of food her mother lifted towards her and guiding it into her own mouth. As she grew older, a neighbour commented that at the age when babies usually drop and throw things on the floor, the baby did not do this as if she knew that this would be difficult for her mother.

Early on, babies respond to people's moods, tending to laugh back at happy faces and to become quiet and anxious at sad faces (Murray and Andrews 2000). In their second year, children often enjoy teasing others, taking a toy and stirring up trouble and then seeming amused when they watch the adults rush in to the rescue to try to sort out the problems (Dunn 1987). The sensitive ways in which children sort out and 'repair' their differences are seen in early years centres (Danby and Barker 1998). Some very young children offer help and comfort to other children in distress, whereas others seem indifferent and some, who have been abused, seem pleased when others are unhappy (Bråten 1996).

Sisterly love. This newspaper headline was about twins who were born 11 weeks early. Chelsea was soon well enough to go home and she visited Daniel regularly and lay next to him in his special care cot at a Newcastle hospital. The babies cuddled up together and a photograph showed Daniel curling his fingers around Chelsea's hand. Their parents were convinced that the twins missed each other, and that Chelsea gave Daniel strength to get better during his months in hospital (*London Metro*, 20 August 1999).

Adults play key roles in helping babies to become responsible for their own health care, and to be adventurous yet cautious enough to avoid injuries (Mayall 1994a). This may involve waiting, a kind of silent consulting, sometimes while children test and decide whether to take a risk in climbing and balancing. They can do this very skilfully while they gradually increase their strength and mobility.

Ruby and the chocolates. While healthy children can share in managing their own health care, can young children understand and share in controlling a serious condition? Children aged 3 to 12 years who have type I diabetes were asked this question. They have to have finger-prick blood tests and insulin injections at least twice a day, keep to a strict low sugar and carbohydrate diet, and be careful about 'hypers' and 'hypos' when their blood sugar is too high or too low.

Maisie, aged three years, shook to show how a 'hypo' felt and how she warned her mother. When adults cannot always be around, the children hold their health in their own hands. Ruby's friend found a box of chocolates and she ate some and offered some to Ruby. Ruby said 'no', as her blood tests later showed. Aged only four years old, she knew the kinds of rules she had to keep. She was upset when there was birthday cake at her nursery but the staff would not let her have a piece. She asked her mother to remind the staff that she was allowed one piece. When she was five years old she knew how to test her blood sugar and decide for herself how much birthday cake she could eat (Sutcliffe, Sutcliffe and Alderson 2004; Alderson, Sutcliffe and Curtis 2006b).

This section has reviewed how young children can not only become major partners in their own health care, but they can also contribute to the emotional health and wellbeing of their families and friends. Their share in decision-making will be reviewed in Chapters 3 and 8.

Review, when looked after (by the local authority)

Any child cared for by authorities has the right to 'periodic review of the treatment provided to the child and all other circumstances relevant to his or her placement' (25). Children's views should be attended to carefully. This right applies to disabled, sick and other children in long-term health or social services care. From as early as possible, the young child's feelings should be considered. There are now many publications on the practical methods and benefits of consulting these children (Gardner 1989; Willow 1996; Masson, Harrison and Pavlovic 1997; Cavet 1998; Knight 1998; Morris 1998; Noyes 1999; Thomas 2002). However, there are still large areas where young children's views are ignored, such as in the courts, and this will only change when all adults realise that young children can have valid, realistic views about their best interests (Winter 2006a, 2006b).

An adequate standard of living

Every child has the right 'to a standard of living adequate for the child's physical, mental, spiritual and social development...State parties...within their means' shall assist families when in need with, for example, food, clothing and housing (27). An adequate standard of living involves spaces to play freely and to learn, and economics can play a vital part in how children are consulted and involved in these areas. A review of nurseries in Italy, Spain and England showed great differences in the quality of the play and relationships, between the nurseries in beautiful centres which are honoured in their community, and the low-budget ones in poorer districts (Penn 1997a). There are creative nurseries in both kinds of areas, but many factors make it harder for the disadvantaged ones to be like the highest standard nurseries. Early years centres reflect and express their political setting and the adults' sense, and so indirectly the children's sense, of how much children are citizens with a right to be consulted and respected (Edwards, Gandini and Forman 1998; Dahlberg, Moss and Pence 1999).

Young children express themselves through 'hundreds of languages' – all kinds of drama, dance, story, art and music. With varied materials and the sensitive support of skilled adults, children create things, which delight and amaze, such as in Reggio Emilia, Italy (Edwards *et al.* 1998). This prosperous city is renowned for spending over 10 per cent of its budget on the education of the children aged from four months to six years.

Although this cannot be measured exactly, in 1993 it was estimated that for every £100 spent on leisure activities for adults, the English Department of National Heritage spent three pence on activities for children, one-fifth of the population (Laing 1993). Children cannot easily enjoy resources if they find them hard to reach. As one six-year-old pointed out: 'We need more bridges over the roads so we can get to the park' (Lansdown and Newell 1994, p.13; and see National Voluntary Council for Children's Play (NVCCP) Charter 1992; Shier 1995).

Hundreds of English playgrounds and playing fields have been closed. The Government's policy that parents can move their children into the most popular schools involves building new classrooms on shrinking playgrounds, which have to contain more children. When new, and smaller, houses and flats cover over the green areas in cities, there are even fewer spaces where children can play and work off their energy after sitting still for hours in school. Policies for play and space need to be linked to those for antisocial behaviour (see Chapter 2).

Poverty can exclude people and silence them when it is harder for them to belong to those groups that are involved, respected and heard (Bradshaw and Mayhew 2005). One in three children in Britain lives in poverty, and 1.3 million children live in families with an average annual income of £7000 or less, compared to the UK average family income of £19,000 (Save the Children 2007). Over half the children in inner London live in poverty, and one in seven lives in substandard housing (End Child Poverty (ECP) and Association of London Government (ALG) 2005). Poor housing usually means no garden, noisy crowded streets, no nearby safe clean play spaces, traffic dangers, and possibly violent and drunken behaviour on the streets. Children then tend to be cooped up at home with few chances to let off energy, meet other people, and make friends. They are even more confined when families live in bed-sitting rooms, hostels or when homeless families squeeze into friends' or relatives' housing. There may even be no safe space for a baby to crawl.

In Britain, the main route out of child poverty is seen as ensuring that parents do paid work (HM Treasury *et al.* 2003; Joseph Rowntree Foundation (JRF) 2006). Yet this does not solve the problem when many parents work long hours for low pay and have to pay high childcare, housing and other costs. Children then lose out on family life as well as having to live on a low income. Scandinavian countries, with the lowest child poverty rates, have higher child benefits and supports for working parents, and a much narrower range from highest to lowest incomes (Mayhew *et al.* 2005). Marked inequality of incomes in Britain is a major threat to child welfare when, for example, the richest people can buy several homes to let and the poorest can barely afford to pay their rent (Maidment 2006).

The *State of London's Children* reports (Hood 2002, 2004; McNeish 2007) show close links between poverty and lower standards of economic wellbeing, health, enjoyment (play, arts, sports, leisure), education, transport and road safety, family life and care, racism and violence, housing and children's participation. The reports also show how all of these areas need to be addressed together if children's rights to an adequate standard of living are to be respected. The UNCRC helps to advance justice and equal rights for all children.

An adequate standard of living: the global scene

This section looks at poverty in rich and poor countries, at relative and absolute poverty, and at children's potential standard of living over the next decades.

A survey of child wellbeing in 21 rich countries had six main measures (UNICEF 2007b). These were: material wellbeing; health and safety; educational wellbeing; family and peer relations (trust, 'just talking with parents', 'kind and helpful peers'); health and risk behaviours; violence; subjective wellbeing (health, liking school, personal satisfaction). The survey found that two of the richest countries, Britain and the United States (USA), had the worst responses (see Table 1.1). For example, British children were least likely to expect their peers to be kind and helpful. These two countries have the greatest inequalities between highest and lowest earners.

Table 1.1 An overview of child wellbeing in rich countries.

Country	Average of total replies[1]	Country	Average of total replies[1]
Netherlands	4.2	Canada	11.8
Sweden	5.0	Greece	11.8
Denmark	7.2	Poland	12.3
Finland	7.5	Czech Republic	12.5
Spain	8.0	France	13.0
Switzerland	8.3	Portugal	13.7
Norway	8.7	Austria	13.8
Italy	10.0	Hungary	14.5
Ireland	10.2	USA	18.0
Belgium	10.7	UK	18.2
Germany	11.2		

1   Higher figures denote more adverse results.

There is further evidence that the richest countries with the highest Gross Domestic Products (GDPs) can be less happy places for children than poorer countries. GDPs measure economic growth and success in terms of goods and also 'bads', including the costs of crime, prisons, illness, disasters, accidents, advertising, waste, excess packaging and commuting. A US annual Index of Social Health has 16 measures which include infant mortality, child abuse and poverty, teenage suicides, drug use, mental illness and high-school drop-out rates. The Index shows how between 1977 and 1994 (the latest available records in Douthwaite 1999), the GDP steadily rose, and so too did the reported 'bads'. This trend is found in other wealthy countries. Ironically, the more costly the 'bads' become, the healthier the GDP appears to be.

Why should children in the richest countries seem to be less happy than those in poorer countries? One possible reason is the 'commercialisation of childhood' (Williams 2006). Children are seen as obsessed with advertisements and marketing messages, which shape how they see themselves, their values and hopes. They are anxious to appear cool with the latest fashions, accessories, computer games and junk food items in order to avoid being bullied and excluded. Anxiety about commercialisation is extended into transferring the adult-generated markets, advertising and gimmicks on to children (Palmer 2006). Palmer's muddled title, *Toxic Childhood*, indicates contradictions through the book, which suggest that children themselves, and not adults, are the main source and site of these 'poisons', from which adults rescue and 'detox' deluded children. While it is informative, Palmer's book needs to be read with care. Almost every reference to childhood, commercialised or not, is negative, whereas references to 'grown-ups' are positive. A typical example is: 'Any child can regress to the level of a two-year-old on a bad day…in a civilised society we expect a decline in self-obsession and an increase in grown-up behaviour as the years go by [although] children then enter that long dark tunnel known as adolescence' (Palmer 2006, p.6). This stereotyping of age groups appears to deter Palmer from seeing when adults are possible sources of problems, or when children are possible sources of solutions. The stereotyping follows a long history: from Puritan beliefs in original sin through Kant, Freud and Piaget to today's age–stage child development theories (Hardyment 1984) and images of the greedy foolish child. These beliefs undermine children's human rights when children are seen as not yet fully human. The UNCRC is about children's rights to basic necessities and to an 'adequate standard of living', but not to luxuries and passing fads. Everyone deplores the abject long-term poverty that traps millions of children in poorer countries (UNICEF 2007a). The UNCRC basic rights to clean safe water, good food, shelter, clothing, education and health care are vital tools towards reducing *absolute* poverty.

Yet many authors also argue that children in richer countries need a high family income and that many 'luxuries' become necessities, when *relative poverty* can be painful, excluding and life-limiting in richer countries, although different from the suffering of *absolute poverty*, mainly in poor countries. However, as mentioned, some children in Britain are extremely deprived. Relatively poor children, it is argued, are cut off from friends and from equal opportunities so that poverty and disadvantage persist through the generations (Millar and Gardiner 2004; Bradshaw and Mayhew 2005; Pantazis, Gordon and Levitas 2006).

Yet do we have to question the idea that the only way to help relatively poorer children is to enable them to become richer, for several reasons? First, the researchers tend to assume that all the children are miserable and lonely, even when most children in an area live in poverty and enjoy some solidarity and friendships. Second, are the accounts of relative poverty as so miserable realistic, when many of our great-grandparents seem to have enjoyed childhoods with far fewer resources? And are the researchers reflecting and reinforcing negative beliefs about less-than-wealthy lives? Third, the children are shown as trapped and helpless, and only rarely are they shown as strong and resourceful (Seaman *et al.* 2006). Disabled people protested against being portrayed in lonely negative images, saying that this only added to their social exclusion. Is the same thing happening to poor children? Fourth, poverty tends to be linked to crime, drugs, obesity, low grades at school and other problems. Yet many poor children do not have these problems. They risk being unfairly blamed and stigmatised, and perhaps falling into these predicted problem lives. Teachers and others may blame failure on general poverty and poor children, instead of looking at potential problems in the services for these children. Fifth, is it realistic to suppose that the solution is for everyone to become richer? There will always be even richer children to catch up with. And even if this could be achieved would they all be happier? Sixth, in a fragile finite planet where are the resources to support this dream?

Millions of people already consume much more than their fair share. Justice demands, and sooner or later nature will force, the use of fewer and not more resources. Since 2000 when the first edition of this book was published, there have been great changes in knowledge about climate change and resources, and soon there may be further huge changes in thinking and policies. Floods and droughts, fires and rising sea levels are reducing food supplies and habitable land space. At the same time, supplies of fossil fuels and fresh water are dwindling while wars fought over them intensify (Lynas 2007; Monbiot 2007). The richer minority world is being urged to consume less (Hillman and Fawcett 2004; Kennet and Heinemann 2005). Feminists are working out new kinds of economics to take account of climate change and to respect both women's rights and the finite planet (Mellor 2006; Mies 2007). We need to work out new eco-friendly policies on the equal rights of every child to an adequate standard of living, without some children having an excessive standard. This involves respecting thrifty indigenous cultures and ending efforts to impose Western values across the world (Penn 2002, 2005). Some Indian villagers believe they lived happier, more fulfilled, and socially and spiritually richer lives in older traditional ways, before Western schooling was introduced in their village. They worry that schools make young people discontented with rural and Indian life and values, so that they go off to live in cities in more Western ways (Gupta 2005, and see section on poverty in Chapter 2).

Education and childcare

Primary education shall be 'compulsory and free to all' (28) and involves 'the preparation of the child for responsible life in a free society, in the spirit of understanding, peace, tolerance, equality of the sexes, and friendship among all peoples' (29).

Informal education starts from birth and includes adults listening and responding to children's views. Education includes learning about local cultures, traditions and work in and around the home that sustains families and communities (Katz 2004; Gupta 2005), as well as formal schooling and more abstract knowledge. Western education emphasises the latter, although for decades researchers have pointed out that many children and adults find abstract thinking very difficult and restricting (Donaldson 1978).

Learning skills. While studying 16 four-year-old children to investigate why Bangladeshi children did less well than white children during their first year at school in London, Liz Brooker (2002, p.51) visited the children's homes. Knives were kept away from some Anglo children. 'In many Bangladeshi households, however, a razor sharp *dar* stood on the kitchen floor for slicing food and children knew to make their way carefully past it. In Jelika's house, I came across her standing on a chair using a heavy knife to chop onions. As I moved towards her to intervene, her grandmother mildly stepped forward and tidied the chopped onions leaving Jelika to continue chopping. On another occasion I found Abdul Rahman, under his father's instruction, using two hands to manipulate a large meat cleaver.' The children showed big contrasts between how they were apprenticed and how their skills, to cook or to play, were encouraged at home and at school.

The British Government aims to compete in global markets by producing highly educated and qualified adults. There is concern that even when only 22 months old, disadvantaged children fall behind others in certain learning skills (Feinstein 2003). Other research often quoted by the UK Government comes from the American Perry High/Scope studies in the 1960s (Schweinhart and Weikart 1997), which is said to 'prove' that young children in nurseries, whose mothers do paid work, later achieve more than those who stay at home. For every $1 spent on nurseries, $7 will be saved later on juvenile justice and other social problems, it is claimed. Researchers question the 'highly conjectural figure' in the Perry High/Scope trial about saving later costs (Penn et al. 2006). This is because the trial involved very disadvantaged black children. They did badly on average whether they attended nursery (very part-time) or not at all, and the boys were likely to end up in prison, so that the trial results do not extrapolate well to Britain in the twenty-first century. Penn (2005, pp.29–30) considers that the claims 'border on the fantastic'. The supposed high savings by the successful children include potential payments to victims and justice system costs of crimes not committed, reduced need for welfare and special needs support, and the higher taxes paid when they were employed as adults. Most of the reports of the trials are in promotional material from the Perry High/Scope Foundation.

The use of such tenuous data suggests ideological rather than scientific foundations for current child policies, including extended schools (see Chapter 2). The Government's Children's Agenda involves detailed early years curriculum and inspection. Billions of pounds are being spent on new buildings, new staff and on more than 25 layers of advisory, planning and inspection agencies (HM Treasury et al. 2003). The result is that, from their early months, children can enjoy dedicated well-equipped centres, interesting activities, the company of other children and caring adults, and general respect for their right to education. Similar universal early years childcare and education services are being promoted for every country (Woodhead 2005).

Yet how far do these policies serve children's rights? The policies' first aim is to increase adult employment and serve 'local employment needs' (HM Treasury et al. 2003). While mothers and young children tend to welcome part-time nursery care, many of them are not happy about the 50-hour week at nursery when parents have to work long hours. These young children hardly see their parents, and may not eat one meal with them through the working week, which does not respect their rights to contact with their family. The view that nurseries promote learning and language skills better than mothers can, and therefore they can help disadvantaged children to 'catch up', is questionable (Tizard and Hughes 1984). And in any case, the childcare is so expensive that the centres tend to be used by middle-class families more than by the disadvantaged ones.

Early years experts advise consistent care for each child by one or two key workers in small groups (Elfer, Goldschmied and Selleck 2003; Lindon 2006; *Birth to Three Matters* 2007), like the constant mothering care on which babies thrive (Gerhard 2004) and with family style meals (Robb 2007). Care and education combine, the experts consider, with all learning led by the child (Cousins 2003). Discipline should be kind, firm and consistent. Yet many nurseries cannot achieve these high aims, especially when staff work eight-hour shifts and children stay for ten hours a day. Most staff are low paid, with few qualifications. Although many are very dedicated, hardworking and affectionate, they often do not have the support needed to achieve the experts' standards. The Effective Provision of Pre-school Education (EPPE) trial (2007) on the benefits of early years care raises concerns that children who spent most of their time in nurseries as babies may later have more emotional and behavioural problems.

The Early Years curriculum offers a wealth of ideas to respect children's equal rights to care and education. The aims include supporting early communication, literacy and numeracy skills, and children's personal, social and emotional wellbeing, and fostering positive attitudes towards their learning, social skills and persistence (Qualification and Curriculum Authority (QCA) 2000). However Dickens, Emerson and Gordon-Smith (2004) point out potential problems for disabled children that could apply to all children if there is undue concern with goals and targets. Adults may then: de-value children's activities and achievements that seem unrelated to the goals; perceive children with difficulties as disadvantaged; focus on what children cannot do more than on what they can do; neglect children's own contributions; be less spontaneous, flexible and sensitive to individual children; put formal learning before play, and then be more likely to exclude disabled children from these formal sessions. Even children who are 'included' may not feel confident that they are, when there is a more competitive school-like approach. It is therefore vital, given that staff have to observe the goals, that they adapt them freely, and also that parents, staff and children share in planning and reviewing the services.

In efforts to raise maths and literacy rates, the British Government promotes earlier formal schooling and longer hours; four-year-olds now attend school all day and have homework, although its benefits are unclear (Hallam 2004). During recent years, schools have cut play and meal times in order to fit in more lessons based on the national curriculum. In European countries with higher literacy rates, however, children start formal schooling later, aged six, seven or eight years, and they may have part-time schooling. British children up to 14 years stay all week in extended schools, 8.00 a.m. to 6.00 p.m., 50 hours a week, longer than European working hours for adults. Children in Norway and Finland from about seven years upwards enjoy being at home while their parents are at work (Solberg 1997). They also play with friends until their parents arrive home in the late afternoon, often after dark in the winter. Norwegian children have more hours away from adult supervision, and a slightly higher accident rate than other European children, which the Norwegians consider is worth risking for the benefits of freely enjoying the country-side (Frönes 1994). German children aged ten years old attend school for five hours a day and play out on their own or with friends all afternoon (Zeiher 2001). Might the respectful early years policy that children learn through play rather than through formal teaching apply in later childhood too?

In contrast to perhaps too much schooling, thousands of children, mainly boys and including some 4-year-olds, are permanently excluded from school: a total of 9440 in the period 2004–2005, and 60 were aged four years or under (Children's Rights Alliance for England (CRAE) 2006). That year there were also 389,560 fixed period exclusions. In 2006, children were at last allowed to speak at exclusion hearings if they wish to 'and the parent agrees' but they do not yet have the right to be heard or to appeal, as the UN Committee on the Rights of the Child keeps recommending. Excluded children have no right to education. During the first five days of an exclusion, if children do not stay at home during school hours, their parents can be fined up to £1000 or imprisoned (CRAE 2006, s. 44), although many parents are also expected to be at work. In Britain, children have no say in planning or reviewing the national curriculum, unlike children in many other countries, where they are then likely to be more willing to learn. Children in Rajasthan show the great potential that British children are not allowed to show, as shown in the next example.

Education or work? It is often said that no child should do paid work because this stops attendance at school. Yet children around the world combine work and schooling. In Rajasthan, one of the poorest regions in the world, the Children's Parliament has run night schools since 1993. Children aged 6 to 14 years elect their MPs who are aged 11 to 14 years. The Parliament monitors the schools and can fire teachers. The children work from around dawn to dusk before attending school. Unusually, the night schools emphasise skills over abstract learning, rural and working class language over urban middle class approaches, small local schools rather than larger distant ones, and skills over exams. Everyone learns and teaches (a model for every school). The young teachers are former students of their school. Sustainable education helps everyone to understand and enrich their self-reliant local community instead of wanting to move to a distant city. By 2001, there were 150 night schools with nearly 3000 children, and two-thirds of them were girls. The Parliament organises a travelling puppet show to warn people against money-lenders, and to promote women's and children's rights and the value of good teachers. So the children teach the adults about citizens' power, even in this very traditional community (John 2003).

Cultural life and the arts

The child has the right 'to rest and leisure, to engage in play...and to participate freely in cultural life and the arts' (31). Babies take part in cultural life as soon as they are wrapped or clothed, hear a lullaby or taste breast milk flavoured with their mother's food. Children's centres and schools are involving more varied music, art, books, fabrics and food to reflect children's diverse cultures. Exhibitions of adults' art now often include creative spaces for children to work with clay and paint, sometimes with professional artists. Many poets and other writers, actors and dancers, musicians, artists and gardeners work with children in schools and other centres.

Far from being escapism, the arts enable children to develop and express their concerns and values. The Wheelworks mobile community arts programme in Belfast, for instance, helps them to overcome barriers when children from different communities work together. The group *Children 2000* worked with children to increase their profile at all levels of funding and planning in the arts, media, sports, leisure, education, environment, health and wellbeing, building and transport. They wanted all national lottery applications to have clauses on children's needs and equal rights, for all applicants and assessors to consider (Cox 1997).

Kids Company involves hundreds of disadvantaged children in South London (Batmanghelidjh 2006). They mounted a visual and aural exhibition at Tate Modern art gallery in 2005. This included a life-sized pretty but sinister pink bedroom with obvious hints that the girl who slept in the room was abused. Among many brilliant and powerful works was a life-size wire outline of a child's body. The lungs were stuffed with cigarette ends and the stomach with crushed cans.

Publicising the UNCRC

Rights can only be claimed and respected when people know that they are rights holders. State parties should undertake to make the principles of the UNCRC 'widely known, by appropriate and active means, to adults and children alike' (42).

The British Government has hardly publicised the UNCRC to children or adults. Ideas from the expressive South African photograph posters, with pictures of children next to UNCRC rights, could be copied in this country. Posters drawn by children could be displayed in health, early years settings and other public places to promote children's rights (Save the Children 1999). The Government has not yet met the requirement to develop human rights training for all professionals working with children. Indeed, when they are asked at meetings if they know about the UNCRC, very often almost no-one does. Although Scotland, Wales and Northern Ireland have Children's Rights Commissioners 'to promote and protect the rights of children', England has only a Children's Commissioner 'to raise awareness of the views and interests of children', which he sees as a constraining mandate (11 Million 2007, p.57). He would prefer to report to Parliament, instead of to the Department for Children, Schools and Families. Like the other child advocacy groups, he considers that greater awareness of the UNCRC will help adults and children throughout Britain to work together to increase practical respect for children's rights.

Protection, provision and participation rights overlap, and some topics raised in this chapter will be reviewed further in the next chapter on protection.

CHAPTER TWO

Children's Protection Rights

This chapter reviews how children have both more and fewer protection rights than adults. The chapter begins with a brief history of rights, and then reviews, mainly in the English context, UNCRC articles on protection from neglect, abuse, violence, cruel and degrading treatment, discrimination, invasion of privacy, exploitation and hazardous work, armed conflict, invasive research and ecological change. There are sections on protective justice and problems of over-protection and under-protection.

There is only space to refer to international matters briefly, if at all. But to outline the global context, the annual UNICEF report, *The State of The World's Children* (2007a), reviews in extensive detail the suffering of the world's children, and the urgent need to increase protection for them, from drought and famine, floods, poverty, infections including HIV/AIDS and their effects on daily life, armed conflict, forced migration, persecution and torture, physical, mental and sexual abuse and trafficking. Sanctions are another policy intended to achieve good ends, but through drastic means that hugely increase the suffering and death of children (Pilger 1998). Children in England include migrants and those who have international family ties. Today's global childhoods also involve countless cross-influences: British children's clothes are stitched by children in Asia and Africa; their food is grown by farming families in every continent; their rubbish may be sorted by children in Asia; their parents may work to make peace or to make arms, intimately affecting children's lives, protections or harms and risks across the world.

The final section will briefly review links between global policies and protection. *The United Nations Secretary General's Study on Violence against Children* (UN 2006) reports that much violence is hidden, unreported and under-recorded (paragraphs 25–7). Violence occurs in homes, schools, care and justice systems, workplaces and communities. Almost 53,000 children died in 2002 as a result of homicide, with younger and disabled children being most at risk. Up to 98 per cent of children suffer physical punishment at home and 305 million of them are severely punished with implements (28). In 2002, it is estimated, 150 million girls and 73 million boys were sexually abused, and 30 million girls and women had some form of genital mutilation performed, adding to the total of 100–150 million affected girls and women. The report is packed with information, and it concludes that all forms of violence must be prohibited, none is justified and all forms are preventable. States should promote non-violent values, enhance the capacity of all those who work with children, and ensure children's participation in all aspects of prevention and monitoring of all forms of violence against them (103).

A brief history of rights

Protection is central to rights. Modern ideas about individual human rights began only around 400 years ago. Before that, duties to God, the monarch and feudal lords came first. John Locke in the seventeenth century and Thomas Paine and Immanuel Kant in the eighteenth century wrote about Man's autonomy rights to personal privacy, to own property and to have freedoms, for example, of thought, conscience and religion. Property owning Man was seen as having pure reason and therefore as being the best person to make his own personal wise decisions. Bioethics debates about the key question of informed consent hinge on who is competent to give valid consent (see Chapter 8). The original rights emphasised the protection of freedoms from interference by other individuals or the state. Women and children were seen as too dependent and irrational to have these rights, and Man's privacy rights included unlimited control over his family (Mendus 1987). In the nineteenth century, John Stuart Mill contended that men and women cannot always make wise decisions. Yet whether they make wise or foolish decisions (and who is to judge what is wise?) adults, but not children, should have the precious freedoms of autonomy and liberty and the right to make personal decisions or best guesses.

Most opposition to children's rights draws on two main concepts: Kant's view that they do not have the reason or wisdom to make informed correct decisions (strong autonomy); Mill's view that they do not have the courage, maturity or responsibility to cope with the risks of liberty and of making and standing by their own mistakes (weak autonomy). This book investigates whether young children can have either form of autonomy, or the complex mixture of both forms, called competence (for more details on children's human and legal rights, see Alderson 1993, pp.30–56, 143–174).

Slowly, women, other minority groups and, later, children also gained rights. In eighteenth century London, Thomas Coram persuaded benefactors to believe that abandoned babies and children were worth rescuing, recognising their right to life. He was followed by Dr Barnardo and others in the nineteenth century. There are controversies about Barnardo's policies to part children from their families, and to export many of them to the colonies, showing how it can be harmful to protect and provide for children without listening to them and involving them in decisions about their care. Gradually the state began to provide a whole infrastructure from administration and planning to transport and plumbing, with many services including education, health visiting and protection of children from neglect and abuse by taking them into care. Cooter (1992) and Hendrick (2003) review the history of the benefits, problems and controversies in services for children. Early ideas of *autonomy* rights to protect men from state interference changed into seeing the state as a *provider* (pensions, insurance, benefits, services and amenities) and as a *protector* (armed and police services, child protection, domestic violence, health and safety laws, such as on seat belts, non-smoking, and banning harmful substances in foods). Objectors to the 'nanny state' worry that over-protection can treat adults as if they are children without rights.

Eglantyne Jebb, who founded Save the Children in 1919, prompted by concern about starving children in Europe, initiated international children's rights. She wrote: 'Help should not be a gift from above but rather help aimed at self-help between equals, where everyone contributes according to their ability from a feeling of human fellowship across racial, ethnic and national borders' (Jebb 1906).

The League of Nations adopted Jebb's 'International Charter of Children's Rights' in 1924, and the United Nation's 'Declaration of the Rights of Children' in 1959 similarly promoted provision and protection rights. During the 1960s civil rights movements, concepts of children's autonomy began to be advocated. Holt (1975) argued that children should be able to exercise their rights as soon as they understood how to and wanted to do so. Freeman (1983) considered that Holt's liberationist views were politically naïve and helped to bring ridicule on notions of children's rights. But Freeman called for respect for children as persons by not treating them as property for others to dispose of. (In Kant's philosophy this is to treat persons as ends in themselves and not as means towards other people's ends.) Freeman also wanted respect for children's competencies, for their share in decision-making processes when they can participate meaningfully, and he wanted all public policy-making to take children's interests into account. He did not want children to be treated 'as adults' but endorsed encouragement of their growing rational independence.

The UN Year of the Child in 1979 initiated many projects, including the ten-year task of writing the UNCRC. This was proposed by the Polish Government, and drew on the writings of the Polish and Jewish paediatrician, Janusz Korczak, who chose to remain with his patients and die with them in a concentration camp during World War II. His 'Declaration of Children's Rights' in 1924 included autonomy rights: to respect, to optimal conditions in which to grow and develop, to live in the present (they are people today), to be himself or herself (not a lottery ticket marked to win the main prize), to make mistakes, to fail, to be taken seriously, to be appreciated for what he is, to desire, to claim, to ask, to have secrets, to respect for his possessions and budget, to education, to resist educational influence and what conflicts with his or her own beliefs, to protest an injustice, to a Children's Court where he can judge and be judged by his peers, to be defended in the juvenile justice court, to respect for his grief (even though it be for the loss of a pebble), to commune with God, to die prematurely (Joseph 1999).

The 1989 UNCRC added children's participation rights or freedoms to the already endorsed protection and provision ones. Today, Article 8 of the Human Rights Act (1998), on protection and autonomy rights, is among the most widely cited Articles: 'Everyone has the right to respect for his private and family life, his home and correspondence.' On the one hand, governments tend to argue that their first duty is to defend citizens from external attacks, from 'terror', crime and violence. In order to protect our rights to life, our values and way of life, they argue that control and surveillance need to keep increasing, for example, with closed circuit televisions (CCTVs) and identity cards. On the other hand, liberal, liberty and civil rights bodies argue that over-control undermines our values and way of life and basic rights and freedoms. So while one side aims to protect our safety, the other side wants to protect our freedoms.

There is growing concern about the 'protective invasion of children's autonomy' (Lyon 2007), silencing and controlling children in the name of safety. Children's protection rights play a complicated part within these tensions. Children have many of the legal protections that adults have, with extra measures, such as health visitors and social workers, security around 'fortress' schools, and criminal bureau record checks for people who work with children. When governments allow or encourage adults to drink and gamble (and so to pay more taxes), they can claim to be moral by insisting that they protect children from such risks. Yet this can have the effect of making it criminal to be young, in that if people aged under 17 or 18 drink or smoke or drive they are in trouble for breaking the law for doing things which adults can do legally. This is not to argue that children should be allowed to do these things, but to comment that attempts to protect them with restrictive laws, which do not always fully work, can expose them to the risks of being drawn into a punitive criminal justice system. The next sections consider how well children today are protected.

Abuse and neglect

Of the 11 million children in England, each year about 50–100 die from neglect and abuse; 25,700 children (in 2003), 26,400 (in 2006), were on child protection registers; 59,700 are 'looked after' by local authorities; 3–400,000 are 'in need'; and 3–4 million are 'vulnerable' (HM Treasury *et al.* 2003). These are likely to be massive under-estimates (CRAE 2007, para 127).

> States Parties shall take all appropriate legislative, administrative, social and educational measures to protect the child from all forms of physical or mental violence, injury or abuse, neglect or negligent treatment,

maltreatment or exploitation, including sexual abuse, while in the care of parent(s), legal guardian(s) or any other person who has the care of the child (19.1).[1]

Such protective measures should, as appropriate, include effective procedures for the establishment of social programmes to provide necessary support for the child and for those who have the care of the child, as well as for other forms of prevention and for identification, reporting, referral, investigation, treatment and follow-up of instances of child maltreatment described heretofore, and, as appropriate, for judicial involvement (19.2).

No child shall be subjected to torture or other cruel, inhuman or degrading treatment or punishment (37a)

The balance for social workers between removing children from risky families too often and too soon, or leaving them until it is too late to prevent severe harm, is especially complicated with the youngest children, who are most dependent on their parents and carers, and least able to speak for themselves, or to be heard, or taken seriously. Some professionals are anxious not to undermine fragile parent–child relationships with critical 'support' that can deskill parents and increase their stress and anxiety. Yet half of all parents with learning difficulties have their children taken away, not necessarily because the children are at risk, but because to have learning difficulties does not fit social services' concepts of being a good enough parent (Chinn 2006).

The UNCRC emphasises support for families and for the child within the family.

States Parties undertake to ensure the child such protection and care as is necessary for his or her well-being, taking into account the rights and duties of his or her parents, legal guardians, or other individuals legally responsible for him or her, and, to this end, shall take all appropriate legislative and administrative measures (3.2).

1   Figures in brackets refer to the relevant article in the 1989 Convention.

States Parties shall ensure that a child shall not be separated from his or her parents against their will, except when competent authorities subject to judicial review determine, in accordance with applicable law and procedures, that such separation is necessary for the best interests of the child. Such determination may be necessary in a particular case such as one involving abuse or neglect of the child by the parents, or one where the parents are living separately and a decision must be made as to the child's place of residence (9.1).

Many children are not adequately protected, and current social, health and education services appear to be unable to meet the basic needs of many abused children living within or apart from their family. Batmanghelidjh (2006) contends that this is because law, policy and services assume a baseline of children being well protected and cared for by loving parents. She reviews how, when parents are not able to be the advocate and to obtain services for their child, there is often no-one else who will or can do so for children in greatest need.

Every Child Matters (ECM)

The Government might seem to have made great steps forward in child protection with its Green Paper *Every Child Matters* (HM Treasury *et al.* 2003) followed by the 2004 Children Act. Both documents emphasise protection. ECM's central symbol for every child is Victoria Climbié, who was killed by her great-aunt. However, she is in the rarest group at highest risk, and ECM was mainly drafted before the Laming Inquiry about Victoria's death was published in 2003. ECM treats all children as potentially at risk – of becoming criminals, of not fulfilling their (economic) potential, and of being abused, with the implication that they must all be protected. ECM emphasises five outcomes: being healthy, staying safe, enjoying and achieving, making a positive contribution and achieving economic wellbeing.

By 2010, there will be 3500 Children's Centres linked to extended schools (see Chapter 1). They will enable the 'childcare market' to meet the 'needs of the area' for fully employable parents. The schools will be 'one-stop shops', offering education, health, social and employment-seeking services for parents. Multidisciplinary teams based in the schools will provide all-round care for families, to detect, identify, prevent and treat emerging problems.

The State used to hold back from intervening in families, not wanting to undermine parents' rights and responsibilities, and possibly weaken family ties, and end up having to pay for the children's care. But now there is intense *intervention* in families (Hendrick 2003; CRAE 2007), for example, extended day care from the early months onwards, parenting classes and punishments for parents whose young children offend. However, there is less direct social and financial *support* for families. For example, as mentioned earlier, most parents have to pay for childcare in the Children's Centres. Parents' employment is seen as the solution to poverty, rather than benefits and redistribution of wealth, as in some northern European countries. The pressures on many parents to do tedious work for long hours on low pay, and to control and contain their children, are liable to add to parents' stress, fatigue and anxiety, and their impatience and irritation with their children. ECM, which is led by HM Treasury and other government finance departments, including the Department for Trade and Industry, renamed in 2007 the Department for Business, Enterprise and Regulatory Reform, appears to be more concerned with the welfare of the national economy than with the welfare and protection of young children (CRAE 2007).

Smacking

The Government continues (summer 2007) to refuse to give children equal legal protection from assault by banning physical punishment. In the UK, children are the only people who can, in law, be hit (renewed by the Government as 'reasonable punishment', in the Children Act 2004, s.58). Private foster parents may also hit children. In 2007, New Zealand was the eighteenth country to ban physical punishment, as the UN Committee on the Rights of the Child urges every state to do.

The Adoption and Children Act 2005, s.120 refers to children's suffering in seeing their mother assaulted, but there are very different standards for women assaulted in domestic violence and for child protection (Phillips and Alderson 2003). The Child Contact and Adoption Act 2006 enables courts to make a risk assessment before they order children to have contact with a parent who may be violent, although this does not necessarily protect children from such visits or ensure that the courts hear their views (CRAE 2007, s.29).

Over 90 per cent of British babies are smacked (Newson and Newson 1990), and babies and the youngest children are hit the most often (Smith 1995; Leach 1999). Smacking does not prevent wrong-doing (Miller 1983), although many adults think they cannot reason with young children and that 'a smack is the only language they understand'. Consulting young children about their behaviour and about positive discipline, as soon as they begin to understand, is the way to avoid physical punishment (Newell 1989). Occasionally smacking escalates into lethal violence. Of the 58 child homicides in England in the period 2004–2005, 23 were of babies under one year (CRAE 2006).

Smacking hurts you inside. The views of 76 five- to seven-year old children on smacking vividly show the pain and fear they feel, and the many reasons for which they are hit. These can include, for example, being accidentally clumsy, so that for some children a smack can just happen at any moment and is not something which the child knows how to prevent. This is counterproductive if smacking is meant to be a deterrent. A few children said they felt so sad 'it makes you not like your parents' or 'you feel like you want to run away' (Willow and Hyder 1998).

The UK's record on Article 19 has been one of the main criticisms in the responses by the UN Committee on the Rights of the Child to the UK regular reports (UN Committee on the Rights of the Child 1995, 2002).

Listening to abused children

A vital way to protect children is to listen to them, as repeated inquiries after the death of a child endorse. In the year ending 31 March 2005, 27 per cent of four- to nine-year-old looked after children did not even have their views conveyed to the review considering their future care, although 22 per cent of four- to nine-year-olds attended the review and spoke for themselves, demonstrating that this is possible (CRAE 2007, s. 63). Karen Winter's research in Northern Ireland (2006a, 2006b, in progress) with looked after children aged four to seven years, shows the need for unusual skill and psychological strength, if adults are to listen to abused young children seriously. Winter gave the children boxes to decorate with craft materials, encouraging them to express in words and images their views about themselves and their wishes and feelings. The children could control the pace and topics of the interview by concentrating on the artwork when they did not wish to reply. From four years old, children could describe and comment on relationships, extreme deprivation, fear, anxiety, and also on security and choices about where to live.

Despite the meticulous data-collecting methods, the reports tended to be dismissed by the authorities, who frequently believe that children aged under 12, certainly under seven years, cannot have views worth hearing (Winter 2006a, 2006b). Reluctance to listen to abused children may partly be because the social workers and lawyers who are supposed to protect them (Children Act 1989, s.8; Adoption and Children Act 2002; Children Act 2004, s.53; Childcare Act 2006, s.3(5)) need to protect themselves, by refusing to believe that young children can be so aware and can suffer so much (Miller 1983; Batmanghelidjh 2006). Child development theory that children are slowly growing towards being complete people endorses these kinds of dismissals. If children's rights and protection are to be taken seriously, then children first have to be understood as real people (Winter 2006a, 2006b; and see Chapter 4).

Children separated from their family 'shall be entitled to special protection and assistance' from the State (20), which shall ensure safeguards and high standards in cases of adoption (21), and special protections for refugee and asylum seeker children (see p.71).

Unfortunately, if children leave abusive families and become looked after by the local authority or private agencies, their problems do not end. In the year up to 31 March 2005, 13 per cent of children had had three or more placements during that year, and as they grow older, looked after children have far above-average rates of failing to gain 5 A–C grade GCSEs, of becoming homeless, or going to prison. Despite the importance of contact with family, siblings and friends, over 10,000 of the children live further than 20 miles from their family home (CRAE 2007, s.49).

Bullying

Since ChildLine was set up in 1986, it has counselled over 1.5 million children, 140,000 in 2006 alone. More children are talking about bullying at and near school, and the Government tends to propose punitive responses as protections from bullying. A DfES press release dated 2 April 2007 was headed 'New disciplinary powers lay down the law for school trouble makers' and stated 'Tough new powers giving teachers' [*sic*] clear and unequivocal authority to discipline badly behaved pupils became law this week. Designed to combat disruptive, bullying or offensive behaviour, they give teachers a clear statutory right to restrain, detain and remove unruly pupils…and punish pupils for poor behaviour, not just in school, but also on the way to and from school.' During the summer of 2007, the Government published plans for school children to choose punishments for bullies, like the plans for adult communities to choose punishments for local offenders. To punish bullying with bullying tactics contravenes the UNCRC's concepts of mutual respect for everyone's worth and dignity, and reinforces cultures of violence, in contrast to positive and effective approaches reviewed later.

Non-discrimination

All the UNCRC rights apply 'without discrimination of any kind' and children shall be 'protected against all forms of discrimination or punishment on the basis of the status, activities, expressed opinions, or beliefs of the child's parents, legal guardians, or family members' (2). In cases of adoption and other alternative care, 'due regard shall be paid to the desirability of continuity in a child's upbringing and to the child's ethnic, religious, cultural and linguistic background' (20).

This right also relates to settings where babies and young children are cared for, partly to ensure reasonable continuity between home and day-care. Anti-racist measures, in matters such as books, dolls, music, pictures and home corner equipment, are also important in centres attended only by white children and adults, who otherwise learn racist attitudes (Commission for Racial Equality (CRE) 1996; Siraj-Blatchford 1996; Lane 1999; Save the Children 2000). Emily and Pauline, aged three and four years, illustrate how deeply early years centres can affect how children feel about their personal and cultural identity (Brown 1998).

Emily, Pauline and Cinderella

Emily: Let's play Cinderella.

Pauline: That's a good idea. Can I be Cinderella?

Emily: No, you can't.

Pauline: Why not?

Emily: Because you're black.

Pauline: Why can't I be Cinderella because I'm black?

Emily: 'Cos Cinderella is white in my story book and on my video.

In Northern Ireland, interviews with 352 children aged three to six years found that, from the age of three years, catholic and protestant children showed small but significant differences in their preferences for people's names and the flags that are identified with their own side, as well as in their attitudes to Orange marches and the police. And 51 per cent of three-year-olds showed they were aware of the cultural/political signifi-cance of at least one event or symbol, rising to 90 per cent of six-year-olds, particularly parades, flags and Irish dancing. Fewer children, however, clearly identified themselves with either religious community or made sec-tarian comments, although these tended to increase when they began to attend the segregated schools educating 96 per cent of children. Given this very early awareness, the researchers (Connolly, Smith and Kelly 2002) recommended education about respecting differences, and from five years onwards about understanding their own attitudes to the negative effects of prejudice in those schools which encourage cultural diversity. The London borough of Newham policy of inclusive education partly works well because disabled and able children are educated together and accept one another from the earliest years onwards (Alderson and Goodey 1998).

Children as young as four years make comments like: 'I don't like black people because they are bad on television'. Very young children are not immune to racism but can feel deeply hurt and excluded, bewildered or angry, unless they know they are valued. Black and Asian children can feel troubled about their identity in a 'white' world.

Anti-racist education aims to increase contact between people from different ethnic and cultural backgrounds by helping them to listen to one another respectfully, and to feel liked for who they are. Many young children in refugee and asylum-seeker families live in temporary housing and move on frequently, so that rapid and flexible ways of welcoming these children and their parents are especially important (Rutter and Hyder 1998).

Anti-racist practice in early years settings has been summarised (Brown 1989) as care staff promoting health and happiness by helping all young children to: feel relaxed, confident and secure; feel good about themselves and their families; feel that adults expect them to achieve and that these expectations are realistic; feel accepted and valued by other children and, in turn, to be able to reciprocate these feelings; be able to respond cooperatively to adults and to other children; trust and to feel at ease with adults; be exposed to as wide a range of suitable learning materials and situations as possible; be given encouragement and praise; be in an atmosphere in which they can feel a sense of belonging. 'When children's needs are met they blossom; when they are not, they suffer. Where there is an anti-racist approach, all children benefit. Where racism is allowed to flourish unchallenged, all children are disadvantaged' (Brown 1989).

Anti-racism can be encouraged or discouraged in many subtle ways. For example, staff may try to stop children from speaking their first language, although research suggests that they learn English more quickly when they can use both languages. Or staff may try to insist that children who eat with their fingers at home use utensils at school (Lane 1999).

Children's and parents' rights to privacy

> No child shall be subjected to arbitrary or unlawful interference with his or her privacy, family, home or correspondence, nor to unlawful attacks on his or her honour and reputation. (16.1)

> The child has the right to the protection of the law against such interference or attacks. (16.2)

The original rights to privacy and freedom from interference in personal and family life involve a balance between respecting family privacy and protecting children in families where they are neglected or abused. As mentioned earlier, in recent years there has been more state intrusion into family life, in attempts to regulate parenting and prevent early problems. In 2007 there were plans for midwives to be assigned to make extra visits to mothers from before birth onwards if their future child was expected to fail in the five Every Child Matters (ECM) outcomes (www.pm.gov.uk/ output/Page10033.asp, accessed 12 December 2007). There are questions about how far state intervention, to support but also vet parents, succeeds in protecting children and promoting better parenting. There is a long history of the state providing advice for 'feckless' mothers but failing to relieve poverty (Mayall and Foster 1989; Hendrick 2003). There are reports of mothers fearing to ask health and social services for help, because they are afraid their children will be taken away from them (Robinson 2004). There are also concerns that parents' intuition and confidence are undermined by professional advisers (Ferudi 2001; House 2003) and that standardised advice is too crude and disrespectful of delicate, individual, complex parent–child relationships (Mayall 1993; Brooker 2006).

A major part of ECM is comprehensive databases. ContactPoint (Children Act 2004, s.12) will hold personal and family details of every child. Around 330,000 practitioners will have access to the data, to promote effective care and information-sharing across education, health, welfare and youth justice services (HM Treasury *et al.* 2003). It is said that the database will prevent tragedies such as Victoria Climbié's. However, she was known to, and had records kept by, several services, and this did not prevent her death. Local authorities will also keep electronic Common Assessment Frameworks (eCAFs), for possibly one-third of all children, if they do not seem to be progressing towards the ECM five outcomes. CAFs record data on all aspects of the child's life and assess parental competence. They aim to promote integrated multidisciplinary care and to provide early interventions for potential problems.

Among the critics of the database plans are the Parliamentary Joint Committee on Human Rights, the Information Commissioner, and Action on Rights for Children (ARCH) which raised the following concerns (Dowty 2007):

- ContactPoint will interfere with rights under the 1998 Human Rights Act Article 8 on privacy and family human rights, and the 1998 Data Protection Act. from which the databases will be exempt.

- Surveys show that many children do not want teachers, social workers and others sharing details about them. When they do not trust adults to respect confidentiality, and are unwilling to confide in them, children have less access to help and protection.

- Some children in greatest need will not be protected or entered on the database when, like Victoria Climbié, they do not have a settled address and are expected to leave this country soon.

- Practitioners will be too busy entering, updating and scanning endless data to notice the children most at risk, or to have time to meet and work with them.

- Government databases are unreliable, so it would be dangerous to rely on ContactPoint to protect children.

- The databases are hugely expensive to set up, repair, maintain and to keep all entries accurate and up to date. They exceed their initial budgets by billions of pounds, and soak up funds needed for direct care.

- ContactPoint plans involve health visitors, midwives and social workers reporting early problems more often. Yet already these services are 'stretched to breaking point', seriously understaffed and under-funded, facing funding cuts, and unable to give enough support to families with severe and complex needs.

- 'At risk' no longer means 'at risk of significant harm from abuse or neglect' (child-centred protection), but 'at risk' of poor outcomes, or of committing crime (society-centred protection).

To summarise, ContactPoint and ECM appear to centre less on child protection than on protecting society from the costs of failing children who may become low earning, dependent or criminal adults. 'There is little point in investing in IT systems to facilitate assessment of an estimated 3–4 million children's needs if the required services are inadequately funded or unobtainable' (Dowty 2007).

There are also concerns that ContactPoint will be so expensive that, to help to fund it, data may be sold to commercial and research interests, and also that it will be linked to other huge databases. This could increase

far the UNCRC endorses appropriate or unhelpful and abusive
consult, protect and provide for them. I am not going to attempt
in this short book extremely serious and extensive global ques-
but children's conditions, in this case hazardous and exploitative
though a few examples will be reviewed later.

andards of health and safety

xt examples may seem comparatively parochial and trivial. Adults
easingly worried about many risks, not only actual but also count-
ential dangers. A broad range of 'green' risks is linked to nature and
outside: getting cold or wet or dirty; picking up infections from the
d, water, animals, dog dirt, or dirty needles hidden in fallen leaves;
s from falls, bites and stings, conkers or poisonous berries.

n safety standards, an important problem in many, perhaps most,
ries is when working conditions illustrate the differences between
ctions for adults and for children. Children at school, because they do
ount as workers or have trade unions and laws to defend them, have
r standards for health and safety than their teachers would tolerate.
example is school toilets. The Welsh Children's Rights Commissioner
nsored research which found that 40 per cent of children tended to
until they arrived home to use the toilet because they found the ones
hool too dirty or dangerous (Barnes and Maddocks 2002). Children in
gland have similar problems. For example, in order to stop reported
lying or vandalism in the toilets, some schools insist that children sign a
m whenever they use the toilet, but many children feel too embarrassed
do so. Their discomfort is increased when they avoid drinking fluids all
y too, and is not conducive to being able to concentrate on schoolwork
Mayall et al. 1996). Some children do not dare to raise their hand and ask
r permission to go to the toilet during class, a ritual that is not necessary
all schools. Teachers sometimes dismiss school councils as a waste of
ime: 'All they want to talk about is the toilets'. Yet the teachers would
robably react in the same way if their toilets were of a similar low
standard. One comment might be, 'Teachers keep their toilets clean and
children should too'. Children do so in many schools where there are
enough well designed and well situated toilets.

government surveillance, along with the detection and prevention of crime
and fraud. Critics question whether the benefits of ContactPoint will be far
outweighed by the risks, costs and loss of personal rights and freedoms.
During the week this page was written, the headline news included the
trial of a mother who had allegedly murdered her young child. Social
services had been by alerted by neighbours, and visited the house but
failed to save her life, suggesting that they are already so over-burdened
that the extra workload demanded by ContactPoint could reduce rather
than increase their efficiency.

Further invasions of privacy are that Britain has the most dense CCTV
cover in the world. Monitors are even placed in school toilets. Schools use
biometric systems, such as fingerprints in canteens and libraries, to
monitor children's choices of meals and book. As this book is published in
2008, there is no statutory regulation of the use of these devices. ARCH
(2007) and others question the disregard for children's civil rights, the lack
of children's and parents' informed consent, and the risks of habituating
children to the use of their biometrics when this is not essential. There are
also risks of identity theft and fraud, and of records being corrupted or
used in organised crime when every day at least one school is burgled.

Drugs and sex

> States Parties shall take all appropriate measures, including legisla-
> tive, administrative, social and educational measures, to protect
> children from the illicit use of narcotic drugs and psychotropic sub-
> stances as defined in the relevant international treaties, and to prevent
> the use of children in the illicit production and trafficking of such
> substances. (33)

These are matters that might seem remote from babies and young children.
However, illicit drugs affect children in several ways, including: the
poverty and violence which trading with drugs brings into homes and
local communities; the difficulties that some, but not all, addicted parents
have in caring for their children; and the serious medical problems for
babies born to addicted mothers.

The UNCRC includes rights to protection from sexual abuse, exploitation and pornography (34), trafficking and abduction (35), and all other

forms of exploitation (36). Young children are vulnerable to all these abuses; babies may be trafficked from before birth and also used in pornography. CRAE (2007) criticises the Government for putting immigration control before the protection of extremely distressed children.

Hazardous work

The UNCRC is criticised for not recognising sufficiently the rights of children who work in and around the home doing domestic work and caring for younger children and for sick and disabled relatives, those who work on the streets, in factories, shops, markets and restaurants, and those who sort through rubbish tips. In all countries, young children do many kinds of 'adult' work and help to support their families (Ennew and Morrow 1994; Mizen, Pole and Bolton 2001; Punch 2001; Qvortrup 2001; Katz 2004; Liebel 2004; Qvortrup 2005). Their hard work at school (on which all societies' future depends) and at home is often not recognised or valued as 'work'.

However, the UNCRC does not specifically ban child work, although this is often alleged.

> 1. States Parties recognize the right of the child to be protected from economic exploitation and from performing any work that is likely to be hazardous or to interfere with the child's education, or to be harmful to the child's health or physical, mental, spiritual, moral or social development. 2. States Parties shall take legislative, administrative, social and educational measures to ensure the implementation of the present article. To this end, and having regard to the relevant provisions of other international instruments, States Parties shall in particular: (a) Provide for a minimum age or minimum ages for admission to employment; (b) Provide for appropriate regulation of the hours and conditions of employment; (c) Provide for appropriate penalties or other sanctions to ensure the effective enforcement of the present article.' (32)

'Child labour' is a vague term ranging from hazardous exploitative labour to work that children in every country want and need to do (Ingenhorst 2001; Mansurov 2001; Mizen et al. 2001). Campaigns to end all child labour and all importing of goods made by children ignore several reali-

ties. Millions of children need to work v their parents do not earn a living wage t needs. Many children combine work and school if they earn enough to pay for scho tend to prefer to work in factories, making than beg, pick rubbish heaps or do sex wo work is the International Labour Organisat adults' trade unions. The campaigns against 'n have more to do with protecting adult workers by child workers than with directly protectin achieved by campaigning first for all parents to trying to end children's paid employment. Work shown by the history of trade unions' long working conditions and fair pay. The useful p working age (32, 2a) can unfortunately mean t workers who are below that age do not have any that older children and adult workers have (Hanso Invernizzi and Milne (2002) explore complication child workers and also to respect and involve them.

Ennew (2002) contends that the ILO and UNCI concept of helpless dependent domesticated children sets working and street children 'outside childhood' a She explains how the rights in 27 out of 40 UNCRC a street children, and she critically reviews Hart's (1992) paigning political work of the Brazilian movement of st 8 to 16 years. Ennew proposes new rights for street include rights: not to be labelled; to be correctly describec counted; to fair work conditions and wages; to have th systems respected; to have appropriate and relevant serv tected from secondary exploitation (voyeurism) and from ha 'caring' social agencies. A separate convention could im children do not need these rights and that they are someho able when 'inside' this constructed childhood. Ennew's im highlights the concerns of especially disadvantaged children vance of the UNCRC to them, and therefore to all chil depends, however, on how narrowly or broadly the UNCRC interpreted when assessing their relevance to particular groups o

and how efforts to to cover tions ab work, a

Basic s
The ne are inc less po being groun injurie
O count prote not lowe
One spo wai at s En bu fo to d (N fo i t

Armed conflict

> Children under 15 years should be protected from taking a direct part in armed hostilities. (38.2)

Being a child soldier is an extremely hazardous form of child labour. The UNCRC aims for protection of all children affected by armed conflict (38.4), and support for the recovery of children who have been victims of any form of harm in order to foster the 'health, self-respect and dignity of the child' (39). War zones have moved from battlefields and into villages, towns and cities, and war mainly occurs in countries with the highest proportion of young people. Over 60 per cent of Baghdad residents are aged under 21, and the hospitals keep filling with injured and dying children.

Some children aged seven or eight years join as child soldiers, and many older girl soldiers have babies who have to live an army life if they survive. Some children are abducted and forced to become soldiers, but others join armies in order to escape from poverty or violence at home, or in the hope of earning money for their family, or to revenge relatives murdered by an opposing army, sometimes to fight for justice, or in search of a group to belong to. Protecting children from becoming soldiers therefore involves addressing all these reasons that feed children and young people into armies all over the world (Brett and Specht 2004).

Research on children

Another hazard can come from research on children. While the results of much research, if implemented, can benefit countless children, the process of collecting data and testing medicines or services may pose risks. In the past, children tended to be protected from social research by being excluded and therefore silenced. Today they are much more able to comment on and influence policies and services and they are more involved in testing new drugs, as well as drugs prescribed for adults but with as yet unclear evidence about their effects on babies and children. Alderson and Morrow (2004) review a wide range of ethics guidelines and also risks and benefits that can arise at every stage of research on children from first plans to final dissemination, how to review these, and how to protect children through enabling them and/or their parents to give voluntary and informed consent.

Ecological change

There is growing concern that climate change will soon be the greatest
threat to everyone's wellbeing and survival (Lynas 2007; Monbiot 2007).
Already, mainly in poorer societies, people are facing unprecedented
droughts, fires and floods that can destroy their homes, animals and crops.
The present 6.5 billion people on the planet are set to increase to 9 billion
by 2050, while dwindling supplies of fresh water, oil and habitable and ag-
ricultural land are already leading to increasing poverty, armed conflict and
forced migration. There is not space here to cover this huge topic, but it is
too crucial to omit and it has added effects on children – the 10 per cent of
the world's population aged 0–4 years, the 10 per cent aged 5–9 years, and
the 19 per cent aged 10–19 years. These are estimates, given that over 40
million births per annum are never registered. The youngest children are
likely to have the fewest years in which to enjoy present standards of life,
but a longer future lifespan in which to try to cope with the many predicted
destructive effects of climate change. The Green Economics Institute
and Journal provides useful multidisciplinary analysis and introductory
contacts, meetings and further reading (see www.greeneconomics.org.uk).

Protective justice

Rights are devices to safeguard governments' respect for citizens, through
the law courts if necessary. Protection rights are especially vital for the
victims of crime, and also for those alleged or accused of committing
crimes. Children aged ten years can be tried in the English adult Crown
Courts and imprisoned, and this book is about children aged eight years
and under. However, many of the UNCRC protective justice rights also
apply to younger children, and it seems that growing concern about 'criminal' ten-year-olds is transferring down towards younger children.

In the UNCRC, children who are alleged or accused of offending have
the adult rights: 'to be presumed innocent until proved guilty' (40.2.b.i);
'to have parental and legal support before and during a hearing' (40.2.b.ii);
'to have the matter determined without delay by a competent, independent
and impartial authority or judicial body in a fair hearing according to law'
(40.2.b.iii); 'not to be compelled to give testimony or to confess guilt; to
examine or have examined adverse witnesses and to obtain the participation and examination of witnesses on his or her behalf under conditions of

equality' (40.2.b.iv); 'to have the free assistance of an interpreter if the child cannot understand or speak the language used' (40.2.b.vi); 'to have his or her privacy fully respected at all stages of the proceedings' (40.2.b.vii).

> Whenever appropriate and desirable, [there shall be] measures for dealing with such children without resorting to judicial proceedings, providing that human rights and legal safeguards are fully respected. (40.3.b)

> A variety of dispositions, such as care, guidance and supervision orders; counselling; probation; foster care; education and vocational training programmes and other alternatives to institutional care shall be available to ensure that children are dealt with in a manner appropriate to their well-being and proportionate both to their circumstances and the offence. (40.4)

These formal rights may seem rather extreme for young children, but when they face serious inquiries in schools or the family courts about their behaviour or residence, they surely need at least as much protection as older children and respect for their UNCRC rights, in articles 12 and 40, to be heard, to question witnesses, and to have an independent hearing. For centuries these human rights were fought for by adults who knew the severe and even fatal effects of injustice, and the vital need for due process of law to protect victims of crime and also people who might be unfairly accused, tried, imprisoned and punished.

The UNCRC states that children who are alleged to have committed, or accused of committing, an offence shall 'be treated in a manner consistent with the promotion of the child's sense of dignity and worth, which reinforces the child's respect for the human rights and fundamental freedoms of others and which takes into account the child's age and the desirability of promoting the child's reintegration and the child's assuming a constructive role in society' (40.1). 'The establishment of a minimum age below which children shall be presumed not to have the capacity to infringe the penal law' is required (40.3.a). At ten years, England has one of the lowest minimum ages in the world. Since the Bulger case in 1993, when two ten-year-olds murdered a younger boy, there has been much discussion about young children being capable of evil and requiring harsh punishments and deterrents. This is in contrast to far less punitive and more rehabilitative approaches, for example, in Norway where a similar murder occurred at about the same time (James and Jenks 1996).

'Tough on crime'

There is concern that children are being over-regulated and criminalised, that is, unduly regarded as potentially or actually criminals with the increased risk that they will become criminals (Goldson and Peters 2000; James and James 2004, pp.169–88; Davies and McMahon 2007). Levels of crime in the UK have fallen over the past three decades while punishment and imprisonment rates have soared. The Government is being 'tough on crime', but less so on 'the causes of crime', such as poverty, cramped housing and violent estates, failing schools, poor employment prospects, and lack of the activities and safe, interesting spaces for children and young people to meet that are to be found in low-crime affluent areas. Paradoxically, the Government's policies to reduce crime appear to increase anxiety and complaints about crime, as well as conflicts between neighbours, and between age groups, with predominantly older people complaining about children's noise and behaviour. Children are often the victims of crime, but 95 per cent of crimes committed against children and young people are not reported (Hall 2001).

Antisocial behaviour

Since 1997, over 3000 new offences have been created in English law, stretching crime to include antisocial behaviour such as dropping litter. Children can be found guilty following hearsay from absent witnesses who claim to *feel* anxious or harassed – claims that require no supporting evidence. Parents of these children aged under ten years who have been found to misbehave can be fined, given parenting orders, even imprisoned, and whole familes can be evicted. The Antisocial Behaviour Act 2003 allows fast-track eviction of families for the very vaguely and broadly defined anti-social behaviour. From October 2003 to September 2006, there were 1720 such evictions (CRAE 2007, s.195).

Laws appear to protect older citizens and commercial interests before children's interests. For example, although children aged under ten years cannot be served with Antisocial Behaviour Orders (ASBOs), they can incur crime safety orders, piloted parental compensation orders with fines of up to £5000, even if their child is being looked after by the local authority, and local child curfew schemes (Crime and Disorder Act 1998, s.14) if they are not under the supervision of a responsible adult between 9 p.m. and 6 a.m. In 2000, blanket curfews were introduced on areas, even for innocent children. If children breach the curfew, parents face fines of up to £1000 and possible imprisonment, with children being looked after by the local authority. Curfew rules were extended in the Antisocial Behaviour Act 2003, s.30. The 'mosquito antisocial device', used in shopping centres to reduce crime by deterring young people, emits a high-pitched sound, too high for adults to hear, but heard by young people who quickly leave the area, and 3300 devices were sold by March 2007 (Ward 2007). Babies may be even more distressed by the noise than older children, but adults may be unaware of the problem.

The 2004 Antisocial Behaviour Act allows fast-track evictions of families if any member, in the terms of the Crime and Disorder Act 1998 s.1, has acted 'in a manner that caused or was likely to cause harassment, alarm or distress to one or more persons' in another household. The family is deemed 'intentionally homeless' with no obligation for the local authority to find them housing (CRAE 2007, s. 62). Evictions may follow neighbours' complaints about children's noise or ball games, and parents report being afraid to let their children play outside, although children say that their first preference is playing with friends in the street (Children's Play Council and The Children's Society 2003). Evictions, and the threat of evictions, apply only to tenants, not to mortgage holders, and therefore mainly affect disadvantaged families.

The courts

Children's cases, including decisions about adoption, and where children will live when families separate, are heard in family courts in order to protect children from very intimidating adult courtrooms, adversarial inquiry, and public reporting. This can be a benefit when specialists take account of children's youth, their fear, inexperience and heavily dependent status. Yet, despite these protections, research reviews have found that the views of children aged under eight years are seldom heard during family court cases (Thomas 2002; Winter 2006a, 2006b; CRAE 2007). And there is a paradox that, although adversarial barristers are frightening, they can also be protective, when they insist on justice by scrutinising and challenging evidence and hearing different viewpoints.

This was shown during 2006, with expert medical witnesses to the family courts. They advise, for example, when a child might or might not have been injured or killed by the parents, and therefore if parents should be imprisoned or their other children adopted. Professor Meadows' expert medical opinion was found to be incorrect, and innocent mothers were wrongly imprisoned. (Some have since been released.) It was argued that these cases could have been served more justly if they had been heard in the adult criminal courts, with critical barristers, mass media reporting, more transparent open inquiry and higher standards demanded of the evidence, instead of in the secretive family courts. Parents may not discuss their case in public.

Stricter inquiry, while carefully protecting children's anonymity, might also assist in the rising numbers of adoptions. There were 3800 adoptions in England in the period 2003–4 and also in 2004–5, a rise of 37 per cent per annum since 1998. In 2002, the Government set a target of a 50 per cent increase in adoptions of looked after children by 2006, a huge cost saving for tax payers. The aim was to find families for children who might spend years being looked after by local authorities. However, it is alleged that in attempts to meet the targets, social workers are increasing the numbers of newborn babies removed from their parents. CRAE (2007, s. 49) challenges this target, which can involve removing children from parents when they long to stay together. Children have no power to veto their adoption, and no right to information about their birth family until they are 18 years old, a breach of UNCRC articles 3 and 9, among others.

Prisons

'No child shall be deprived of his or her liberty unlawfully or arbitrarily' (37.b). 'Every child deprived of liberty shall be treated with humanity and respect for the inherent dignity of the human person' (37). State parties shall 'take all appropriate measures to promote physical and psychological recovery and social reintegration of a child victim' after neglect or abuse, cruel treatment or armed conflict (39).

Prison sentencing of adults takes no account that prisoners' children may suffer even more punishment and deprivation than their parents, and with subsequent increased risks that they too will be led into crime. (These points are not made to excuse crimes, or to dismiss the agency of many adults and children and their ability to make informed moral choices, but to try to understand and explain crime, the pressures that limit people's choices, and possible ways to prevent further crime through UNCRC principles.) Although babies can stay in prison with their mother, they have to leave at an age when close contact with their mother is still crucial, and families are not helped in their 'social reintegration'. In 2007, only 5 per cent of the 18,000 children whose mothers were in prison could remain in their own home (Corston 2007). Often they lose their siblings, school, neighbourhood, friendships, belongings and, presumably, their sense of identity. Many of the soaring numbers of young people who are in prison are also parents (Katz 2002), and many women are imprisoned for reasons such as debt or petty theft, associated with poverty among young and single parent families. One-quarter of women in British prisons are 'drug mules', smuggling drugs into this country for payment, which they usually need urgently in order to repay debts and provide for their children who live mainly in the Caribbean or Africa (Durendt 2007).

Ramsden (1998) interviewed children aged four to 14 years who had one parent in prison. They spoke of their worry about being teased, losing friends, and being labelled themselves as bad. Children react differently. One six-year-old painted a face behind bars, suggesting perhaps that she wanted to talk to her teacher; another seemed to want to ignore the reality that her mother was in prison as much as she could; others were tearful or angry, showing that adults who hope to help them must first listen to children about how they would like to be supported.

Refugees and asylum seekers and trafficked children

Protective justice rights in the UNCRC also apply to refugees and detained asylum seekers of all ages. However, each government is allowed to have a reservation against certain UNCRC articles, and the UK Government rejects article 22, which respects the rights of refugee children to special protection and to be with their family. The Government, when ratifying the UNCRC, stated that it 'reserves the right' to control 'entry into, stay in, 're from' the UK. Refugee children may be separated by their parents, kept in detention centres and deported (CRAE , s. 47–50; CRAE 2007, s. 36–41, 156–8). In 2004, failed asylum seekers began to be charged for health care, including maternity care. Immigration control takes priority over children's rights in articles 22, 30, 32–6, 37b–d, 38, 39 and 40 (CRAE 2007, s. 221–45), over their rights to education, an adequate standard of living, welfare support and protection. Their parents' right to work was removed in 2003. The most vulnerable are the unaccompanied children, those whose parents are imprisoned without them, and trafficked children. They may not have a social worker. For many, accommodation is inadequate, and local authorities say that funding from the Home Office is also inadequate (Save the Children 2005c). The Refugee Council reported in 2007 that 2000 children who have fled persecution are locked up in UK detention centres each year. In March and April 2006, two breastfeeding mothers were held at Yarl's Wood immigration removal centre for days without their babies. For a series of other severe problems for young refugees and asylum seekers, which breach the UNCRC, see Candappa (2002), and CRAE (2006, 2007).

Are children being overprotected?

Many children need stronger protections from neglect and abuse. However, in the daily lives of well cared for children, the examples in the Introduction of Albert Parr, able at four years old to walk around his town, and Kevin and Alan, afraid to walk down their own street alone, illustrate their lost freedoms. When children and adults feel that it is wrong for children to walk around freely, then children may not know how to find their way around their local area. I recently met a 'lost' child aged about five years and walked around the streets with her to help her to find her way home. I was not sure if she was more terrified of being lost, or of me as a stranger, or of being found and then being blamed and punished. Her mother was very anxious and angry when we met her. In Britain and the USA, older generations remember having more freedoms, and younger generations assume adults must constantly control young children (Hillman 2003), whereas children in many other countries tend to be able to roam more freely.

If children aged four and five years are mainly confined to home, nursery, school and car, seldom allowed to learn to cope on their own, their inability to cope could be said to be imposed on them, or ascribed to them. It may then be assumed to be inevitable, part of their slow biological maturing, instead of part of social inexperience. Media panics about the very few lost or murdered young children make responsible adults, and also children, very anxious. I was surprised at some of the responses, when interviewing children, about their fears of being kidnapped or killed on their local streets. Some children in fortress schools seemed uncertain whether the security was to keep bad adults out or bad children in. Parents in the UK and US are increasingly using 'nanny-cams' and fitments on mobile phones to keep guard on their children by remote control (Katz 2005).

Who benefits from this anxious vigilance? The murder rate of young children outside their homes has hardly changed over 30 years whereas, inside the home, each week one or two children die from abuse or neglect, and they need neighbours and friends to listen to them before it is too late. Efforts to protect children with 'say no to strangers' campaigns can un-helpfully discourage children from approaching helpful neighbours.

Another paradox is when parents protect their children by driving them around in cars, but add to traffic levels and dangers, and reduce the children's chances to learn about road safety skills and their neighbour-hood. Britain has the highest rate of serious injury and death of children on the roads in Europe. With the increase in paid childcare, young children spend more time in groups, and with paid carers who are liable to be even more anxious about safety than parents have to be. These factors can further reduce children's freedoms to roam, to play out with friends on their own, to explore, climb, run, take small risks and test out their growing physical strength and skills, have adventures and fun and feel fully alive with excitement and growing confidence. 'Don't run, watch out you'll fall', 'Don't go on that [very low] ledge, it's dangerous', are constant refrains in childcare settings. While safety is extremely important, no one appears to benefit when over-restriction and anxiety can undermine adults' and children's confidence in children's abilities, skills and good sense, leaving children bored and frustrated, timid or rebellious (Lindon 2003).

Why are children overprotected?

If the benefits to children of reasonable protection are at times overtaken by the dis-benefits of overprotection, well beyond protections in other countries or in Britain in the past, why is this happening? One possible pressure is psychological, when overprotection is part of the triangle game made up of rescuer, victim, persecutor (Berne 1968). An adult rescues a victim child from bullying and then blames the bully, who was the persecutor but now becomes the victim, and so the game goes round. Berne suggested that authentic relationships move beyond games and respect everyone equally as strong and reliable as far as possible. When children are respected and have space and freedom to play, schools have found that bullying does not occur (Cleves School 1999; Vaughan 2006). Iona Opie (1993), who spent decades observing countless children playing, saw that crowded playgrounds incite bullying, but in the open countryside children of different ages and away from adults tend to play together peacefully.

Berne's analysis can also refer to the feelings of parents and staff, who tend to feel highly responsible but fairly powerless, and potential victims of hostile publicity and blame if they take risks. Adults are then liable to confine children still more. Vulnerable children can be seen as threatened by dangers but also as threats to adults' security. Adults' over-vigilance protects children, and also adults themselves, from their own fears of risk and blame, of being sacked or sued.

Fears are increased by commercial pressures from advertising and mass media articles and programmes about child safety, from firms that produce security and safety equipment, insurance, and childcare services (Ball 2007), which 'responsible' teachers and parents are made to feel they must buy. There are policies to keep children out of public spaces, such as the use of mosquito devices, in order to increase commercial efficiency and adult convenience. Parents and children alike hear frightening news on the radio and television at all hours of children being lost, abducted, tortured and murdered. Behind each caring protector and protected child are powerful commercial, media and political pressures, which are not necessarily interested in children's rights.

Why are children under-protected?

In contrast to 'the terrors of hyper-vigilance' (Katz 2005), often against small risks, the death, injury and loss for countless children across the world signify that many of them lack protection against great dangers. Why are these children's protection rights still so often disrespected? At the personal level, as already mentioned, parents are expected to be the primary protectors, and when they do not, or cannot, protect their child there may be no adequate alternative protector. At the global level, millions of adults are not safe from severe harm and injustice, and children can be still more vulnerable – as members of poor, minority, excluded and immigrant groups; missing out on education and the prospects of secure well paid work; lacking the confidence, authority, contacts and sometimes the language, the cultural capital (Bourdieu 1997), which help when challenging injustice and inequality.

Individuals and groups can be harmed, either deliberately by *commission*, or indirectly, perhaps unintentionally, by *omission*. Would anyone deliberately plan for 1.2 billion people to live in dire poverty, for example? The Nobel laureate economist Joseph Stiglitz (2002) reviews how poor people, including billions of children, are extremely harmed by much global policy making controlled by the International Monetary Fund (IMF). Set up in 1944 to help to prevent and reduce poverty, the IMF, in Stiglitz's view, increases rather than reduces poverty. He outlines the dominant 'neo-liberal' policy, which aims as quickly as possible to: privatise banks, industry and services (such as water, health care and phone lines); reduce 'interference' from government policies, industries, services and supports; raise interest rates, taxes, school and health care fees; ensure low wages for workers and clear inequality between rich and poor. People are blamed for being poor because of personal limitations, accused of being lazy, inept, dishonest, criminal, lacking intelligence, or because of a 'culture of poverty' through their negative beliefs and behaviours and welfare dependence (Penn 2005). Stiglitz explains how IMF policies (and those of the USA and to some extent the UK) therefore aim to make everyone want and need to work hard, and so to promote social stability, employment, production, trade, exports, profits and wealth, which in time will trickle down from rich to poor and benefit everyone.

However, Stiglitz himself advocates more caution, still aiming to promote social stability, employment, production, trade, exports, profits and wealth, but in the following ways. Let industry and markets grow more slowly as new jobs are created. Keep some government control, both to ensure some equality and supports (benefits, pension) for the poorest groups, and to guide the growing economy in everyone's best interests. Keep down income gaps between the very rich and very poor in order to promote social harmony. Invest in free schooling and in universities so that future workers can enter more highly paid knowledge and technology careers.

Stiglitz shows how the extreme and dominant IMF policies have terrible effects on poor countries. He argues that the IMF sets its aims, to promote wealth tomorrow, far above thinking about the suffering of poor people today. The IMF even sees social suffering as evidence of progress – 'no pain, no gain' – and as the only way forward. Many global and national economic policies harm poor groups, including children.

Penn (2005, pp.19–44) criticises Northern policies to reduce poverty by early childhood interventions forced on to poorer peoples in the North and the South. Children can be desperately poor in the rich USA and UK, whereas some of the poorest countries – Mongolia and Cuba – can provide high quality early years services. Some people living in absolute life-threatening chronic poverty can live with hope and dignity, whereas others feel overcome with despair or anger. People's agency matters, as well as the political and economic stuctures and contexts. We need to know far more about the complex, varied, local patterns of poverty in order to avoid 'Alice in Wonderland logic', and 'evidence' and generalisations (Penn 2005, p.41). When poverty is structured by social class, early years education targeted at poor children, especially if it is low quality, can bring little economic change.

UNCRC Article 3 states: 'In all actions concerning children, whether undertaken by public or private social welfare institutions, courts of law, administrative authorities or legislative bodies, the best interests of the child shall be a primary consideration'. While respecting the rights and duties of parents and other responsible adults, 'State Parties undertake to ensure the child such protection and care as is necessary for his or her well-being…and, to this end, shall take all appropriate legislative and administrative measures' (3). They shall also 'undertake all appropriate legislative, administrative and other measures, for the implementation of the rights [in the UNCRC]. With regard to economic, social and cultural rights, State Parties shall undertake such measures to the maximum extent of their available resources and, where needed, within the framework of international co-operation' (4).

The power of UNCRC lies in each of the 192 states that have ratified the Convention being answerable to honour and implement it in all matters affecting children. This means practically every policy made, every law passed and every service provided. Yet today, so much policy is regional (European, African) or global (IMF, World Bank, ILO, multinational companies) that a government's powers are limited. Real protection from poverty, neglect and abuse will begin when children are recognised as valued world citizens with UNCRC rights in all international, as well as national, economic policies. Alston, Tobin and Darrow (2005, p.xii) advise that agencies such as the IMF and World Bank 'should adopt official policy statements affirming their commitments to children's rights and the CRC'. However, the first step, at both local and global levels, is to recognise each child as a person who matters as much as each adult – the topic for the next two chapters.

CHAPTER THREE

Children's
Participation Rights

The first time we talk to them they don't listen. The second time we talk they start listening. The third time we talk they start to act. (A Dalit child in Nepal working to promote access to primary school, Save the Children 2003)

Provision and protection rights enjoy wide support, but participation rights are seen as more controversial, although all three kinds of rights can overlap and be complementary. Children's rights are carefully qualified in the UNCRC to defend the interests of children, adults and society. As formal entitlements, rights protect children from having to rely on adults happening to be kind, although rights also support such kindness. Rights complement welfare measures, and they show how young children can actively participate in their family and community life.

The African Charter on the Rights and Welfare of the Child, adopted by the Organisation of African Unity (OAU) (1990) and entered into force in 1999, goes beyond the UNCRC in saying 'Every child shall have responsibilities towards his family and society, the State and other legally recognised communities and the international community'. 'The duty' is explained in detail, for example, '(a) To work for the cohesion of the family, to respect his parents, superiors and elders at all times and to assist them in case of need... (c) To preserve and strengthen social and national solidarity...' (article 31). The Charter complements the UNCRC, but lays greater emphasis on the UNCRC's principles of solidarity and interdependence, as discussed, for example, in the special issue about the Charter of the *International Journal of Children's Rights* (2002, 10, 2).

Later chapters will consider methods, stages, levels and further examples of participation, besides the risks of involving young children. This chapter briefly reviews a range of UNCRC participation rights, their importance and advantages, including the rights: to life and optimal development; to a name, identity and family; to form and express views; to respect for the child's evolving capacities; to be heard during procedures; to freedom of expression and information; to freedom of thought, conscience and religion; to freedom of association and peaceful assembly; to respectful mass media; to inclusive communities.

What is participation?

Participation means taking part, and is a very broad concept. Children take part in countless activities and relationships, in pairs or groups – playing games, digging ponds, acting, learning, cooking and caring for other people and animals. However, reports about participation often reduce it into two main areas: being consulted and making decisions. This narrows participation down from generally *doing* into specifically *talking, thinking and deciding*.

The transfer during the twentieth century for most adults in the richer minority world[1] from manual work to desk and computer-based and committee work is reflected in children's schooling (Qvortrup 1997, 2005). Practical lessons have been replaced with theory, text, talk and virtual or computer-based ones. So to define participation mainly in terms of children influencing or making decisions is part of the general minority world transfer from doing to talking.

There is an assumed format that adults are mainly in control. They choose the questions to be decided, sometimes raise funding for formal consultation, and they instruct and control the process of deciding. The

---

1   The terms 'minority world' for the 17 per cent of people who live in the richer nations, and 'majority world' for the rest, avoid and question the assumptions behind the terms 'first and third world' or 'developed and undeveloped/developing' world.

success of participation is seen to depend on the *process* of how far adults allow children to contribute to, influence and perhaps make decisions, and the *outcome* of how far decisions are acted on – mainly by adults. Like adults, children tend to have more influence over their own personal decisions than over group decisions and efforts to change the world. However, large agencies, such as government departments and non-governmental organisations (NGOs), are increasingly concerned to consult and involve children in effective and fair ways. Each UK government department now has an action plan on involving children in policy and service development, though no-one coordinates or monitors these the plans (CRAE 2007, s. 64). For example, the main Department concerned – for Children, Schools and Families – issued a report *Every Parent Matters* (DfES/DCSF 2007a), which mentions the rights only of working parents, not of children. Thinking, talking and deciding will be covered later, but the first participation rights in this chapter are mainly about being and doing.

Right to life and to optimal development

'Every child has the inherent right to life' (6)[2] and to 'care as is necessary for his or her well-being' (3). State parties 'shall ensure to the maximum extent possible the survival and development of the child' (6).

These rights, to participate as a member of the human race, make all other rights possible. Rights are conditional rather than absolute. Sadly, even the right to life is counterbalanced, for example, by rights to maximum survival and development and to protection from torture. Such conflicts occur when babies and children are so ill or impaired, or their medical treatment is so painful, that the responsible adults may have to consider when to allow the child to die (Wyatt and Alderson 2005; Alderson, Hawthorne and Killen, 2006). Article 6 overlaps with provision rights (Chapter 1).

2   Figures in brackets refer to the relevant article of the 1989 Convention.

Name, identity and family

Name

'The child shall be registered immediately after birth and shall have the right to a name, the right to acquire a nationality and, as far as possible, the right to know and be cared for by his or her parents' (7).

The right to a name involves other people in respecting the child's full name and not altering it, such as by shortening it or using a nickname against the child's wishes. Respect includes spelling and pronouncing the name properly, and not mixing up the personal and family name, as European people sometimes do with Asian names. The Muslim name Tahir, for example, begins with a sound between Th and D so that it takes some practice for European people to pronounce the name well. Mispronunciation can be especially offensive if it creates another word in the original language, and if the name has a religious meaning (Lane 1999).

Identity

The child has the right 'to preserve his or her identity, including nationality, name and family relations' (8). And if the child is illegally deprived of these, there should be help 'with a view to speedily re-establishing his or her identity' (8). Children have the right to know about their birth parents' identity after separation, adoption or assisted reproduction (7–10).

Do babies have identities? What does identity mean? How can identity be a legal right? Identity is often thought of as being gradually formed and changed over a lifetime, which suggests that babies start from zero without an identity. The UNCRC Preamble recognises that: 'for the full and harmonious development of [their] personality [children] should grow up in a family environment...of happiness, love and understanding'. The UNCRC is about helping parents to provide these good things, but cannot enforce them as rights. So what are the enforceable rights relating to identity?

Identity means the condition of being a specified, identifiable person, in two opposite senses: being identified as a member of a group (such as the whole human family, or an ethnic or cultural group) and also as a unique separate individual (Jenkins 2004). The UNCRC rights to a name and a nationality identify each child as a unique individual (first name) and a group member (family name).

In the legal UNCRC meaning, identity is mainly a conferred status in how other people recognise and identify – or ignore – the child. For centuries, the law tended to treat children as their father's property, not as identified separate persons. In order to be able to respect, protect and provide for the rights of all their children, states must first identify and register them.

When does identity begin? The UNCRC Preamble recognises 'the inherent dignity, and the equal and inalienable rights of all members of the human family'. A legal identity is the key or passport to state services, and is fully developed from birth; it is not earned or developed. Besides providing services to children and their families, states must hold back from harming or interfering with them. They must 'respect the right of the child to preserve his or her identity…without unlawful interference' (article 8), a basic privacy right (Woodiwiss 2005, p.xii). The UNCRC mentions children's identity solely in terms of preserving and respecting it (articles 8 and 29).

> Where a child is illegally deprived of some or all of the elements of his or her identity, State Parties shall provide appropriate assistance and protection, with a view to speedily re-establishing his or her identity. (article 8)

In contrast, the UNCRC speaks of the development of the child's personality and abilities, and of 'physical, mental, spiritual, moral and social development' (Preamble, articles 18, 23, 27, 29, 32). Personality and personhood are closely linked to how people perceive and relate to, respect or disrespect, people's identities. Unfortunately, respect tends to correlate with age and maturity, unlike the UNCRC's vision of equal respect for everyone. Some philosophers even see babies as non-persons, whose lives are of no value because they do not know how to value them (Harris 1985) and there has been little research into babies' personalities. However, here are one mother's memories:

> I didn't see my third child until he was 30 hours old. The doctors said he might not survive. As soon as I saw him, yellow, hunched up in his incubator, I knew he would live and always be a strong loving support to me. I watched my fourth child being born by caesarean section, very annoyed to be interrupted, stubbornly protesting about being hurried, but within half an hour doing things with great energy and enthusi-

asm. Around 30 years later, they have the same personalities. (Personal communication, 2007)

Our research in neonatal units found that parents and nurses believed that premature babies had personalities and relationships, and clearly preferred some adults to others. Als (1999, pp.35–9) speaks of the baby as an agent and 'an active structure and participant in his or her development'. One mother described how she first came into the unit and saw her daughter, born 15 weeks early:

> She was looking so helpless and tiny, but then I say something to her and then it was so, she was moving her hands and legs so quickly and right, like trying to recognise you... 'Yes go on', [the nurse] was saying... 'this is the one voice she has known for a long time, now she can have a sense that she has not been abandoned that you are still here'.

And a doctor commented:

> I think it is remarkable. I have enormous respect for these little babies, and sometimes the way they cling on to life is extraordinary...he nearly died about three or four times. It was extraordinary how this little body, this little soul kept winning through... (Alderson *et al.* 2005a, 2005b)

Video records show how, from the moment of birth, babies struggle to turn towards and relate to their parents' faces and voices (Murray and Andrews 2000, pp.18–35). From birth, babies are active members of their family and community, a union of their parents' families, and engaging in the 'micro dance', by nodding in time to speech patterns, pausing, vocalising and turn-taking with the person talking to them (Stern 1977). Such examples raise questions, which there is not space to consider here, about how personality with its unique set of genes is inborn and already complex early in life, and/or gradually unfolds or is acquired or constructed from external influences. Undue stress on development risks devaluing babies' humanity, identity and personality as 'undeveloped' and not worthy of respect.

Yet ideas are changing fast. A group of doctors, philosophers, researchers, and people with related personal experiences held meetings on 'cosmetic' surgery on children. Is it ever ethical and who should make the decisions? Many children are born with ambiguous genitalia and surgeons tend to rush in to 'correct' the problem, and assign a clear gender identity to the child. Adults, represented in the group, often later felt they were assigned to the wrong gender, and many have had further corrective surgery to restore their original identity. The group concluded that in most cases there is no need for emergency treatment, except for counselling support for distressed parents, and instead the adults should wait until the child clearly demonstrates his or her gender identity and also clearly requests surgery (Parens 2006).

A book debating cochlear implants for deaf children suggests that young childen's views should be taken very seriously. Deaf adults tend to oppose implants. The children should be informed and involved in making decisions as far as possible from their expert knowledge as deaf people, knowledge which their hearing parent cannot have (Komesaroff 2002). The history of conjoined twins suggests that twins prefer to remain joined and not to be separated by surgery, and Dreger (2004) concludes that respect for their personal identity involves expanding society's concepts of what is acceptable and 'normal' to include the person's own concepts of normality. Our research found the same message from disabled children, who identitfied themselves as normal (Alderson and Goodey 1998).

Family

States should 'ensure recognition of the principles that both parents have common responsibilities for the upbringing and development of the child' (18). The child and parents should not be separated 'unless this is in the best interests of the child' (9). States must avoid unlawful detention or imprisonment. It is vital for babies that they and their parents are not separated, or persecuted, or arbitrarily imprisoned. Separation should only be a last resort in the best interests and safety of the child. Again, these kinds of 'inalienable' or inherent UNCRC civil identity rights are fully developed from birth.

A main objection to children's rights is the fear that they disrupt 'intimate' family life and parents' rightful authority (Ross 1998). However, UNCRC articles repeatedly (5, 7, 8, 9, 10, 11, 18, 20, 22, 24, 27) stress the importance of the family and state support for parents. The Preamble is:

...convinced that the family, as the fundamental group of society and the natural environment for the growth and wellbeing of all its members, and particularly children, should be afforded the necessary protection and assistance so that it can fully assume its responsibilities within the community.

Beliefs about rights as mainly sources of conflict or of mutual respect depend on whether they are perceived as zero–sum (the more rights children have, the fewer their parents can have) or win–win (where everyone gains). Lansdown (1995a, 1995b, 2005b) analyses how respect for children's rights can promote harmonious, enriching family life for all the members. Although most of the literature is about problems and dysfunction, Brooks (2006) describes in subtle detail children's experiences of 'ordinary' complex family life today. When parents separate, frequently the children are the most loyal, loving and forgiving family members, trying hard to sustain relationships with both parents unless there has been severe violence. Children tend to blame themselves after their parents reject them, showing that it is vital to help them to talk about their experiences and sense of guilt and shame (Miller 1983; Winter in progress).

Loneliness. Taking part in a study of families after divorce were two young boys, Pete and Paddy, who lived with their authoritarian father and were afraid of the violent man who lived with their mother. Pete was asked, 'Who would you include in your family?'

Pete (aged 6): Nobody.

Paddy (aged 8): Not even me?

Pete: My brother...

Q: What's it like living in your family?

Pete: Horrible.

Q: Can you tell me why?

Pete: Because people smack people...

Q: What happens if something goes wrong?

Pete: I pay for it…

Q: Are there things you'd like to change about your family?

Pete: That we could have got on better.

Paddy drew a tall blank house, with a tiny window in each corner. The boys' pictures were bereft of people, and there was a significant discrepancy between their ideals about family life and their experiences (Smart, Neale and Wade 2001, pp.62–3).

The sense of identity, which grows through continuing relationships, is the basis for children to be seen, and to see themselves, as people to be consulted – the topic of the sections which follow.

Respect for the child's evolving capacities

When babies are seen as respected persons from the start, as members of their family and their community, participation rights are a life-long process taking 'due account of the importance of the traditions and cultural values of each people for the protection and harmonious development of the child' (Preamble). This includes attention to the culture of each child, such as in language, dress, music, art, food and religious ceremonies (30).

State Parties shall respect the responsibilities, rights and duties of parents [and other legally responsible adults] to provide, in a manner consistent with the evolving capacities of the child, appropriate direction and guidance in the exercise by the child of the [UNCRC] rights. (5)

'Evolving capacities' can be interpreted in repressive ways (children do not fully evolve until they are adults when they may acquire adult rights and freedoms) or in quite emancipating ways (as children gradually become more competent and independent there is a 'dwindling' (Denning 1970) need for adult control). Lansdown (2005a) concludes that the UNCRC recognises diverse childhoods, and children acquire different kinds of competencies, at different ages, according to circumstances. Children's understanding and competence depend more on their experiences, culture and family life than on their age (Alderson 1993). 'Children, therefore, require varying degrees of protection, participation and opportunity for autonomous decision-making in different contexts and across different areas of decision-making' (Lansdown 2005a, p.ix). 'Appropriate direction and guidance' involves balancing between: protection and respect for the child's autonomy; providing too little or too much adult support; helping children towards independence too early or too slowly; the child's and the parents' and other people's rights, interests and welfare (and see Smart *et al.* 2001). 'The best interests of the child will be their basic concern' (18), and there may be conflict between the parents' and the child's views about 'best interests'.

Lansdown (2005a) observes that the UNCRC, for the first time in international law, establishes a direct relationship between the child and the State. This challenges the presumption that parents 'own' their child, and respects the child as a citizen and rights holder. While all children have UNCRC rights, whatever their capacity, the question is where responsibility for the exercise of the rights lies, and whether there should be set age limits. There are many complications in attempts to prescribe universal age-based standards, to define competence, to determine the degree of competence required to make each kind of decision, and to assess how competent each child is. These questions are reviewed later.

Having a say

'State parties shall assure to the child who is capable of forming his or her own views the right to express those views freely in all matters affecting the child, the views of the child being given due weight in accordance with the age and maturity of the child' (12).

The key participation right is the right to express a view. As reviewed earlier, newborn babies clearly 'express their views' by making contented or unhappy noises, and asking to be fed. Amy, aged 10 days old, while being handed gently around a group of adults, kept her gaze fixed on her mother and began to suck her fist hard, signifying that she wanted to be fed.

Children are said to be egocentric, and therefore incapable of making valid decisions, which include being morally responsible. Everyone is self-centred to some extent, but the word does not fit much that babies do. They watch intently, react to other people's moods very sensitively, absorb and copy their behaviours such as facial expressions, and initiate interactions with them from their first days. Children are also said to be pre-rational and unable to reason. Babies aged one month seem able to match shapes they have sucked with ones they look at (touch with vision); from four months they notice differences in numbers of objects; and at six months they seem able to perceive cause and effect and be surprised (staring hard, widening their eyes) at effects that appear to have no cause (Siegal 1997). These abilities are, of course, not described here as full competencies to make valid decisions, or as 'mile stones' which babies should reach. Everyone varies and Einstein was said not to begin to talk until he was three years old. Instead, this book aims to show how babies are people with early forms of thoughts and feelings, as people who are close to them know.

Besides looking outwards and reacting to people and things around them, well before it used to be thought possible, babies express their views strongly and clearly through sounds and gestures, and in play when they make choices and show intense concentration and enjoyment. One video showed a 21-day-old baby at play with an older baby for 20 minutes as they made sounds and touched each other (Goldschmeid and Selleck 1996). As infants start to use words, they make their views and wishes still more clearly known. The right to express a view (12) through any 'media of the child's choice' (13.1) and to be responded to begins to be honoured or withheld from birth and is soon expressed through sophisticated activities.

Henry, Harriet and Natalie. Henry (six months) sat watching Harriet (six years) patting her legs and clapping her hands, and he patted his own legs and clapped his hands. As she rolled a ball to him he held out his hands ready to take the ball, held and sucked it, and then jerked his arms to push it away, as if trying to throw, and watched where the ball rolled. His rocking music box stopped playing music so he casually batted it to restart the music. Harriet looked at something behind Henry and he turned to follow her gaze. Then she pulled a caterpillar on a string towards him. Henry grasped the string and drew the toy towards himself. Harriet passed him a coloured box covered with shapes which make different sounds when pressed. Henry looked very pleased and banged the shapes, smiling at the sounds. Later, he grabbed his teddy, cuddled it and chewed its ear. He leaned forwards and sideways to reach other toys as if trying to work out how to crawl to them. When given a piece of apple he held it carefully and bit off a lump. Often placid and watchful, Henry became excited when his friend Natalie (five months) arrived. Natalie waved her arms up and down with pleasure, smiled and made happy noises at Henry. Natalie's mother sat her near to Henry and the babies reached eagerly towards each other.

Henry shows a few of the many ways in which babies 'form and express a view' (12), in responding differently to each object and event, showing his interest and pleasure and, perhaps most importantly, constantly creating and recreating his relationships with other people through copying them, playing, greeting, and sensitively responding in many other ways. Later, as tape recordings of four-year-old girls show, young children hold rich, deeply thoughtful daily conversations. Frequently they ask questions such as, 'Why do ships float?' and 'Does the queen always wear a crown?' (Tizard and Hughes 1984). Four-year-old Robbie, when told about Dutch elm disease, wanted to know exactly how the beetles destroyed the trees, and later he asked how buried corpses decompose, questions that his grandmother was unable to answer in sufficient detail. This is not to say that young children can reason and argue as well as most adults, but that their reasoning and their views about their own and other people's interests cannot wholly be dismissed or discredited.

Participation

Adults provide funding, research, evaluations and reports that advise on methods and standards of involving children (Kirby *et al.* 2003; Dickins *et al.* 2004; Lansdown 2005a, 2005b). O'Kane (2003), for example, identifies four key ingredients to effective participation: children's sustained

Body language. Hasid, aged four, who does not speak, was having difficulty at meal times. The speech therapist working with his helper at school suggested better seating positions and liquidising his food slightly more. That helped to improve his feeding skills and reduced the risk of choking. The therapist advised his helper to remember to go slowly, and give him time to respond, to wait for signs from him that he wanted more food. He has always enjoyed having his food, but he had just been in hospital having surgery, and was uncomfortable and still adjusting to coming back to school. The school staff thought: 'Maybe he's taken a few steps back after making a lot of progress. So maybe we have to go a few steps back with him in every area, in order to move on' (Cleves School 1999).

active involvement in making decisions at different levels in all matters that affect them; information sharing, dialogue, mutual respect and sharing; power for children to shape both process and outcome; acknowledgement of the key influence of children's evolving capacity, experience and interest.

There is disappointment that, although there is so much consultation, there is relatively little action or practical effect afterwards (Morrow 1999b; Kirby *et al.* 2003; Sinclair 2004; Cairns 2006; Tisdall *et al.* 2006). Participation, or at least consultation, is now much more widely understood, accepted and practised, partly through the influence of the UNCRC. However, there is concern that, in practice, participation and 'empowerment' are often too formal, managerial and vague, too controlled by adults and committee formats, too top-down and naïve about power, conflicting interests and the politics of how to manage, prevent or achieve change (Cleaver 2001; Matthews 2003). Participants are too often selected and not representative. (All these problems also apply to adult 'lay' participants who find an imbalance of power between themselves and paid professionals.) Thomas (2007) proposes paying greater attention to the range of sites of participation, from private to public, the range of types of decisions, from personal to collective, the varying contexts of intergenerational relations, the law, children's political rights, and other vital variations, in order to develop a politics, a sociology and a theory of children's democratic participation.

The activities listed earlier, such as playing games or cooking, all involve countless minor formal or informal decisions and rules, which many children enjoy discussing and negotiating among themselves. However 'participation' tends to be discussed in its political sense of being involved in formal explicit decision-making. Article 12 is often misquoted as 'children can express their opinions about decisions that affect them'. Yet Article 12 is about 'views' – a stronger word than 'opinions' – and about 'all matters affecting the child'. These matters could be relationships, the built or natural setting, imaginary ideas, games, meals, clothes, school work and countless other matters that extend far beyond formal decisions. Concealed within daily taken-for-granted routines are endless decisions that have already been made and are no longer seen as decisions: 'we always do it this way'; 'that is the rule'; 'there is no alternative'; 'don't be silly'; 'because I say so'. When children begin to talk and to question matters that affect them, these hidden decisions may become clearer and perhaps become negotiable. For example: 'Can traffic be banned from our road to turn it into a play area?' 'All matters' can open the way for children to raise their own questions and decisions, with less reliance on adults to choose which decisions should be made.

Decision-making

Do children have the right to make decisions? The right to make personal decisions and, as far as possible, to be in charge of one's own life is a central autonomy right for adults. The UNCRC, however, is less about children's autonomy rights than about a diluted version, their participation rights. Do children have the right only to express views, but not to make decisions? Article 12 mentions the first, but not the second right. And if children do have any decision-making rights, are these fairly open or quite closed in the types of decisions that they may make?

Children can participate in decision-making at four levels (Alderson and Montgomery 1996):

1. Being informed.

2. Expressing a view.

3.   Influencing the decision-making.

4.   Being the main decider.

Participation is sometimes defined solely as stage 4, leaving the child to decide, and this is then often dismissed as too risky. But each of the other stages are important forms of participation in their own right, and they precede the fourth stage if the child is to be able to make informed decisions. The first three levels are in the UNCRC (12, 13) which adds, 'the views of the child being given due weight in accordance with the age and maturity of the child' (12), although giving no age guidance. The first three levels include any child who can: first, understand information; or second, form a view; or third, is considered to be able to form a view, which can usefully inform adults' decisions. The 1989 Children Act advises local authorities to inform and consult with children on 'their wishes and feelings' about plans which affect them.

The UNCRC aims to bring national laws up to its own standards, but also respects national laws 'which are more conducive [than the UNCRC] to the realisation of the rights of the child' (41). English law explicitly goes beyond the UNCRC in specifically respecting the right of children not simply to contribute to decision-making, but also to be the main decider, and to make serious personal decisions in their own right. If this fourth level of participation is taken to mean children's rights 'to do whatever they want', 'to divorce their parents' or 'to refuse to go to school' then all participation, even expressing a view or being informed, is easily dismissed as dangerous nonsense.

Some critics worry that, especially when parents and children disagree, children's rights harm children, break up families and could bring chaos into schools (Archard and MacLeod 2002; Guggenheim 2005). However, children can only make legally valid decisions if they are able to understand the relevant information and have the discretion to make a wise choice in their best interests (*Gillick* v. *Wisbech & W. Norfolk AHA*, 1985). In English law, this fourth-level right has no set lower age limit, but it does have strict competence limits; children have to convince the responsible adults that they can make an informed, sensible decision. The UNCRC and English law agree that 'the best interests of the child shall be a primary consideration' (1, 3, 21) and the UNCRC qualifies children's rights in other ways (see Introduction). Adults take competent children's decisions seriously when these are 'wise' as well as informed.

Lansdown (2005a, 2005b, 2006) contends that children do have the UNCRC right to decide, and to shape the process and outcome of decision-making, through mutual respect and power-sharing with adults, through Article 5 on evolving capacities (see above). All the UNCRC rights cohere, so therefore all relate to Article 5, which involves the gradual transfer of rights from the adults' to the child's right to exercise rights and, as quoted earlier, English law endorses this (Denning 1970). Lansdown contrasts how majority world children tend to be more highly respected for their practical competencies, whereas children's decision-making is more valued in the richer minority world.

Thomas (2002) reviewed the participation of looked after children in decision-making processes. He emphasised that adults must ensure that the children have: choice over whether they participate; sufficient information; some control; a voice in discussions; support to speak; and some autonomy and independence. These practical standards attend to the politics of sharing power and adults' obligations.

In contrast, most of the detailed research about children's decision-making is medico-legal and emphasises children's competencies. The research mainly investigates informed and voluntary consent to medical treatment and surgery. Alderson, et al. (2006a, 2006b) interviewed children aged 3–12 years who have diabetes, and adults caring for them. They explored the criteria for valid consent set by English law and international medico-legal guidance (*Nuremberg Code* 1947; *Declaration of Helsinki* 1964/2000; *Gillick* 1985). The criteria for *informed consent* are the abilities to understand: the proposed intervention and its hoped for benefits, risks and costs; the likely effects on the child's health and person; and any alternative interventions. *Valid consent* includes the ability to weigh the information, to make an enlightened or wise decision in the child's best interests, and to express the decision. *Voluntary, unpressured consent* includes having autonomy, courage and resolve. These involve resisting any pressures and standing by the decision, even if the warnings of risks turn into real harms. The person giving consent has understood and accepted these potential harms and does not blame other people if they occur.

Finally, the person giving consent must have *legal status*. English law gives no lower age bar to *Gillick* competence. So, in theory, any child who meets these earlier criteria could give consent to treatment, but probably not to research where the law is uncertain. In many countries, the law does not allow children to consent at all. Most children prefer to share major decisions or to have their parents decide for them, but some can and want to give or withhold consent. For examples, see Samantha and Amy in Chapter 8.

A newer standard is being set by government guidelines, children's and youth and social services. To count as competent, children must refuse to have their parents involved in the decision. There are at least four serious problems with this standard. First, it is not a test of competence because wanting their parents to be involved or not tells us nothing about the children's reasoning competencies. Second, it can be used as an excuse by practitioners to exclude parents, and so to increase their power over getting inexperienced children and young people to consent to interventions. Third, young children, who are most likely to want to involve their parents, may then be wrongly judged and dismissed as incompetent. Fourth, whenever parents are involved, practitioners may only inform and ask consent from the parents, leaving the child not properly informed, consulted, involved or assessed for potential competence. Immensely important gains since the 1980s in informing and involving young children in serious decision-making, listening to them and preparing them for interventions, may be undermined. Finally, the standard misunderstands *Gillick*, which went through three courts with nine judges. Only one judge, Fraser, mentioned excluding parents, and four of his five points are about contraception (Kennedy 1988; Wheeler 2006). Fraser was very concerned that young people should have access to treatment and advice, even if their parents were not informed or involved. He wanted to protect and enable doctors to help the girls. The Government also wanted to provide treatments to prevent unwanted pregnancies and sexual infections. These are useful reasons for respecting young people's, and children's, decisions if their parents might not support their best interests. The danger is that this standard is being misused as an essential competence criterion. It is even more ironic that the Fraser ruling, with its potential misuse and exclusion of young children, was originally about contraception, a health service they do not use. This criterion of competence needs to be challenged.

Who should consult young children?

Clear communication is vital when adults consult children about care and services provided for them, and about involving children as more active partners in caring for themselves and for one another. Parents can be valuable advocates and advisers for, and interpreters of, their child's views. In children's services, are visiting researchers more useful than adults who know the children well, but who may doubt they have the skill or time to consult children? Researchers report that after they get to know a group of young children well, and a new researcher arrives, some children become quieter and take time to get used to the new person. Familiarity is important. Working in small close groups, and taking time for the children to become used to the consulter, also help to draw out fuller responses from the children. Rapport grows through enjoying shared experiences and through playful methods of enquiry. In one project, outside expert researchers worked with the staff, until the staff took over doing the consulting routinely, convinced and confident that this was a worthwhile use of their time (National Early Years Network 1998). This is a more efficient use of outside advisers, to train and work with the staff, instead of working as if children can only be consulted when experts are called in, leaving the staff and children less confident and more distant from one another. Consulting works best when it becomes a routine part of everyday work with children (Kirby *et al.* 2003; Willow *et al.* 2004).

Right to be heard during proceedings

The child shall in particular be provided the opportunity to be heard in any judicial or administrative proceedings affecting the child, either directly, or through a representative or appropriate body...'(12.2)

Part of the right to express a view is the right to explain and to appeal in serious matters, such as being excluded from school. Even some four-year-olds are among the thousands of children each year permanently excluded from school (CRAE 2007; Children's Society 1998), with no right in English law to speak to the adults who decide to exclude them, or to appeal. The UN Committee on the Rights of the Child was disturbed about this omission (UN Committee on the Rights of the Child 1995, 2002). Jeffs (2002) reviews the paradox of schools excluding thousands of children, often against their will, while also enforcing attendance on all other enrolled children, and he argues for voluntary schooling. Schools would then have to raise their standards in many ways, working with children, in order to attract students, an unusual example of how market forces really might bring improvements. It is fairly certain that almost everyone would attend willingly – to see their friends and for lack of alternative activities, as well as to gain an education and qualifications (Alderson and Arnold 1999; Mayall 2002; and many other education researchers, usually with older children, although the youngest ones are among the keenest to attend school initially). Instead of so much energy and time being spent on forcing everyone to attend, they could be diverted into extra support for the few who do not want to attend from boredom, fear, problems at home or other reasons (Alderson 2003; Vaughan 2006).

As numbers of exclusions from similar schools vary so greatly, some excluding no children at all, it seems that this is a reflection of school policy rather than of children's behaviour. Centres in London and Bradford, for example, help to prevent exclusions by working with many three- and four-year-olds who find it extra hard to settle into their schools. The next example shows how listening to children can helpfully expand well beyond formal disciplinary hearings into working with children on changing their distressed behaviour.

Janet illustrates how behaviour problems, even ones with serious medical names, can be greatly relieved (or increased) by the ways in which the adults consult and learn from the child and adapt their minute-by-minute care.

Disruptive and distressed behaviour. Janet (22 months) ran around frenetically at home and all around the whole nursery, making everyone anxious. Her key worker, Helen, listed the many things Janet could do, which helped the staff to feel more hopeful. Helen began by running with Janet in the garden, holding her hand. She wanted to slow Janet down and help her to gain more skill and control in movement, in close relationship to her adult. Helen would hold Janet in her arms until she relaxed and was able to enjoy the treasure basket, mouthing objects as if she were a much younger child. Later Janet began to put objects in and out of containers, while the nursery organiser discussed these approaches with Janet's mother. After a few days of intensive attention, Janet became more like an ordinary energetic child, and the staff found there were many ways of helping her to be more calm and attentive. The staff had decided not to wait for weeks until Janet saw a paediatrician before beginning their programme to help her. Even when a doctor had seen her, a medical diagnosis would still leave the staff to have to devise practical ways of helping Janet (Goldschmeid and Jackson 2004).

Freedom of expression and information

The child shall have the right: to freedom of expression [including] freedom to seek, receive and impart information and ideas of all kinds, regardless of frontiers, either orally, in writing or in print, in the form of art, or through any other media of the child's choice. (13)

Jacqueline. Jacqueline (17 months) sat with her legs stretched in front of her near a heap of ribbons and chains. She chose a red ribbon and laid it across her ankles, then laid a chain two inches higher and parallel, then a yellow ribbon, repeatedly alternating a ribbon and a chain to just above her knees. She looked at them intently and smiled to herself (Goldschmeid and Jackson 2004).

In this playing, babies make choices, are independent and creative. They cannot do it 'wrong' or make mistakes. Jacqueline devised her own rules and purposes, and concentrated on creating. Babies can be deeply satisfied with colours, shapes and patterns and with rearranging them. The following examples about the treasure basket show babies' fascination with objects and with using things to express and deepen these relationships with other people. The treasure basket is a low basket filled with ordinary objects for babies to select and handle. When only a few months old babies can be propped up to play with it.

A ten-month-old boy, sitting at his mother's feet, played with the treasure basket. He tried to pick up a large pebble with one hand and then managed that with two. He lightly gnawed the roughish surface, making a grating noise which made the watching adults shudder. Seeing this, the baby gnawed again while watching the adults who began to laugh. During the next 40 minutes, he gnawed again twice, watching the adults' amusement intently. The interchange of intense looking, of glances, smiles, proverbial noises of great variety, touching each other and sharing objects, all spring directly from the experiences babies have with their close adults (Goldschmeid and Jackson 2004).

If children's instincts to explore have been strongly discouraged, it may take much gentle encouragement before they are confident enough to express themselves, such as by reaching out to grasp objects.

For people to be able to have informed views, adequate information is essential. Children gather information in many ways, through their senses, by watching and copying others, by testing objects and people, as well as by being informed and taught by others (Selleck and Griffin 1996). Babies develop trust (or mistrust) in their carers and willingness to cooperate with them (or not), through their experiences of being treated gently or roughly. They respond to reassuring explanations before they understand words, and they learn to talk by being spoken to for months beforehand, as if they can already talk. 'Information' includes physical contact and other body language, games, pointing and holding objects and pictures, feeding and playing, and many other means of supplementing or replacing words. Information surrounds babies in the constant examples they see of how other people interact, which they soon imitate.

From the second year, telling a story can help children to understand and cooperate with stressful experiences like having hospital treatment. It is as if the story format describing the treatment and how they will go home afterwards helps children to make sense of the ordeal. A story with toys and pictures can help children as young as three years to cope, for example, with major surgery (Alderson 1993). One way that children help one another to digest and come to terms with new information and experiences is through playing partly imaginative games together, such as one about a new baby arriving or a daddy leaving. The Qualifications and Curriculum Authority (QCA) (1998) advises that by the end of Key Stage 4, 14-year-olds should be able to express and understand another person's point of view, and yet young children do this daily when, for example, they play in the home corner (Dunn 2004).

Extra information. Some children need extra information. For example, blind babies lie very still in order to hear intently when someone enters the room. If they are suddenly picked up, they become very distressed. Their parents are upset because they expect the baby to be pleased when they arrive. If the parents talk to the baby as they enter the room, the baby understands, enjoys their arrival, and wants to be picked up.

Freedom of expression may require extra aids such as Makaton signing for children who do not talk, or double bikes so that children of different physical abilities can ride around in pairs. Many ideas increase the scope for all children to express themselves more fully, as shown at Save the Children's Equal Opportunity Centre in London (and Cleves School 1999). In a sense, information is power, helping the child to have security through some understanding and sense of control, instead of feeling suspended in helpless uncertainty, at the mercy of unknown powers. Children are then better able to see how to cooperate, instead of making fearful protests. Like other rights, the child's right to information is qualified to prevent harm to the child and to others.

Freedom of thought, conscience and religion

The child has the right to 'freedom of thought, conscience and religion' (14), subject to conditions listed in the Introduction.

Freedom of thought and conscience

These rights raise questions about respecting young children's sense of awe and wonder, and their understanding of right and wrong, and of making moral choices which are shown from the second year (Dunn 1995). Since writing 'from the second year' I have watched a nine-month-old boy absorbed for hours in watching a JCB, which he calls 'dig dig', with awe and wonder at its power. Again, these capacities cannot be linked to an age; newborn babies' intense feelings of pleasure or fear can also be seen as awe and wonder.

Children learn more in their first four years than at any other time of life. Neuro scanning and research have greatly added to knowledge of fetal and infant brain development. Within five months of conception, all the 80 billion neurons for the mature human brain have been formed. At peak growth times, 250,000 neurons are 'born' each minute. The cells grow, migrate, mature, and are selectively 'pruned' as the infant brain develops into the fully integrated adult brain. Billions of synapses, which connect neurons, develop in the first years through great 'overproduction' and then through 'pruning'. Although adults may have 10 to the power of 14 cortical synapses, this is 40 per cent fewer than they had in infancy. Too little pruning is associated with learning difficulties (Fox, Leavitt and Warhol 1999). This suggests that infants have huge learning potential; their abilities possibly become stronger in the 'parts of the brain they use' and weaker in the 'parts they use less'. Some experts think formal teaching and learning are vital in the first years. However, most people believe that children themselves, with parents and carers, are the best teachers, and that encouragement, talk and play within a rich environment are the best aids to learning.

From the early months, through playing with other children, children learn about moral relationships, other people's feelings and needs, sharing, turn-taking, caring intimately for others, sympathy, sustaining a relationship through conflict and disagreement, managing frustration and anger, and enjoying pleasure and affection. They learn through imitating each other and, perhaps most vital of all, through imaginative play, make-believe and story-telling, realising what the other child is imagining. From 18 months, they make this 'great leap forward' (Dunn 2004) in cooperative imaginative play, illustrated, for example, by Johnny aged 24 months on a pretend picnic with his friend aged three years. 'Johnny, on instruction from Kevin, fills the car with petrol, "drives" the car, then gets the "food" out, pretends to eat it, says he doesn't like it! Both boys pretend to spit out the food, saying "yuck!" and laughing.' The younger boy doesn't simply copy, but invents and adds humour and drama to the game.

Barnes (2003) reviews how through their friendships, children experience affection, intimacy, many kinds of communication and sharing, cooperation and also anger, jealously and exclusion, shaping their sense of self. Pritchard (1996) argues for respecting the moral actions and reasoning of children (aged over four years), which are based in their strong emotional relationships, and sees their morality on a continuum with adult morality, not essentially different. Pritchard (1996) and Paley (1999) explore morality with young children through telling and discussing stories. Gordon-Smith (2007) observed and talked with four-year-olds about being kind and fair at nursery, and found clear awareness of what it means to be kind – or unkind – as also Danby and Barker (1998) found, from the age of three years. Mayall (2002) reviews children's moral status in the context of respect for children's rights and agency. I have found that passing round a plate of big and little biscuits reveals that even two-year-olds have a strong sense of justice and merit when they protest, 'that's not fair'. Respecting children involves reserving judgement about whether they are 'good or bad', trying to understand their behaviours from their point of view, and encouraging their respect for other people's thoughts and feelings. I have heard examples of children younger than 14 months (in the next example) who appear to be aware of 'conscience', and readers may like to reflect on when they think moral awareness and choices begin to emerge.

Freedom of conscience. Emma (14 months) usually did as she was asked, and as she became more mobile, dangerous things were lifted out of her reach. One day she touched a gas-fire tap in a house she was visiting. Her mother said: 'No, no, don't touch that, it will hurt you, please come over here, come on'. For the first time, Emma looked as if she realised that she had freedom to choose whether to cooperate with her mother or not. She paused, with a look of surprise, interest and perhaps of pleasure and alarm. Her mother felt this was a great moment in their relationship, when she had to choose whether to appeal to Emma's new capacity to make decisions, her conscience, or else firmly overrule her, by force if necessary. Emma touched the tap again, as if to test her mother, who repeated her words very firmly and seriously. Emma looked as if she decided to believe her mother's tone and look of great concern for her welfare, and she moved away from the tap. These can be decisive moments when, in new ways, parents try pleading that can sound too weak, or force that is too strong, or else a kind of confident consulting, a direct appeal to the child's reason, sense and trust.

The main aspects of citizenship have been defined as social and moral responsibility, community involvement and political knowledge (QCA 1998) (politics involves how power and resources are shared out). Children learn about these through doing them, such as talking about how to share, take turns, or plan events they can enjoy together. Research with children about their rights found direct, practical and responsible understanding among all age groups in the survey of 7- to 17-year-olds (Alderson and Arnold 1999).

Participation is counterproductive when children see tokenism and no change, for example, with school councils. Children can see when rights are ignored or overridden in schools, and trivialised or distanced. One eight-year-old succinctly complained, 'It's so boring when they keep telling you that making the world a better place means picking up litter and not killing whales' (Alderson 1999).

Incidentally, children showed their interest in rights, besides their ability to complete a 20-page questionnaire; the youngest group was most likely to say that they found the booklet interesting (88 per cent). They were sceptical when rhetoric about democracy did not fit the reality in their schools, and knew whether their school council was token or genuine. Eight-year-olds said: 'The council meetings aren't much good because we have to write the newsletter then, and we can't discuss things'. In another school, pupils this age kept notes and reported between their classes and the effective council meetings. Primary schools councils have helped to raise standards of behaviour in schools, reduce bullying and other problems, end the need for exclusions, train pupils in other schools and run a farm (QCA 1998).

Sharing responsibility. With a group of 20 children aged up to four years, the staff decided that the children could help themselves to fruit and water when they wanted to. At first, the children asked for permission until they learned they could help themselves. Some spilt the water but they helped to mop up the spills and learned to pour more carefully, as they became used to doing so. In being consulted in this practical way about what they actually preferred and could do, the children were able to behave more responsibly and the staff were free to do other things (Miller 2003).

Freedom of religion

Freedom of religion is often seen in liberal democracies as freedom to choose a preferred religion and, for children, the right not to follow their parents' religion. However, in most countries, freedom of religion means the right to practise the family religion without being persecuted, imprisoned, tortured and possibly killed, and this second meaning is most relevant to young children. History tends to show how people of very different religions often lived peacefully together until invading and colonial powers incited conflict and hatred between different ethnic and religious groups, following a divide and rule policy. De Bernier (2005) analyses how intolerance is introduced into formerly peaceful multi-religious communities with tragic results for the children and adults. Children in early years centres tend to be accepting of one another, although very early they begin to identify symbols with friendly or hostile religious groups (Connolly *et al.* 2002), indicating the importance of educating children from different religious groups together and not apart.

Freedom of religion enables children and their families to live as members of free communities, enjoying religious rites, including post-birth welcoming ceremonies such as baptism, and also weddings and funerals. As symbols of hope and renewal, babies can bring profound meaning to these ceremonies. Moral awareness begins very early. When children are aware of the difference between hurting and fighting versus helping and sharing with other people, or when they argue about who should have the biggest biscuit, they negotiate concepts of kindness and justice.

Freedom of association and peaceful assembly

The child has the right to 'freedom of association and peaceful assembly' (15), subject to conditions listed in the Introduction.

To walk freely out of their home and go round to see friends or attend a meeting is a basic right for adults, which most young children used to enjoy. When there are conflicts and curfews, people are frustrated, angry and afraid when they are denied this right. But fear of traffic and stranger danger now imprisons many children in their homes for long periods. Adults who live with young children know that it is vital for them to be outside playing as much as possible, and that restlessness, tensions, rows and the risk of violence quickly increase if children have to spend too long in small spaces. Chapter 2 noted that the welcome fall in numbers of child deaths on UK roads was gained at the cost of children's freedom to roam and meet together. Photographs in the 1900s show streets and roads filled with children playing; photos in the 2000s show streets filled with traffic. Denmark resolved the problem of road injuries in the opposite way: by restricting cars instead of children and creating spaces to walk, cycle and play. The demand for housing in Britain results in smaller homes and gardens, and thousands of children lack this safe space to play with friends. Children without gardens are more prone to traffic injuries, neighbours' hostility, control by police, and families' fear that they will be evicted (see Chapter 2). In families who have to move frequently, the children's freedom of association is limited when they lose old friends and have to try to make new ones. CRAE (2007) lists many of these current limitations on children's rights. Although mainly about older children, much research on this topic relates to younger ones too (Morrow 2002; Christensen and O'Brien 2003). Morrow (2003) makes useful critiques of problems with 'social capital' theories in relation to children and their neighbourhoods.

Mass media

State Parties shall 'encourage the mass media to disseminate information and material of social and cultural benefit to the child and in accordance with the spirit of the [UNCRC]…especially [materials] aimed at the promotion of his or her social, spiritual and moral well-being and physical and mental health…[and protect] the child from information and materials injurious to his or her well-being…' (17).

This article can be interpreted in two main ways: individual benefit (or harm) to children from the rich resources of the mass media, and benefit (or harm) to children collectively in the way they are presented and reported through the media.

There is a debate about whether the mass media – mainly television – harm children and 'poison' or 'take away' their innocent childhoods, turning them into greedy passive consumers (for example, Palmer 2006), or else enrich children's lives, liberate and 'empower' them through their active engagement, mainly through the internet, and also fashion, magazines and music (Kehily 2003). Buckingham (2003) cautions that both

sides have some truth but are oversimplified, and children are sophisticated, discriminating and critical consumers. However, the immense
anxiety of many children and adults about not being fashionable enough
would seem to challenge this optimism, and researchers of children's
cultures tend to ignore the wider political and economic contexts of
poverty and globalisation.

Besides providing children with entertainment and information to
enlarge their understanding, the media have a strong influence through
promoting positive images of children, or unfairly negative images which,
by frequently denigrating children, make it harder for adults to take them
seriously. An article picked at random illustrates common themes, which
journalists presumably find appeal to the public. Called 'Want a baby?
Read this first', the article describes how a mother's 'romantic notions of
family life' were destroyed by the strain of having a baby whose father has
now left the home. The mother works part time as a model, is taking a
degree course, cares for her baby, and 'has no time left for herself', as if
somehow she is not herself while doing these things. The baby is implicitly blamed for increasing the strains that existed between her parents
before she was born (Morris 1999). The media reflect and reinforce public
attitudes and policies, such as cutting benefits to single mothers and ex-
horting them to find paid work. Implicit in this policy is that any paid
work, however menial, pointless or mechanical, is better than caring for
children. Even when child-care workers are paid, they tend to be seen as
having low social status. College students, when asked to name 'masculine'
work that compares with 'feminine' childcare work, said 'rubbish collection' and rated being a car park attendant above caring for children (Penn
1997b).

The media contribute to driving young children away from enjoying
public places, partly through sensational stories about strangers and
dangers, partly because adults fear being publicly blamed through the
mass media if children they care for get into danger. Children and teenagers are the last groups still to be dismissed in adverse stereotypes, in ways
which journalists would no longer risk applying to women, or black, or
gay people.

Headliners (Children's Express), an international movement. The staff on UK Headliners work as peer-trainers, reporters aged 8–13 who conduct penetrating interviews, and as editors and managers aged 14–18. Most of them come from disadvantaged backgrounds, and they publish reports in many leading newspapers and magazines and on radio and television (see their website for details). When 27 of them monitored 400 stories in the national press, they found that every article stereotyped children – as victims, cute, evil, exceptionally excelling, corrupted, as accessories to adults, or as 'brave little angels', reported in a seminar in 1998 'Kids These Days...' (Neustatter 1998). These children also speak at policy conferences, and in 2000 held a conference at the House of Lords on how to promote children's safe use of the internet (Williams 2002).

Inclusive schools and communities

'A mentally or physically disabled child should enjoy a full and decent life, in conditions which ensure dignity, promote self-reliance, and facilitate the child's active participation in the community'. The eventual aim for all services for disabled children should 'be conducive to the child's achieving the fullest possible social integration and individual development' (23). International understanding, skills and capabilities in the care of these children should be improved, according to the UNCRC.

The Article on disabled children is here, in the participation chapter, because of its important emphasis on inclusion rather than protection or provision. Although it is said that special schools promote eventual inclusion by preparing many disabled children for adult life better than mainstream schools, this is a doubtful claim. Mainstream schools often fail disabled children, as they fail other children, and great improvements need to be made to raise standards of education for all kinds of children. An important way to do so is to include and support disabled children, the largest group being those with emotional and behavioural difficulties, in ways that also help the great numbers of borderline children with unacknowledged needs. Segregating disabled children into often isolated special schools can make them even more vulnerable to abuse (Lansdown 2001, 2005b). In 2006, 3790 children aged up to four years were in special schools or units (CRAE 2007, s.4). Many disabled adults deplore their own segregated education. Disabled children learn many subtle social skills from mixing with other children, who learn to accept their disabled peers as an integral part of 'ordinary' everyday life. Both these benefits are lost in special schools. Children bussed to special schools are less likely to have local friends at home, increasing their loneliness and sense of difference. Northern Ireland's schools, segregated by religion, tend to increase fear and hostility between the two separate groups, and this is just as likely through separation on ability. 'Able' children educated away from their disabled peers are less likely, when adults, to employ or socialise with them.

Siobhan. Siobhan's mother, June, 'fought' to get her into mainstream nursery school, and felt criticised by teachers and other parents. 'They looked at me as if I was crazy... Somebody said to me: "I don't think you've accepted your daughter's disability," and I said: "Well I live with it, of course I've accepted it." So it was harder for me to take Siobhan to mainstream than to special because I had people [adults] staring at me. But once they got to know me, all that was gone... As far as I was concerned, the *children* were accepting her. I think because she was in from the age of three, the children didn't have the hang-ups that the adults had. I think they found it easier and that made me more determined then to keep Siobhan at mainstream... Things that the teachers or even me as a parent would be frightened to attempt for Siobhan, such as climbing on the frames, getting on the swings, they saw a way round it. And she'd manage to get up the top of the slide and there would be people around saying "Oh God, no," but the children always saw a way round and got her down, where adults were frightened to master that part.'

Perhaps the confidence she gained during her early years through playing and taking risks helped Siobhan during the 'kind of horrible time', when she started at her secondary school, to wait for months in the school entrance until lessons were rearranged and a lift installed for her to reach the classrooms. Now, she is happier about the teachers: 'I suppose they wasn't really sure how to approach me and what to say,

> kind of, if they said something would they hurt my feelings…talking down to you, would I understand. [Now] they talk to me more personal, suiting my age.' June added: 'It would be nice to protect Siobhan, I mean I'd love it as [her] mum, but that's not what I wanted. I wanted Siobhan to face the world as it was going to be' (Alderson and Goodey 1998).

One reason for referring disabled and disturbed children to special schools is that 'other children will be cruel to them'. Yet there are many examples of young children helping disabled children to learn and play (Lewis 1994), to climb, explore and take reasonable risks. Disabled children, like any children, are often outgoing, friendly and adventurous, and they have much to offer to people in mainstream schools (Audit Commission 1992; Herbert and Moir 1996; Cleves School 1999). An inclusive borough, Newham in East London, which gradually closed its special schools and brought their resources and expertise into mainstream schools, succeeded by beginning with the early years and slowly maintaining integration up through the age groups. This works better than trying to reintegrate children who have already been segregated. It is sometimes said that young children do not notice difference or disability, but it seems that they are aware of differences, and make allowances without judging others as better or worse, more or less able. It often seems that the children who are seen as difficult, or 'tougher' and 'harder', lead in making their groups or classes more inclusive, uniting with the disabled children themselves (Cleves School 1999).

Other excluded groups

The above points about ability also apply to segregation or inclusion on grounds of race, ethnicity, gender (Osler and Vincent 2003), religion and socioeconomic status, all of which can all apply to young immigrants, refugees and asylum seekers (Osler and Starkey 2005). These groups are especially excluded and denied rights in Britain (Candappa 2002; CRAE 2007). This chapter has only briefly covered some aspects of participation, and some groups of children, with many omissions. Instead of attempting to review these other important groups separately, I suggest readers consider them in relation to all the UNCRC rights in Chapters 1–3.

Ennew (2002) advocates rewriting the UNCRC for street children. Another approach is to see how the broad UNCRC principles might apply comprehensively, and how reviewing the UNCRC in detail in relation to children living 'outside' childhood can increase understanding of the rights of all children.

Advantages of young children's participation

For centuries, authors have warned that respecting children's (and women's) rights can only bring harm, chaos and unhappiness. In contrast, recent researchers report the following advantages of informing children, listening to them, involving them in making decisions, and working to put these into practice. Adults' examples and children's experiences of participation offer three main kinds of benefits:

1. They can benefit society, by informing and improving communities, services and daily life through advocacy (Lansdown 2005b) and through increasing adults' understanding about optimal regional policies (Hood, 2002, 2004, see Chapter 8), optimal health care (Alderson *et al.* 2005a, 2005b), education (Cleves School 1999; Highfield School 1997; Jeffs 2002; Burke and Grosvenor 2003), social and legal services (Winter 2006a, 2006b) and caring family life (Lansdown 1995b; Morrow 1998; Aldred and Becker 2002; Mayall 2002; Neale 2002; Lansdown 2005b).

2. They can prevent and reduce neglect and abuse.

3. They can benefit and change adult–child relations and individuals when they work to talk and negotiate instead of trying force and violence (Highfield School 1997), when they understand and value democratic processes (Matthews 2003), when they respect others through being respected, and when they gain in confidence, skill and self-esteem.

I have given only a very few of the many examples from around the world. There are also far more reported examples about the benefits of involving children aged nine years and over, beyond this book's remit unless younger children are involved too. The London-wide work (Hood 2002, 2004, see

Chapter 8) shows how young children can share in complicated ambitious projects, especially when they join with older children. Despite the reports of the benefits of respecting children's participation rights, cautious, hostile or dismissive voices still dominate public, professional and policy debates. They emphasise the risks and problems, follies and failures of efforts to respect children's participation rights. Participation is constrained by 'rules, routines and regimentation' (Sherman 1996). The hard casing of powerful and rigid old systems and beliefs prevent new ideas from breaking out and flourishing, as many of the authors already referred to critically analyse. Adult control where the real decisions are taken elsewhere, adults' reluctance to share power with children, and children's resulting cynicism are further barriers in community regeneration (Thomas 2002; Matthews 2003). Many adult citizens share these frustrations too. Even when good outcomes are reported, there can be problems with evaluating them and showing how they derived from the participation (Kirby *et al.* 2003) Later chapters in this book will review further ways in which the UNCRC supports young children's participation rights – and respects them as people, the topic of the next chapter.

CHAPTER FOUR

Young Children as People

Images of childhood

People sometimes ask, 'Do you mean children should have adult rights?'. This chapter looks at meanings of child, adult and human being, beginning with examples of varied childhoods, followed by theories of child development. Further examples of children's abilities lead on to considering their status as human beings.

Histories of childhood, and reports of research today across the world, show how greatly varied childhoods are (Aries 1962; Hardyment 1984; Hendrick 1990/1997, 2003). Here is one historical example.

William Blake, England c.1800. 'At seven years of age I was set to work in the silk mills, where I toiled from five o'clock in the morning till seven at night for the weekly sum of one shilling. This paid for my board and lodging, and rendered me independent of my father except for the clothes I wore.

There, a remarkable circumstance occurred to me. Afraid of being past my hour in the morning, and deceived by a clouded moon, I frequently rose in the night mistaking it for day. At one of these times, I found all was silent in the mill, and I knew that I was too early. As I stood leaning pensively on the parapet of the bridge, I heard the clattering of horses' feet; and, without turning my head, I asked what it was o'clock. No answer being given I turned to look, and I distinctly saw the appearance of a man, riding one horse and leading another, on the mill wheel. The clock then struck four, and the apparition vanished' (Rosen 1998).

The example shows the high demands made on working children's energy and time in the belief that this was normal. Today in Outer Mongolia, children start school at eight years. Before that, they work as herders and some spend all day wandering alone with their goats in very high or low temperatures. Again, this is seen as normal in the accounts of both children and adults (Penn 1998a, 2001).

These examples tend to be compared with the lives of children in the UK today, as if we now know how to treat children properly because we understand what it really means to be a child. Yet the examples say far more than this. They show how our images of childhood are no more real than those examples are, except in the way our images construct and reflect the lives of children in our society, just as other images reflect other societies. Children's health and perhaps the happiness of most children have improved in the UK since the 1800s, but they have lost independence and status – William Blake thought it right to be independent at seven.

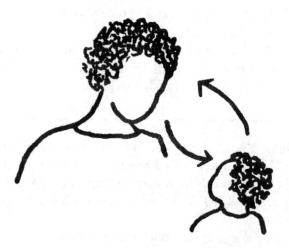

Figure 4.1. Adults and children construct and reconstruct one another, for example, either as having very different levels of understanding, or as sharing more equal insights.

The images of childhood also show how adults and children continuously construct and reconstruct their beliefs about childhood in their daily talk and behaviour (Figure 4.1) (James and Prout 1997). Each of the three kinds of rights involve a child–adult dyad: the providing adult and the needy child; the protective adult and the victim child; mutual respect between the participating child and adult.

Another colouring of adults' views of children comes from adults' memories of their own happy or unhappy childhoods and, for example, their delight or envy when seeing happy children. William Blake, quoted earlier aged seven years, as an adult wrote pairs of happy and sad poems about childhood, including two nurses' songs (Blake 1958, pp.37, 47). At sunset the nurses call the children home to bed and the children say they want to go on playing. The first nurse lets the children play until the light fades:

> The little ones leaped & shouted & laugh'd
>
> And all the hills echoed.

The second nurse, her 'face green and pale', tells the children to come home saying,

> Your spring & your day are wasted in play,
>
> And your winter and night in disguise.

In another poem 'The Echoing Green' (Blake 1958, pp.27–8), old people remembering their own childhoods laugh while the children play. Children's voices echo through the ages, respected or repressed by adults, heard clearly or misheard, heard with pleasure or pain, interest or irritation. Children's echoes are blurred by the echoes of the listening adults' own childhood memories and present values, and by resounding myths about young children's inabilities.

Developing children

Public and academic discussions about children are dominated by notions of 'development', and of 'early experiences as the path to the whole person'. People still repeat theories of the developing mind as if these are factual, and as if children's minds develop like their bodies through one universal pattern of ascending growth marked out by 'mile stones' from zero to adult maturity. These views strongly influence public opinion, as well as all the professions that work with children or advise or comment on their care. Developed mainly since the 1900s, these theories have had positive effects on children's lives, but they also misunderstand and dismiss young children's capacities, and so discourage adults from trusting and consulting children.

A book about how to fit observations of children to 23 pages about milestones of development sums up ten whole months in these words: 'Key features of 9–18 months. Growing independence can lead to rage when thwarted. Shows anxiety when left alone. Emotionally more stable but can be jealous of adults' attention to other children. Can be defiant – learns NO' (Sharman, Cross and Vennis 1995). Students are instructed to conduct case studies of children but without asking for consent, another example of seeing children more as objects than as real people with rights. And if the study were explained to parents, would they be happy about their children being observed in such negative ways? The text concentrates on children's unreasonableness and limitations, which makes trusting them impossible.

Similarly, television programmes when a nanny arrives to sort out a dysfunctional family, and many of the parenting programmes now so much promoted by the Government, tend to construct children as either naughty or helpless, but not as reasonable agents who can make positive contributions and share with adults in resolving problems. Again, if parents and children were shown the final film about them, would they consent to it being televised? Brooker (2006) contends that experts who attempt to discipline and control children deprive them of their rights with covert filming and disapproval of children's (often quite reasonable) non-cooperation with the film makers. They ignore asking for children's agreement, or explaining the process to them, and make them and their parents look foolish. Through tactics to punish and withdraw 'treats', short-term punitive fixes may become long-term battles, which parents must win if they are to control dangerous children.

Another book by many early-years specialists is far more positive, and gives fine examples of competent children, their helpfulness, and imaginative awareness of others (Early Childhood Education Forum 1998):

Yet the book still discusses even children aged three to five years as if they do not yet fully exist with headings such as 'being and becoming'.

> Children learn to belong and connect in their relationships as they explore the possibilities of life in groups…they use all manner of materi-

als...they learn about the constraints and difficulties of joining in...they are learning about choices and boundaries...in all this, children are being and becoming their unique selves...learning that they can make significant contributions to their social relationships...opening new doors and windows on the world [as] they handle bricks and blocks... (Early Childhood Education Forum 1998, pp.32–3)

Max (30 months) is just out of nappies and is expertly washing up his bowl. Suddenly he feels urine running down his legs. He watches anxiously at first and then, when one of the staff smiles at him, he smiles. Unasked, a three and a half-year-old friend brings a small mop, and finishes off the washing up, while Max mops up the puddle.

In one way all this is true, but in three other ways it is false. First, children are not simply learning and practising, they are living and accomplishing. Second, these words do not apply only to this age group; they describe Henry (aged six months in the previous chapter), and adults of any age who learn and relearn in new situations. Third, the words imply that adults are somehow 'developed', complete, so that in conflicts between them and children, adults are dangerously encouraged to assume that they are right and the child is wrong. This encourages and endorses adult control and coercion, instead of humility and reasoned negotiation.

It is as if the new understanding of babies' humanity can still only partly be seen through the lens of older theories about the slowly developing child, formulated by Piaget and others from the 1920s (Piaget 1924). New evidence of babies' abilities cannot be appreciated fully within continuing attempts to distort and squeeze experience into stages, as leading psychologists themselves critically analyse (Burman 2007). For example, Bradley (1989) and John (2003) are concerned with psychological blind spots and the 'genetic fallacy'. This, they consider, is overused, relying on children's genetic origins to explain their present health and abilities and experiences. Such biological determinism predicts rigid futures, which do not allow for diverse individuals, circumstances, choices and potential reactions. Theories of stages of child development have been called 'misleading and oppressive' (Mayall 1994b, p.3) because of the ways they are used to misjudge, control and denigrate children. Psychology is very much a practical, applied discipline, unlike sociology. It attends to the individual case or type, and to deviations from normal development and interventions to restore children to normality.

Although psychology has become more aware of social context, perhaps with all disciplines, whether concerned with adults and/or children, it still finds interactions between agency and structure hard to research. This is shown in sympathetic guidance for parents, as illustrated in the next two examples.

Heather. One BBC programme played a tape of Heather aged two, sister of a new baby, saying 'no' many times. The presenter commented that Heather could be in the Guinness book of records, and emphasised the patience needed by mothers and the huge demands made by children. Yet this ignored the context, and the transcript in the book accompanying the programme (Purves and Selleck 1999) omitted the end of the conversation – which sounded partly like a game. Heather said 'no' to all the comforting and 'babying' offers from her mother, of raisins, a cuddle, and so on. She finally said 'yes' when her mother suggested a shared, more responsible activity. 'Shall we go to the shops?'. Perhaps Heather was partly saying she did not, just then and contrary to the programme's implications, want to be infantilised. Asking children to help in an 'adult' way, respecting their worth and dignity, is often a way to resolve disagreements with them.

The second example, in a best-selling baby book, also blames problems on age–stage and not other factors: 'Temper tantrums. Her ambitions far outreach her abilities. The resulting combination of stubbornness and frustration can be explosive, resulting in the classic temper tantrum' (Stoppard 1998). Yet like anyone, two-year-olds can do lots of things well if other people give them time and do not insist on unrealistic standards. Frustration often arises when fraught rushed adults impose demands and restrictions. But this is not mentioned, and neither are the societies where the 'classic temper tantrum' is hardly known (Penn 2001; Punch 2001).

Notions of inexorable stages of life, such as the 'terrible twos', are like racism except that, instead of blaming skin colour, another part of biology – age – is blamed without reference to context. These theories, with their 'rotten' unscientific foundations in Darwinian philosophy, have been called the 'biologising of childhood' (Morss 1990, 1996; and see Siegal 1997), which diminishes understanding of the humanity of children. It takes at least two people to have a row, which is usually a power struggle. Adults have the most power but 'terrible twos' and other slogans not only absolve adults from questioning their own possible use or abuse of power, but also endorse firmer or harsher adult control, by suggesting that volatile young children are out of control. Young children need responsible adult care and this involves treating them as reasonable people. Many sociologists accept child development theory and reframe it as socialisation theory (Giddens 1991), which is about becoming an adult. However, some sociologists and anthropologists (James and Prout 1997; Mayall 2002) and psychologists (Bradley 1989; John 2003; Burman 2007) question child development theory's over-emphasis on: rationality and children's supposed incompetence; biological taken-for-granted naturalness which overlooks all the social aspects of children's lives and contexts; and universality, as if children in the UK and US develop in the same way as children anywhere in the world.

Multidisciplinary childhood studies involve researching children across the world to see how they grow up in very different ways. Variety across space is mirrored by variety across time in historical studies. Aries (1962) played a key part in showing how childhood is relative and contingent – a set of ideas about what children and child–adult relationships are like and should be like. However, I suggest that many people today, although they accept that childhood was socially constructed in the past, consider that now we know through commonsense and science what childhood is 'really' like, and therefore we can rely on our own evidence and experience as real facts. One theme in this book is how our beliefs and behaviours are as contingent and constructed as those in any other time or place.

Some social psychologists criticise the emphasis in child development on 'normal, natural and needs' and advocate moving from a judging and measuring approach towards 'context, culture and competencies' instead (Woodhead 1998). By 'normal' they mean that a *descriptive* average among an examined group of Anglo-American children, such as their height at a certain age, is turned into a *prescriptive* 'normal' height, which all children are supposed to be near. Being 'too' short is taken as 'subnormal' and a problem, which might need to be treated. Ideas of what is normal are reinforced by assumptions about what is natural and correct, although average heights for the 17 per cent of children in richer countries have been rising throughout this century, and differ from average heights for all the children in the world. Abilities are similarly measured for 'normality', without taking much account of how children's abilities vary depending on how and where they are tested, how much help with the task or previous experience they have, and many other factors. Thus, ability is turned into a static thing, instead of being seen as widely varying responses depending on the context and relationships concerned. Professionals set norms that become the basis for prescribed and sometimes imposed 'needs' (Woodhead 1990/1997). These are defined in the belief that children who are different 'need' adults to restore them to normality, or to compensate for the tested differences, as in special educational needs. Sometimes such help is very useful but it is being defined and given in increasingly rigid ways as young children are subjected to a growing battery of tests by education and health specialists.

Given the great range of childhoods experienced across the world, psychologists who propose a universal pattern of normal child development have been compared with goldfish imagining that their bowl is the whole world (Woodhead 1999). The alternative approach is to see how children's abilities vary according to the expectations and experiences of children and adults in each culture. People have a range of abilities, like warmly welcoming friends or learning a language, which rise and fall and are learned or forgotten throughout their lives, affected by many factors, including experience, context and personality. Instead of assuming that before certain ages it is useless to consult children on some matters, it is possible to see that children might partly understand enough to be consulted on these matters, or on some aspects of them, or they might understand if asked in different ways. Examples of very able young children may be seen as interesting exceptions, which prove the general stages rule, or which slightly stretch age or stage development levels. Alternatively, this evidence is taken to question age–stage theories, and to show the need for new theories which appreciate the capacities and potential in young children, and new methods for nurturing and respecting these capacities. If this is to happen, older theories that block new approaches have to be rethought.

Understanding childhood

The twentieth century saw great changes in how womanhood is understood. At first male priests and doctors tended to be seen as the experts on women's souls and bodies, and on how inferior women were to men. Feminists later succeeded in showing that differences between women and men are worth respecting and valuing instead of regretting. Gender studies reveal how limited, mistaken, misleading, and at times harmful, the former sexist thinking and research, policy and practice can be.

Valuable theories and methods in feminist research can apply to childhood research, to the way children, like women, are measured against a norm and ideal (this time of adulthood) and found wanting, instead of being understood and valued in their own right. For example, feminist standpoint theory, which involves listening to people's accounts, and trying to understand their position in society and their own viewpoints and standpoints, can apply to children (Mayall 2002). The feminist scholarship on the division of labour and respecting the equal moral worth of all workers and their work (*ibid.*), research on the intermediate domain between the public and private, and feminism's concern with women as an oppressed minority group – all these also apply to children. Yet Mayall (*ibid.*) also reviews the uneasy relationships between feminists and childhood when feminists believe that their own rights are the first to be threatened by children's rights. An alternative from this zero–sum win–lose view is a win–win possibility when children and women can both enjoy some emancipation (Lansdown 2002, and see later).

However, a woman philosopher once famously commented (O'Neill 1988), the child's 'main remedy is to grow up'. She showed how developmental theory fits uneasily with children's rights when she advised: 'taking rights as fundamental in ethical deliberation about children has neither theoretical nor political advantage' (O'Neill 1988, p.25). Like the former generic but actually limited 'he' of the past, today's 'we' very often applies to adults only, without the exclusion of children even being recognised and acknowledged. New approaches to childhood research therefore involve analysing generation in similar ways to analysing gender.

Alanen and Mayall (2001) contend that childhood and adulthood have to be understood through their intergenerational relationships, particularly in three main aspects. First, children and adults have to relate across age differences and power inequalities, and the norms and needs and history of the household or school. These have to take account of group as well as individual interests. Second, there are the different status, and positions, interests and concepts of the social group 'children' and the social group 'adults'. They have roots in the past 'which throw long shadows forward' into the future; these can be negotiated and transformed. Third, adults carry extra decades of knowledge, assumptions and experiences. Each generation is subject to different social forces and histories and values. There have been dramatic changes in schools and family life over recent decades. The next box shows how children negotiate family relationships in rural Bolivia.

Interdependence. Although there is unequal power in adult–child relations, children renegotiate adult-imposed boundaries and assert their partial autonomy through controlling their time and space, and taking initiatives and choices, as a detailed study of 18 households in rural Bolivia found. The children work hard and usually do so readily and with pride. Three-year-olds can walk for miles to fetch water or firewood or to do errands. By five years, children acquire responsibilities, skills and competencies, and by six or seven years they can carry two five-litre containers of water. Children found skilful flexible ways to avoid some tedious or arduous tasks. They would get a sibling to do it, or negotiate with their parent to be allowed to do a different task, or they would dawdle, or run off and play. They liked going to the shop as this could allow time for a quick game with friends (Punch 2001).

Mayall (2002) further proposes that before we can respect children and their rights we have to know to some extent where we think children stand in the social order, in relation to adults, and what we mean by 'children' and 'childhood'. Anne Solberg described how four-year-olds showed her that she was talking down to them and infantilising them during research interviews. With their help she established more equal relationships, and she interviewed them for up to an hour about 'what did you do yesterday?' (Solberg 1993).

After their first few weeks or months of life, children are not inevitably and in every way dependent, though many are treated in ways that stop them from becoming independent. The first three examples in this book, of Albert, Margaret and Kevin, show changes over time in the way young children can use the streets. Such examples raise questions about how adults' fear about risk, and their lack of confidence in children, limit how adults can consult and trust children.

One level of research reports the views and experiences of small groups of children. A second level examines how childhood is socially constructed, again usually with quite small groups and on specific aspects of their lives. A vital third level is to collect data from large numbers of children as a distinct social group, to inform national statistical and social accounting. Children are generally invisible, concealed within data on 'the family' or their parents' status, or in birth records, in ways that say little about their own experiences. Once children become the unit of analysis recorded in their own right, surprising statistics emerge. For example, children are more likely than adults to live in overcrowded housing and generally to have a lower housing standard than adults (Qvortrup 1997). The steep fall in the annual numbers of children killed in road traffic accidents in the UK – from around 1000 in 1977 to around 300 in 1990 – looks very encouraging. However, Hillman et al. (1990) showed that this was at the cost of children's freedoms shrinking between 1971 and 1990: the percentage of children aged 7–11 allowed to cross the road on their own fell from 72 to 50 per cent; to walk to the park went down from 63 to 37 per cent; to ride on a bus without an adult from 48 to 15 per cent. The third level of research, in statistical data, is vital for understanding childhood and progress in respect for children's rights.

Spatial, moral and real awareness

A well-known example from child development is used here to show why young children's thinking and morality are so often under-estimated. Piaget set out to prove scientifically Freud's theory that children are self-centred or egocentric (Bradley 1989). He showed a model of three mountains with a doll to Swiss children, and asked them to identify the doll's viewpoint, for example by choosing one picture from ten which fitted the view they would see if they were to stand in the doll's position (Piaget and Inhelder 1956). Few children under eight or nine years could pass this test, and children aged up to seven tended to pick the picture which fitted their own viewpoint, not the doll's.

Piaget concluded that children cannot fully understand that other people have a different viewpoint from their own until they are aged seven or older (Piaget 1932). He thought that young children cannot realise that their own view is one among others, and they cannot separate themselves properly from other people, so they have a false idea of reality and identity, and their reports are unreliable. Piaget's findings were repeated in tests around the world, and were used to validate common beliefs about children's cognitive and moral immaturity. Adults are less likely to respect children's views if they do not believe that children can form worthwhile views.

Scottish researchers rephrased Piaget's question and asked children how a naughty boy could hide from one and then two policemen, and they even added two or three more mountains/partitions to the original three mountains, and a third policeman. They found that children as young as three years could solve these tests. They concluded that the children's seeming inability lay in the original way they were questioned, and not in the children's limitations. The children may have assumed that repeated questions meant that Piaget wanted different answers, and they obliged him (Donaldson 1978). This is contrary to Piaget's assumption that children are unaware of another's viewpoint, and it seemed that the children were more aware than Piaget himself was. This later research about young children's higher abilities is crucial to any discussion about consulting children. Yet it is still much less quoted than Piaget's older work and the myths about young children's incompetence which that work supports. (See also later chapters.)

However, older beliefs about young children's ignorance, inexperience, unawareness, unrealistic and self-centred thinking continue to dominate professional and public beliefs about childhood (Stainton-Rogers and Stainton-Rogers 1992). They still convince many adults that they must protect and control children, without needing to consult them. Children's rights to respect for their worth and dignity cannot be realised while the old theories still dominate public and professional thinking.

Able young children

Much other research supports the value of consulting children, and seeing how much they can achieve with a little help, referred to as scaffolding. This is when children build on hints and cues from helpers, and on vivid direct discussions on their own terms, with the use of human interest stories. It avoids abstractions and impersonal tests that may confuse or intimidate them (Bruner 1966, 1980; Levine 1993).

Children can solve harder puzzles by working together in groups rather than by working on their own (Doise and Myng 1981). Summaries of numerous research studies show that by the age of five, children have very clear understanding of self and others, language and space, music and art, morality, physics and technology, much of which they will rely on for their whole lifetime (Gardner 1993). For example, physics graduates answer questions about trajectory correctly when these are asked through conventional university physics questions. Yet when they are asked questions about physics in unexpected ways, the graduates forget their education and fall back on their basic, life-time knowledge – that of a five-year-old child.

Children are perhaps more likely to be seen as full people and consulted as equal workers in countries where many children work and there are no laws to restrict their involvement.

Water in the village. In Uganda, many children are the first generation to attend school and they become health educators for the community. The 600 children at the primary school became concerned that animals used the village pond which was the main water supply. They spoke with the village leader who called a village meeting where the children presented poems and dramas about the value of clean water. As a result, children and adults worked together on cleaning the well pond and building a fence to keep out the animals, then celebrated with food and music (International Save the Children Alliance 1995, p.236).

These disadvantaged children showed a little of the great untapped capacities which ordinary children have, but which tend to be shown during adversity. Fortunate children who live sheltered lives have less opportunity to show their strengths, and then they are often assumed to lack them.

The restaurant. During their monthly meetings, New Delhi street-boys realised that they spent 75 per cent of their money on food. Twelve boys aged seven to seventeen took an intensive ten-day course on cooking, nutrition, cleanliness, looking after customers and book-keeping, and had help with renting a space for a restaurant. They took half-pay at first, saying: 'You can't expect to be an overnight success in this business, one has to bear losses for a while...and try very hard'. They gave free food to some street children, learned Chinese cooking to expand the menu, and planned to raise money to buy a van to take food to an area where there are many street children, financed by selling snacks in public places. They learned from their difficulties, tested new ways to solve problems, gathered ideas from the surrounding social conditions, and based plans on responses from their young customers (International Save the Children Alliance 1995, p.237).

Katz (2004) researched with children in the Sudan in 1980–81 (before the civil war) and later when they were young adults. She found that many of the skills and former ways of life were being lost to the pressures of globalisation. She describes vividly how they combined work and play with fun, imagination and serious realism. Their play showed how they understood the political and economic context and the differences between subsidence and tenant cultivation.

Work and play. Young children made dolls and elaborate trucks out of natural and discarded materials. They would play families, shops, building small houses and charcoal kilns, farming and trading harvests, creating elaborate miniatures of the fields and buildings around them and of the actual work they already shared with adults.

One day, twelve girls aged 8–15 walked for over an hour, carrying large containers, to find sweet doleib fruit and the branches which burned to a starchy ash for thickening stews. They feasted on the fruit, threw stones at baboons, climbed a termite mound, collected loads of fruit and burned piles of branches for half an hour while they played. Then they washed in the river, drank the water, and while singing they carried water to sprinkle on the hot embers. They gathered the ashes into their buckets then collected more branches to burn. Later they lifted the heavy containers on to their heads and walked home, helped by a boy with a donkey (Katz 2004, pp.90–93). 'The girls loved to go in order to eat their fill of doleibs, to bring fruit home to enjoy later with their families, and to have an outing in the treasured and exotic grove. Work, play and wonder were almost indistinguishable on excursions like these' (Katz 2004, p.93, pp.102–8).

Many children work as child soldiers (see Chapter 2) and here is a summary of Ali's account when he was 20, showing how some young children learn complex skills which will affect their later life (Brett and Specht 2004, pp.6–7).

Work and war. Ali lived in a war zone in Afghanistan when he was seven or eight years. He went to school from 8 to 12 o'clock, and then he helped in a Médecins sans Frontières clinic. He learned to do injections, dress wounds and give first aid, to support the Mojahedin by caring for hundreds of war-injured patients. When he was ten, he fought as a soldier for five to six months, but then all the French staff left the area and he returned to run the clinic; 'there was no one to help the injured soldiers'. When aged 12 and 13, he was a surgical assistant and attended courses on medicine and surgery and how to set bones. Later he passed his exams with very high marks and studied medicine at university. But when aged 20, he said 'due to having a very bad war experience I no longer like medicine'. He said he has seen too many wounded patients, and he is ill, and has hepatitis and poor vision.

Drawing on children's many abilities

In England, the national curriculum provides for broad ways of consulting children in appealing to their many interests and respecting their abilities. Five-year-olds can show how they combine understanding of abstract concepts with practical tasks, from making an electrical circuit to explaining forces such as balance, friction and gravity, from learning about religious faiths to developing awareness of time and maps. Yet to fulfil so many tasks in crowded classrooms involves limiting the time children have to talk and listen to one another and to the adults. There is less time for choices and negotiation. In the interests of the whole group, children often have to wait a long time for their turn, or interrupt activities they are immersed in when everyone has to move on to another activity.

Reading and writing are vital skills, but they hold back young children's thinking. At first, literacy is like Japanese to English children, another language. Talking is far quicker and easier, closer to children's speed and level of thinking than reading or writing are. People need to talk about their plans, activities, perceptions, interpretations, mistakes and speculations. Between what someone clearly knows, and clearly does not know, at the proximal zone of learning where ideas are beginning to be understood (Vygotsky 1978, p.86), it is helpful to put these ideas into words and test them in discussion. When children are constantly stopped from discussing and expected to write, and then to copy out again, their learning becomes slower and more superficial (McNamara and Moreton 1993, 1995, 1997; Nutbrown 1996b), and children are less able to act as valuable resources to one another.

Babies are very good at pacing themselves, working with deep concentration, as long as they feel enthusiastic, and then changing to another activity, and returning to continue with the first one later. They organise their learning, such as by babbling and trying out sounds, repeating tasks over and over again, and picking up vast amounts of knowledge. This self-organisation is respected in many early years centres, but in schools it does not fit the prescribed national model. For example, the termly report for five-year-old Nicola, who read to herself for hours for pleasure at home, criticised her for starting with great enthusiasm but then 'running out of steam', a tellingly mechanical image. At first, she said fervently, 'I love school', but after a few weeks she said sadly: 'You do lots of hard work and you go and ask Miss Mallam if you've done enough, and she says, "Go back and do some more"'. How much harder do children who find learning less easy and enjoyable find this approach? The national literacy hour involves children from four years of age – an hour is a very long time to anyone who feels forced to do something they do not enjoy.

Some schools manage to combine the varied activities within the literacy hour with self-directed learning, in which children plan their day and their chosen order of activities using diaries that they fill in each morning. The children work in large groups with teams of teachers and support staff who can arrange detailed preparation and flexible personal and group support to children throughout the day. Up to age 11, the children's self-directed learning follows patterns taken for granted in many early years settings (Cleves School 1999).

The Free School in Albany for disadvantaged children is charged with energy and intensive noisy learning. The children share in directing their learning and in resolving disputes (John 2003, pp.239–248; and see Vaughan 2006).

For some Italian teachers, 'Our image is of the child rich in potential, strong, powerful, competent and, most of all, connected to adults and other children...co-constructors of their knowledge and identity through relationships' (Edwards *et al.* 1998). These children know that other young children in their centre can create complicated projects, and they are excited and also highly organised during long and difficult tasks. When children's knowledge and motivation are respected, teachers stand back while children question and answer one another and make plans. Children's abilities can then be seen more clearly (see also Griffith 1998). It is disappointing that the early years centres in Reggio Emilia are repeatedly quoted, but do not seem really to have been copied elsewhere in the world. Perhaps the missing elements are the political and economic will to support and trust in young children's amazing abilities.

The dinosaur project. Italian five and six-years-olds spent four months on a dinosaur project, consulting books, drawing, talking and writing about them. In small groups and with many discussions, they built four-foot-high models; the girls used Styrofoam and the boys, because they chose wire and metal, needed more help from adults. The staff 'consulted' children by talking with them and also keeping detailed records of the children's talk, which the staff then read and reread and discussed.

This rereading of the children's concerns led the staff to challenge the six most active children to draw a life-size dinosaur and find a way to hang it so that it would stand on its feet. The children slowly worked out how to enlarge small drawings to scale, they marked out a rectangle 27 by 9 metres on the sports field – someone thought of using toilet paper when they ran out of rods. The girls had decided to use horizontal lines and the boys used vertical lines in their small drawings; so later they used both sets of drawings to map out the larger outline. Then they found they could no longer use the sports ground and they had to design a smaller dinosaur, 13 by 6 metres, in the courtyard.

Most five-year-olds in the pre-school shared in painting the plastic sheeting *Diplodocus*. The six children presented an animated report to the school of all their drawings, and all the stages of creating the dinosaur, and the many problems they had resolved together. The staff arranged pulleys along the sports-field fence and during a festival for the families the dinosaur was hoisted up. The children asked the mayor to find a permanent display place for the dinosaur which he agreed to do (Rankin 1998).

The staff in these Italian centres consult the children continuously, beginning when babies arrive. Staff observe them closely, learn from their eating and sleeping patterns, and talk frequently with their parents. With babies with 'special rights' (who have extra difficulties) the process may go on for weeks or months while they gradually settle in and the staff get to know the baby's 'gifts and contributions' to the centre (Smith, C. 1998, pp.199–214).

Giving and taking

A standard view of children is one of taking: absorbing their parents' time and energy, being expensive dependents, needing many education, health and other professionals to care for them. This view sees the child taking and the adult giving. Yet children bring love and joy into families, they share in household work, thousands of children – a few as young as three years – are the primary carers for a sick or disabled relative in the UK (Becker and Aldridge 1995). In most countries (the majority world of

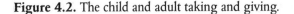

Figure 4.2. The child and adult taking and giving.

poorer countries where 83 per cent of people live) young children have adult-like tasks and responsibilities; they challenge the richer minority world's assumptions that children can only receive goods and services, and do not also contribute. Millions of young children share in field, street and house work and care for babies. Many are grossly exploited, but many prefer to work, at least part-time, giving as well as taking as in Figure 4.2 (Johnson, Hill and Ivan-Smith 1995; White 1996; Punch 2001; John 2003; Katz 2004).

To involve children in daily tasks can be a practical way of consulting them and drawing on their skills, knowledge and ideas, as well as increasing these skills so that children have still more to offer. Young children who are seen as real people are more likely to be consulted and relied on by adults.

An example of research with some of the poorest children in the world, Bangladeshi street children, shows how people who have no formal education and the least rights can value rights to respect and dignity very highly.

Research by street children. Five girls and six boys aged 10 to 15 years were the researchers, and each morning they interviewed one or two people aged 7 to 15, 51 in all, who had been on the streets for years. In the afternoons, they dictated all they could remember to adults who wrote the notes and the report. The young researchers talked though every stage and method of the research and every line of the reports. They copied an earlier project from the UK (West 1995). Gradually the researchers identified 11 priorities. Contrary to experts' views that these children most want and need health, education and care programmes, only two priorities referred to these: dislike of dirty rotten food, and wanting vocational education but not full-time schooling. All the other points were about problems caused by adults: torture, injustice, exploitation, cheating, name-calling, never using the child's own name, forcing the children to do unpleasant and 'bad' work, lack of an adult guardian who is essential for getting a good job and for tackling unjust police and bureaucracies. The children questioned 'why they cannot get a decent life, they should have equal rights'.

The points are about participation rights, keeping dignity and some independence. They illustrate how children's views cannot simply be guessed and assumed by adults and that, in a world controlled by adults, real help and support for children involves working closely with them, giving and taking (Khan 1997).

This chapter began with the question: should children have adult rights? In the UK, children and young people are dependent financially, legally, and in many other ways. Young children cannot have all the same rights, power and freedoms that adults have. However, apart from adults' rights to work, to vote and to found a family, young children share many of the same inalienable human rights which adults enjoy, so these are 'human' rather than 'adult' rights. 'Adult' tends to mean competent, informed, wise, altruistic and reliable, and 'child' to mean incompetent, ignorant, foolish, selfish and unreliable. Earlier examples show how all these qualities can be shared at all ages, so that they challenge assumed sharp differences between child and adult. By showing their shared humanity, the examples strengthen the case for equal respect for the worth and dignity, rights and interdependence of all human beings.

CHAPTER FIVE

Beliefs and Feelings about Consulting Young Children

Only 200 years ago in Britain, the human story looked very different from that of today. After a short infancy, many people joined the working adult population for the rest of their (often short) lives. Society depended on this large working force. Today, the story is decades longer and has many chapters which are assumed to be biological, factual, inevitable: babyhood, infancy, the 'latent' period, adolescence sometimes stretching into the mid-20s, adulthood, retirement, being elderly, old age, frail old age. All the stages except adulthood are also seen as partly dependent. Yet this dependency is not integral to young and old people, who can contribute efficiently. Dependency is imposed by social structures. One example is the debate about child labour, reviewed in Chapter 2, on whether to protect and exclude all young children from being workers, or recognise that all young children 'work', that millions of them need to do hazardous work in order to survive, and at present they need support and protection in doing so.

As structures and routines have changed, so too have attitudes, and it is now commonly believed that children cannot contribute. This chapter further considers some of these entrenched but fairly new ideas. Children today benefit from better provision and protection. Yet, as Chapter 2 showed, protection can expand into coercion and over-rigid harmful control. It can set self-fulfilling low expectations, or increase contagious fear in adults and children about children's supposed inadequacies. Paradoxically, by denying children the chance to become street-wise, overprotection can make children more vulnerable to dangers, and less able to cope with them.

Freeman (2007) reviewed debates about children's rights, including the following:

Pros

- The language of rights (for example, feminism) can make the silent and suppressed heard and visible.

- Rights are inclusive and universal. You do not have to earn them.

- Rights side-step control, rules and exclusion by the powerful.

- Rights are interdependent and reinforcing – civil, political, social, economic and cultural.

- Rights respect the dignity, humanity and integrity of every person as an end in him/her self, not a means to other people's ends.

- The most fundamental right is the right to possess human rights (Arendt 1986) (unlike those destroyed in holocausts).

- Rights are inconvenient to the powerful who want swift, cheap, certain, efficient decisions. They trump all other considerations (Dworkin 1997). Rights therefore have to be fought for.

- Rights holders can exercise agency, make decisions, negotiate, participate and enjoy freedoms.

- Rights ensure advocacy, representation, remedies, resources and change. Rights legitimate campaigns and action to emancipate disadvantaged and excluded people. This involves the new moral 'commonsense' of justice for all with new views about childhood (Mayall 2002).

- Rights offer moral reasoned arguments.

- Rights offer agreed entitlements for action, beyond begging, imploring, making trouble, or having to rely on whim, privilege, charity or kindness.

- Children who can represent themselves and other children increase their resilience and positive self-concept (Grover 2005).

Cons

Freeman (2007) also reviews critiques of children's rights and replies to them.

- Everyone supports some rights – prevention of torture for example – but some authors still over-restrict children's rights into unenforceable non-rights: the right to parents who are autonomous, who represent the child, and who care (Goldstein, Freud and Solnit 1996) or the right to minimally fit and fairly infallible parents (Guggenheim 2005). This is about parents' and not children's rights, reduces children to property and ignores their humanity.

- Children's rights are pointless, and there are better ways to improve their lives, by identifying adults' obligations (O'Neill 1988). But who decides and justifies these obligations, given the history of cruelty to children 'for their own good'?

- Children's 'main remedy is to grow up' (O'Neill 1988, p.39). But children deprived of rights will grow up very differently from those who are respected (Grover 2005), and some will not grow up at all if they have no rights.

- Love, friendship, compassion and altruism are higher ways to relate than rights and duties, so is the ethic of care (Arneil 2002). Yes, they are higher ways to relate than rights, and they work well within happy families, secure childhoods and an ideal world, but many children do not live in ideal contexts.

- Authors who dismiss children's rights passionately defend the 'sacred' rights of even dangerous parents. They are not against rights but against children.

- Children are too incompetent to have rights. Yet many young children and also adults are partially competent. Rights should not depend on being competent but on being powerless and needing protection and respect.

- Infants lack agency, and are like people in a coma or with severe Alzheimer's or mental defects (Griffin 2002). Freeman responds that all these people have rights. Griffin links rights too much to capacity and also ignores the evidence on infant's capacity.

- Children's agency rights to culture (UNCRC 30),[1] religion (14) and freedom of expression (13) are ill-conceived and 'jeopardise the family as an institution' (Brighouse 2002, p.29). Freeman questions the point of these objections.

For his reviews and responses to other cons see Freeman (2007). Basic to Freeman's review are concepts of young children as real persons or as pre-persons. Children's rights are criticised as hostile to intimate family life and loving relationships. However, the UNCRC, in many articles, is framed around practical and political support for the family 'as the natural environment for the growth and well-being of all its members and particularly children' (Preamble). Also, rights are founded within relationships. For decades there has been intricate psychological analysis of how babies' human personhood grows through their dynamic intersubjective relationships with their parents and carers (Newson and Newson 1963; Richards 1974; Newson 1977). When the adult assumes meaning, intention and purpose in the baby's behaviour, that behaviour becomes meaningful. Bion (summarised in Hoxter 1977, p.214) considered that 'the earliest forms of communication take place without any mediation by verbal or nonverbal symbols. In a direct and often raw compelling way the baby conveys its feelings to the mother. If the baby is alarmed or distressed what he does about this is to arouse alarm or distress in the mother. He causes the mother to experience in her own feelings what he cannot yet bear to keep inside himself.'

Bion saw the mother as containing and managing feelings that would otherwise overwhelm the baby. 'The mother who is not too immersed in her own feelings replies to the baby's behaviour [cries, smiles] as though she believes that such behaviour is a meaningful communication which

---

1   Figures in brackets refer to the relevant article of the 1989 Convention.

requires to be understood and responded to. Her response is probably an essential prerequisite enabling the baby gradually to build up some form of realisation of his own that behaviour is meaningful communication' (Hoxter 1977, p.214) – just as babies gradually realise that words are more than sounds and have meaning. These analyses of mother–baby interactions, written decades before the UNCRC, can be rephrased in terms of parents' early 'respect for babies' human rights to form and express views', which can be treated as valid and worthwhile by the adults and therefore by the child. Many researchers trace problems of violence and disrespect in older children and adults back, among other influences, to lack of initial respect for the baby's views and feelings and rights as a human being.

Beliefs and patterns of thinking have been compared with plumbing, in the following ways (Midgley 1996). They tend to be invisible and ignored until something goes obviously wrong, such as leaks or blockages. Then people realise how vitally their lives are affected by the hidden pipes (or beliefs), and see that the most practical thing to do is to sort out the (mental) plumbing. Before assuming that children can or should be consulted, it is vital to examine the beliefs that lead adults either to consult children or stop them from doing so.

Some common beliefs are listed here, so that readers can identify where they stand. Adults who work in pairs or groups could discuss their own positions, in order to reach some broad agreement. If adult colleagues disagree, efforts to consult children and act on what they say are likely not only to fail but also to be seen as proof that it is not worth trying to listen to children. The following lists could be used for group discussions, in which further beliefs could be added and debated. The beliefs are set out under three headings: the principles involved, the benefits or harms which follow consulting children, and how children can learn through being or not being consulted.

Why should young children have the key right to be consulted in all matters which affect them?

1A In principle, it is the right thing to do

- Children, like adults, have the right to be consulted and to express their views (UN 1989). UK government departments and some public services have a duty to consult children.

- Formal consultation methods, like circle times, planning groups, or schools councils, show the adults' good faith and concern for principles of justice and respect.

- To consult children respects them, and thereby sets examples which help them to respect themselves and other people, as part of the duty of care which adults and children have towards others.

- From their second year, children have clear ideas about being fair and being kind to other people (Dunn 1993, 1995, 2004). These ideas can be nurtured early on, partly by involving children in semiformal discussions about making plans or sorting out problems in the groups to which they belong.

- Talking and listening help children and adults to see which plans, problems and values they share, and where they differ, or need to work towards agreement. Through doing so, individuals can see the justice of respecting one another's rights, and sometimes setting other people's wishes before their own.

- Part of responsible adult care is to be willing to explain to children, to be accountable to them, to set the example of negotiating through disagreements, and to expect children to do so too, instead of resorting to pressure or force.

1B There are benefits in consulting young children

- Adults can give more effective care when they use information from children. Encouraging children to share in solving problems can channel their ideas and energy, and their unique viewpoints, into finding better solutions. As one child said on being consulted: 'It would be better to have lots of ideas rather than one' (Mepani and Emerson 1998).

- Some children continue to be abused when no adults are willing to listen to them (Batmanghelidjh 2006).

- Talking together while making decisions can help to prevent misunderstandings or disagreements, and children becoming anxious, or resisting what might 'be done to them'.

- Children who feel respected are likely to respect others and to follow positive examples set by adults and other children. Habits of consulting increase mutual trust, can decrease rivalry, rows, violence and stress, and provide effective ways for groups to cope with problems that arise.

- People are more committed to decisions which they have proposed and agreed, and they will want to make them work well. Otherwise, adults risk working against children, not with them.

- Sharing responsibility for making informed decisions, like how to spend an equipment budget, helps children to know more about the value and the limits of funds and resources. By having to think realistically about ways of working within constraints or disagreements, and choosing what to have and what to do without, they are less likely to blame adults or to expect too much from them.

- Knowing that they can choose sometimes can help people to accept the times when they cannot do so.

1C It is educational to consult children

Besides contributing now, children will also contribute and gain in other ways.

- People learn through talking, putting new ideas into words and checking their own and each other's understanding (McNamara and Moreton 1997).

- When they are consulted, children can learn how to work well in groups, to listen, take turns, explain their views clearly and persuasively, share decision-making and responsibility, and become skilled and confident. Choosing the rules for their group, for example, can teach children to make decisions in a fair and accountable way. Learning to think adventurously involves learning from making mistakes, with protective adult support.

- Part of education is to learn to think creatively, critically and independently, and to know how to question and disagree politely. The best way to learn these skills is through practice.

- Consulting children helps them to be and to become responsible members of their family, peer groups and local community, and to be citizens in their local and national democracy.

Why should young children not be consulted in matters which affect them? These are some of the counter arguments.

2A In principle, it is the wrong thing to do

- Children have the right to be protected by adults and to rely on them; it is wrong to encourage them to question adults' views. A duty to consult children is not sensible, unless it involves simply listening to them with no need to take account of what they say. The child's best interests are paramount and only adults understand these.

- It is hard enough to consult adults and to ensure reports of their views are fair and representative. How can this be done with young children, whose views are unreliable?

- Schools councils often do not work well. Even with adults, school governors' meetings are often undemocratic. Certainly with the youngest children, this pretence of democracy is irrelevant to them and betrays true adult responsibility, justice and respect.

- To consult young children is to confuse and worry them, and the duty of care means just that – adults caring for children by not passing responsibility on to them, but letting them enjoy some years of carefree innocence.

- Young children do not yet have clear sensible views to express. Research shows that children cannot really understand morality until they are at least seven years or eleven years, so their views cannot count.

- If children and adults disagree, children must realise that adults know best and have to set limits and be the judges. Parents are the experts in their child, and other adults who work with children also have expertise through their wider training and experience. Some parents may wish to consult their children, but many parents do not want to, and it is unfair to them if professionals teach children to expect to be consulted. Even if parents can discuss things with their one or two children, adults working with larger groups do not have time.

- Responsible professional staff insist that children keep to the standards expected by the average parent, and they are accountable to parents, tax payers, management and to their colleagues, not to children.

2B There are potential harms in consulting young children

- Letting children imagine they can tell adults what to do, or letting them think they can get away with something once, only leads to trouble for everyone and to lower standards of control, safety and obedience. It wastes time and effort in pointless arguments.

- Pretending to consult children risks raising false expectations. Children will then be disappointed, leading to loss of adult authority, and to rows and stress. Maybe a few insistent children will be given privileges, which is unfair.

- A few articulate children might have useful ideas, but it is favouritism to encourage them. Other quiet children might want something different. A trained professional such as a teacher knows what all the children need, and trying to consult them formally is an admission of failure. Children must learn to trust adults' leadership, and not to follow other children's ideas.

- Children live in a fantasy world of childhood. We should not spoil it by trying to explain budgets, which they will not understand anyway. They need to feel that adults have total control – even if we do not. Children cannot make informed decisions because this involves thinking about more aspects of a question and more viewpoints than they can manage.

2C It is an abuse of education to consult young children

- Children are too self-centred to be able to work well enough in groups to share decision-making and responsibility, and they will be upset when they fail.

- Before anyone can think independently, they need far more knowledge than young children have; the skills they need now are to believe and remember what they are taught.

- Children will become responsible adults if they are set firm examples of responsible adult control.

Deeper feelings

Each side, for and against, raises important discussion questions, about why and whether it is wise or kind to consult young children. But deeper feelings underlie these beliefs. Changes in set routines, such as when adults decide to start up a method of consulting children, involve several levels, from surface behaviour to deep feelings.

Behaviour	Listening to children and acting on their views, or deciding not to.
Knowledge	Gathering, sharing and agreeing on information about consulting, and about children.
Beliefs	The kinds of comments listed above which tend to be stated openly.
Feelings	Deeply held feelings which may not be consciously held.

The more unaware people are about their feelings, the more strongly they may be influenced by them.

The example in the Introduction of the teacher's anxiety about a paper clip illustrates how one approach to such anxiety would be to talk about how serious the risk really might be, and whether it could be worth taking in order to promote mature responsibility among children and young people. Yet this would divert attention from the real barriers, which are the feelings, just listed, that underlie all the pros and cons about consulting children. The feelings can be summarised as set out below.

People in favour of consulting young children tend to feel:

- trust and optimism in young children's ability to think independently and creatively

- respectful faith in each child's unique and important knowledge, and their sense of responsibility and care towards other people

- enjoyment and excitement in working cooperatively and adventurously with children in quite complex ways

- enthusiasm in encouraging children to be self-reliant and interdependent

- confidence that, though it is time-consuming, consulting children and sharing plans with them are vital and rewarding parts of caring for them.

People not in favour of consulting young children tend to feel:

- confidence in adults' superior knowledge and good sense

- conviction that children are very unlike adults and need extremely careful protection and care

- mistrust and a sense that young children cannot understand much, or give reliable accounts, or think sensibly

- deep concern about children's vulnerability

- anxiety that children are volatile, self-centred, and a potential danger to themselves and others

- heavy responsibility and concern that the caring adults will be blamed unless they control children firmly and safely

- worry that it is cruel and wrong to let children take on risks or responsibilities

- scepticism and doubt about consulting children, feeling that it will not work, wastes time, and creates problems which could upset children.

Then there are the children who have been so abused that they defeat even the most highly dedicated and skilled professionals, who come to 'hate them' (Batmanghelidjh 2006, p.20): 'The children made them angry and rageful. The children trod on their dignity as their own dignity had been trodden on. The children terrorised them as they had been terrorised, and we struggled everyday for some safe control'. Much of Batmanghelidjh's book is letters to children telling their story for them. Despite Batmanghelidjh's and Kids Company's high reputation, readers may question how typical these very distressed children are of the whole movement, and how the psychoanalytic approach balances with the social, political and economic analysis, for example, of Ennew (2002).

People tend to have mixed feelings, and do not fall simply into either respecting or else dismissing children's rights. Yet the way they balance their feelings affects how they combine appropriate caution with willingness to trust young children. A study of hospital nurses found that nurses on every level of seniority tended to feel anxious mistrust towards nurses more junior than themselves, seeing them as irresponsible. Yet each nurse also felt angry about being wrongly mistrusted by all the nurses senior to herself (Menzies Lyth 1988). This pattern is common in groups, especially when there are very clear differences in age, experience and responsibility, as in early years settings. Plans to consult children touch on powerful feelings about risk and anxiety, which need to be discussed if they are not to be like Midgley's (1996) blocked pipes.

CHAPTER SIX

Methods and Levels of Involving Young Children

Whereas Chapter 5 was concerned with thoughts and feelings, this chapter is about methods and stages of involving young children through consulting, talking, working and researching with them. It will look at barriers to involving them, and how these might be overcome, and at the levels of working with them from personal to international levels. In this resource book, I will not attempt to explain methods in detail, but will refer to books that do so.

A main way of involving children is by consulting them. Yet 'consulting' tends to mean that the people who do the consulting have the upper hand. They decide what questions to ask, and what they wish to do with the answers. For example, if teachers, play specialists or nurses consult the people who use their services, they may leave out questions which the users would like to raise. The answers may not reflect people's real concerns, and might be used selectively and misleadingly. Children have even less say in services provided for them when only parents are consulted.

In contrast, 'consulting' can mean that the person consulted has the most knowledge and authority to select the correct questions and answers, and decide on the best action, for example a consultant surgeon. Can young children be respected as consultants in this sense? Either meaning of consulting suggests an imbalance. In one the consulter has the main control; in the other the consultant has. With young children, adults always have more control and responsibility, but can they partly share these with children? Can children suggest, and help to make, improvements in their care, ranging from general policies to small daily details, in some kind of partnership with the caring adults? 'Consulting' means 'to sit with' (Skeat 1983), which implies some equality, talking on the same level and sharing time together.

Consulting is easier between small groups when there are flexible options so that children's views can be respected through positive action. On a larger scale, there are no established ways to consult adults properly, let alone young children. The only regular national polls – elections – ask for one cross against numerous known and unknown policies, between a few, little known candidates. No choice is offered on matters on which all the parties agree, and the voting rate may be low. Phone-ins, focus groups and official public consultations publicise a wide range of views, but they neither indicate how representative the responses are, nor how to arbitrate fairly between conflicting interest groups. Like the newspapers, they can undemocratically support an articulate minority in ways that further exclude and silence other groups, including children. On a small or large scale, consulters have to guard against tokenism, poorly designed methods and questions, and misinterpretation of replies. Opinion polls, which do tackle these problems, still contact only relatively small numbers of people, and some elections show how unreliable their reports can be. So the difficulties of consulting children have to be seen as arising largely from the inadequacies of consulting processes, and not of children. The next section reviews some of the main barriers and ways of tackling them.

Practical barriers to consulting children
Lack of time

It can be quicker to consult parents and other adults than to consult children. In large groups of children, one way to increase talking time is to help the children become skilled at talking and working out their ideas in small groups, and the staff can go round listening to the groups in turn. Children tend to baulk at abrupt questioning from strangers. A few moments spent discussing their hobbies or pets first can help them to open up and be far more responsive. Yet busy professionals question whether this is the best way to use their own time. Many education and health care staff worry that they will be criticised for delays if they talk to children, and they learn subtle ways of silencing children. These avoiding tactics can develop into habits and into examples set by experienced staff to junior staff. However, those who make time to talk say that in the longer term this saves time if children are then better able to understand, and sort out mis-understandings, and then to cooperate.

Lack of confidence

This tends to be accompanied with anxiety about making mistakes and looking foolish. Anything worth doing can be risky and involves making mistakes while gaining new skills. Research interviews with children and parents suggest that they are more interested in the goodwill and respect of professionals who work with them, their sincere manner and intentions, than in slick communication skills.

Lack of skill in talking with children

This can be a restriction, though many people may be more competent than they feel, and confidence grows with practice. All adults have been children and have talked with their peers, so this is partly a matter of re-membering former skills. Some adults find that the best teachers are children themselves. The idea that talking to children is so different and complicated that it requires special courses is unhelpful, since it requires similar skills to talking with anyone else of any age. Helpful ways to approach any person (see for example, Ward 1997; Hurley 1998; Morris 1998) include the following:

- Sit at about the same eye level.

- Adapt the volume, tone and pace of talking to suit the other person.

- Use a simple or more complex vocabulary as appropriate.

- Word and rephrase questions clearly.

- Wait attentively for answers.

- Respect what is said and try to pick up and continue themes the person introduces.

- If they do not reply precisely to your question, do not say so, but listen to their reply and then rephrase your question.

- Respond to funny or serious moods.

- Tolerate silences and pauses.

- Try not to interrupt or dismiss what is said, be interested, and thank the other person.

Language can be a barrier

This occurs when the children or adults use pet words, colloquialisms, jargon and any terms which are unfamiliar to the other person. This may happen at all ages, though young children tend to use more personal words. Parents can be helpful two-way interpreters. When English is an additional language for the child and an interpreter is needed, it is important to have someone who respects young children and is skilful at talking with them together with their parents. Some interpreters may wish to 'interpret the culture as well as the language', explaining to you the meaning of words and ideas in the context of country of origin, and advising, for instance, on eye contact or shaking hands, when and how this is acceptable, or not, with your interviewees. Extra time, patience and perseverance may be required. Words are often supplemented by body language, sighs, cries, and laughter. Drawings, acting, games, toys, puppets, taking photographs and making maps can also enrich mutual understanding.

Family dynamics

To address children directly may challenge family dynamics. Although many parents gently encourage their child to take a growing share in the conversation, or are pleased about their child's independence, some parents wish to dominate the interaction. The mid-years alliance, the assumption that adults speak to adults and that children (or elderly people) listen, is powerful. It can require tact and confidence to resist deferring to the parents without offending them when trying to consult the child.

Fear of losing control

This drives some adults to avoid consulting children when they want to get on with their work quickly, in case the child might refuse, dawdle, start an argument or resort to other time-wasting tactics. In schools, for example, some staff worry that if they are too friendly, children will try to play power games – and win. To cope with this, many adults skilfully combine friendly respect with firm confidence.

Anxiety about children's distress

If children have serious difficulties, adults' anxiety can be a major constraint. Adults worry about which topics the child might raise, seemingly unanswerable questions, pleas for help which cannot be promised, long personal accounts which hardly seem relevant, and cries of anguish and despair. Such difficulties span the age groups, and there are books and teaching videos on how to respond (Richman 1993). Another vital support is for adults to be able to share their anxieties with their colleagues so that they can plan helpful responses together.

Because of these anxieties, as shown in the next example, when these are assumed to be routine and inevitable, children's distress and their protests can pass unrecognised, until they are shown in a new light, as in a film. The example also shows how painful it can be for adults to hear children's protests, and to accept them to the extent of questioning and then changing their own policies.

John and Laura. Films of distressed young children, John in a children's home and Laura in hospital, 50 years ago led to great changes which could be said to have followed the voice of the child. Parents gradually came to be encouraged to stay with their child in hospital.

One doctor described his pain on watching a film about two-year-old Laura, made with his permission on his own ward (MacCarthy 1979). At first he could not bear to believe that his well-intentioned policy of banning parents from the ward, because they were thought to upset children, could distress the children so much, and he dismissed the idea. Then the ward sister said that the film made her see everything in a new light and she was determined to change the policy, so he agreed, and became a leading advocate for welcoming parents into children's wards (Robertson and Robertson 1989).

Re-analysis of the Robertsons' films questions the assumption that young children are inevitably distressed in a new setting without their parents

(Barrett 1998). John and Laura initially react quite calmly and stoically and try to adapt. It is only when their efforts to establish relationships with the staff are repeatedly denied, and when Laura has had surgery, that they become more and more distressed. This suggests that young children can have reserves of confidence and willingness to adapt and take part in their new setting, if adults expect them to, and treat them as reasonable partners, not simply as helpless dependents. This also involves recognising how the children can be among each others' greatest asset and friends (Dunn 2004). Children were found to be happier in nurseries when they attended on the same days as their friends and could enjoy close, continuing friendships (Penn 1997a, 1998b).

Prejudice that it is not worthwhile to talk or listen to young children

This is the greatest barrier, and once it is overcome, the rewards of talking with children can help to resolve all the other barriers.

Methods of working and talking with young children

The next two sections mention a few of the books on this topic, rather than repeating the information given by them. A major resource is the practical books about play and games, which extend ways of consulting closely with young children. Careful working together is emphasised, for example, in *Never Too Young* (Miller 2003). This book describes practical techniques, games and creative activities through which young children have serious discussions, and lists the steps adults and children can take together: their manner of talking together, sitting on an equal level, not interrupting, being honest, acknowledging feelings, adults not asking questions when children expect adults already to know the answers. 'Why do you keep asking us questions when you know all the answers? Like 'What colour is it then?' demanded one four-year-old. 'You can see for yourself it's red, so why do you keep asking?' (Cousins 2003, p.16). *An Eye for an Eye Leaves Everyone Blind* (Finch 1998) also gives practical ways of working and playing with young children to resolve conflict, to listen, share and negotiate. There is a section on monitoring and review, which lists ways of checking how different approaches do or do not work over time. Children are asked which ones make them happy or unhappy, and adults check signs of progress such as 'time out' and other sanctions being used less often.

Books about babies communicating with adults and with one another show how early in life they begin to express themselves through their voices and bodies, to share, to join and leave a group, to lead and follow, to create rituals for greetings and farewells (Goldschmeid and Selleck 1996) and to become disturbed if they see another baby is distressed (Eisenberg 1992).

Empowering Children and Young People: A Training Manual for Promoting Involvement in Decision-making (Treseder 1997) is about eight-year-olds plus, but makes many points about consulting groups and individuals of any age. The book covers ways that children can manage consultations: organise meetings; welcome people; agree the agenda; think about timing; take turns when talking; use play for icebreakers and energisers to keep up people's interest and enthusiasm; break up into smaller groups during meetings; use short clear words; have pre-meetings to help new people see more clearly what is going on; and ensure that everyone understands each new point. There are exercises for young people and adults to increase their skill and cooperation. Consultation is seen as a long-term process in which each person gradually becomes more skilled, and groups develop long-standing methods, rather than quick one-off attempts. Slowly, people learn to share responsibility, to overcome barriers, and find which methods work best for them. The book has lists of barriers, tools and skills, and shows what can be gained when things go wrong. Groups of people at any age 'storm, form and norm' while they work through disagreements and while people with different temperaments get to know and trust one another. This process must be allowed for, if groups are not to give up consulting in the early stages.

The planning tree. An example of a method used with teenagers is the planning tree. When in small groups they draw a large tree trunk and talk about 'What can we do?'. Then they write the agreed aims on the trunk. They talk about whom they want to affect, and put the four main types of people on short branches. Then they talk about the good things they want to achieve with the help of these people, and write these on coloured cards to put on the branches. They talk about the bad effects that might happen, and finally about neutral or non-effects, again on coloured cards. The patterns formed by the tree help them to look ahead and put several ideas, which they may already be thinking about, into a helpful order and balance. Young children on school councils might use the tree when solving a problem or planning an activity (Treseder 1997).

The books emphasise that a vital part of consulting children is to respect their decisions. After long, careful discussion, for the staff to say, 'We would like to do what you want but we can't afford it' can be worse than not consulting children at all. It is necessary to explain any financial or other limitations while talking with children. Young children can understand about costs and budgeting.

Talking about budgets. Some children aged two to four years were given a budget of £30, represented by 30 discs, and a toyshop catalogue. They talked about which toys they would choose for their group to have and, with some adult help, they matched their 'money' to the toys they chose. 'They were able to consider the needs of the group as a whole, negotiate with each other, and choose a range of toys that were sensible, good buys.' One staff member said, 'It didn't really take up much time. I wouldn't have believed a child of two and a half could have been able to understand what was being asked of her so easily' (Miller 2003).

Coates (2004) observed children aged three to seven years drawing in their classrooms and weaving symbolism and stories into their drawings. She found that even three-year-olds were spending more time tracing letters than freely drawing, although they could still show how drawing expressed their rich imaginations. Thomas, aged four, drew the machine and pipes in a 'dog factory', explaining the system that produced the dogs while he drew. Tom, aged five, described almost an action picture while he drew the sun going down and the stars coming out over a detailed tall house with a butterfly and a dog kennel.

Methods of research with and by children

Points made in the previous section about practical communication are also useful in research with and by children. In all kinds of settings, children use simple research methods: talking, making a list or a few drawings to summarise the options they have described, and then voting for their most or least liked option by putting a mark, or a sticker or stone by their chosen items. Some groups choose from a set of pictures, or select a sad or happy face to express their response. Some groups use art equipment, make masks or puppets, create dramas and stories and collages to record their experiences, hopes or plans. Some make maps, for example, of their daily round of collecting firewood and animals' food in Nepal (Johnson et al. 1995), or an ecology map of birds sighted in Canada (Hart 1997). Some use cameras, tape recorders, survey sheets or video cameras. A comprehensive and very practical review of methods is to be found in *Children in Focus* (Boyden and Ennew 1997). Methods developed with, rather than on, adults who have little education or rights, through participatory appraisal, paved the way for children to become more involved too (Pratt and Loizos 1992). *Children's Childhoods Observed and Experienced* (Mayall 1994b), *Stepping Forward* (Johnson et al. 1998), Kirby (1999), *Research with Children* (Christensen and James 2008), Alderson (2008) are international collections which discuss research methods partly in the context of children's rights.

Ethics, Social Research and Consulting with Children and Young People (Alderson and Morrow 2004) reviews the legal and ethical background to consulting children. It is based on ten topics, to help adults to check the ethical questions and standards of their work with children in relation to:

- the purpose of the work
- possible costs and benefits
- respecting privacy and confidentiality
- decisions about which children to involve or exclude
- funding

- planning and revising research aims and methods

- informing the children and adults concerned

- consent

- reporting and using the findings

- the possible impact on children.

On the final point, much is written about the impact on children, and protecting and respecting them *during* research and other consultation, but little is written on the likely *after-effects* of research reports, possibly on millions of other children. For example, research is often quoted to 'prove' how vulnerable and dependent all children are, or all children related to the research in question, from looked after children to very young mothers. This book suggests how researchers can take account of the potential impact on all children of their published reports, and can try to ensure that their conclusions are firmly based in the evidence. Researchers respect children's worth and dignity by using positive images, avoiding discrimination, and enabling children to speak directly, in their own terms (Save the Children n.d.).

Interpreting evidence and responding to children's views

Once children have expressed views, there can be further challenges in deciding how to interpret and respond to them. Even when children appear to be talking directly, as in a television programme, it is vital to check how adults may be shaping children's responses. For example, they may confine children's responses to simple issues, and edit out longer words and more complex ideas (Thornborrow 1998). Research material which seems to support an obvious conclusion may have another explanation.

The book corner. Researchers showed children photographs of each main area of their family centre. They asked the children which areas they liked best and least. The book area was the least popular place (Miller 2003).

This example might be seen as evidence of children's immaturity and the need for adults to ensure that the book corner was well used. It could also be seen as a prompt to improve the books. However, through observing and listening, as well as asking direct questions, the researchers found that some children disliked the way the book corner was used – to keep them quiet and constrained, 'squashed on the carpet' as they said, and for reading stories to large groups. The family centre staff and children tried new ways of using the book corner and other areas more freely, and of having smaller story groups.

It is vital to ask wary, critical questions about the process of consulting at every stage of research, and to examine how the context, methods and relationships might shape the replies. Heather saying 'no' on p.116 illustrates how a seemingly obvious interpretation might be a misunderstanding. Examining *why* people think and speak the way they do, their reasoning and values, as well as their yes/no replies, is important.

Qualitative and quantitative research

Quantitative research asks 'How many?' and qualitative research asks 'What kind? What does it mean?'. Most research measures children quantitatively, and the reports emphasise numbers, tables and graphs, standardised and hypothetical questions and tests, and representative samples in controlled or laboratory conditions, to aid statistical analysis. If every child gives a different answer this is hard to quantify, whereas qualitative researchers may see this as useful insights into their diverse views. Quantitative methods tend to find that the children's reported abilities seem to be lower than qualitative reports of their everyday talk. Children may be more confident and articulate when researchers interact with them flexibly and with rapport, listening to each child's concerns as well as to common factors across groups. The leading researcher, Judy Dunn, commented: 'Young children's logical capacities in *conversation* are considerably greater than those reported in test situations' (Dunn 1995). An 'average' group of children in a 'representative' (healthy) sample (Grisso and Vierling 1978) inevitably knows far less about an illness than those selected for their relevant experience of the illness and treatment (Alderson 1993; Alderson *et al.* 2006a, 2006b). So how wise or ignorant children appear to be in certain matters very much depends on the sample of children selected for the research.

Much also depends on the research method. New understandings of babies' and children's immense capacities contradict more cautious, traditional and still dominant research conclusions. The new findings come from detailed research with selected children (Als 1999) and in their own everyday settings (Alderson 1993; Alderson and Goodey 1998; Murray and Andrews 2000; Alderson *et al.* 2006c). Such intensive and contextual research cannot be done with large numbers of children.

Yet the 'hard' methods of larger surveys to support 'scientific' generalisations remain more popular and generally respected than 'softer' approaches such as audiotaped or videotaped findings. High numbers are very important in measurements and generalisations to inform policy, planning and evaluations reliably, for example, about children living in poverty. But numbers can be unhelpful when researching children's capacities because the larger the numbers, the more brief and standardised each encounter, data collection and analysis has to be. Within cost and time constraints, children's diverse and subtle views tend to become lost. However, it does not matter if a few or many very young babies engage in long interactions with one another, or how many six-year-olds share in making decisions about their major surgery, or how many children are extremely distressed if they are smacked. The point is that *some* of them clearly have this capacity. And knowing this opens the way for adults to be more aware of all children's potential, and to search with each child how much he or she can understand and be involved, instead of assuming incapacity.

Qualitative research takes a rainbow approach, exploring many differences between each child and circumstance, while attempting to find common threads and to enlarge understanding and empathy. Quantitative research, by its very reliance on binary computer data recording and analysis, has to take a black and white approach, in order to classify and count similarities. Although many questions and variables may be involved, the computer can only recognise yes/no relies. It can be as dangerous, misleading, and possible to over-generalise about millions of children from a sub-sample of 200,000 children as from a sample of two. Qualitative and quantitative methods can both be used well or badly, appropriately or inappropriately, depending on the kinds of questions and data concerned.

Part of the challenge for researchers who discover unexpected abilities in young children is to gain respect for the qualitative methods they need to use, as well as for their findings. Some critics find fault with the methods used as an excuse to dismiss disturbing and challenging findings. A usual criticism is that the research involves too few children. However, criticisms about numbers may really express political and emotional reservations – the deeper feelings discussed in Chapter 5. Instead of being side-tracked into arguments about research methods, it may be more useful to discuss research politics – whether the critics are worried that emancipatory research findings might offend influential supporters and funders, and if so, why they are worried (for connections between research methods and politics, see Alderson 1998).

Respect for children's participation rights depends on having some confidence that children can be rational and reliable. In the past, research findings tended to prove assumptions about children's incompetence (for example, Grisso and Vierling's much quoted paper of 1978). Studies today find far greater competence, so which types of research are correct? Much depends on the beliefs and values of the researchers. People tend to find what they are looking for and miss what they do not expect to find, in their methods, and in their relationship with the children being researched – a cool detached manner, or warmer rapport.

To sum up the differences: traditional research uses methods that are liable to intimidate children, which can thereby underestimate their actual abilities and appear to confirm their incompetence. Methods that can be offputting or may underestimate abilities include: standardised questionnaires (though with careful design and content they can be very child-friendly); surveys with representative groups (such as asking healthy successful children about illness or crime or other matters outside their experience); testing hypotheses and standardised vignettes; use of 'laboratory conditions', 'objective' observations and assessment without seeking children's views and explanations that might make sense of their responses; 'trick' and covert research that may embarrass or distress the child, such as telling a child not to open a box and then secretly watching until the child does open the box. There is also the 12-minute stranger anxiety test to see how upset a baby becomes if the mother leaves the room and a stranger approaches the baby. The 'very distressing' test is still described in psychology text books with no comment that it is unethical (Harris and Butterworth 2002). The short box about ethics in this textook warns against causing 'prolonged distress' when studying infants (p.52). These two examples breach ethical research standards.

In contrast, some research with children who have chronic illness or disability reveals far higher levels of knowledge and competence relating to their condition (Bluebond-Langner 1978; Bearison 1991; Cousens and Stevens 1997; Alderson and Goodey 1998; Clark 2003; Alderson *et al.* 2006a, 2006b; Winter, in progress). These studies use observations and interactions with children in the context of their everyday lives, examine topics in which the children are expert, use semistructured narrative interviews, toys, games, drawings and other non-verbal media, avoid normative tests and judgements, work to establish friendly rapport and trust with children and to work with them as partners, and aim to understand their perspectives and reasoning. The latter approaches also tend to be informed by critiques of child development theory. They investigate how children's competencies are recognised or denied, encouraged or inhibited (James and Prout 1997; Mayall 2002).

Publishing and disseminating

Much research remains unpublished, which lets down the children and adults who contributed data, the research team, the funders, and everyone who might benefit from the findings. Critical reports and 'negative findings', which show that a technique or system does not work well, are especially liable not to be published. Yet they can be vital in helping to stop useless or harmful practices, and in speaking for young children whose difficulties or suffering may otherwise pass unrecognised. Funders sometimes veto publication. To avoid the serious problem of non-publication, it is useful to have a multidisciplinary advisory group willing to sort out clearly agreed and recorded publishing plans and copyrights in advance (National Children's Bureau (NCB) 1993) and to defend the project publicly if necessary.

Dissemination goes beyond publishing. The word literally means sowing seeds and, more than getting a report into people's hands, it is getting the ideas into their minds and helping them to become intellectually convinced and emotionally committed to the conclusions. Bridging the difficult gaps between research, policy and practice is helped when researchers meet policy-makers and practitioners half way to discuss how links might be made, without dictating how they should be made. Young researchers are very conscious of this crucial task. They tend to begin their projects by talking about whom they want to influence, and how, and what kinds of research will help to achieve these aims (Cockburn, Kenny and Webb 1997; Alan Siddall, Save the Children, 1999, personal communication). The next section look at the levels of involving children from individual personal decisions to international policy making.

Making personal decisions

It can be easier for adults to share in making personal decisions with one child than with larger groups when different children's interests and contributions have to be balanced. Health and social services staff have to consult the individuals they care for. However, children may not be informed properly before or during meetings and may be daunted by the other adults attending. Common Assessment Frameworks in the Children's Agenda increase the numbers of professionals present, and the ways this can intimidate and silence families (and the huge time and costs involved) have not been fully thought through. Genuinely informing, preparing and supporting children through the whole process of consultation especially involves five aspects (Hodgson 1995):

1. Access to those with power – it is unhelpful for junior staff to talk to children if they cannot ensure that reasonable requests will be met.

2. Being provided with relevant information, before, during and after being consulted. In at least some social services departments children are discouraged from attending court hearings ('You'll be bored' – as if their life chances do not matter) and they may not be told until weeks later about a decision where they will live (Masson and Winn 1999).

3. Genuine choice between clear options, but not trivial choices like 'We're moving you on, do you want to go by bus or by train?' (Gardner 1989).

4.   A trusted independent person to give support and be a
      representative if needed, with the child having some choice in
      who this person is.

5.   A means of redress for appeal or complaint.

Beyond the individual level of adults and children working in pairs and
small groups, how can children's views influence policies at a wider level –
in local communities, nationally and internationally? Also, at what levels,
in relation to the degree of involvement, do young children take part in influencing and making decisions? Are children used by adults, or at least
informed by them, or are they more fully consulted, and can they take a
leading part in projects? The following sections consider these questions.

At home and school

Research repeatedly finds that children highly value being with their
families and friends, and pets, and having time to play, to have fun and to
potter about in their own time and space. They report having much more
freedom at home, and that parents and grandparents are mainly more
willing to listen, to negotiate and to take their views seriously than
teachers are able to do (Beck 1997; Morrow 1998, 2003; Neale 2002;
Mayall 2006). In and around their homes, Save the Children (2005b)
worked with 13 young Gypsy/Traveller researchers to interview 109 of
their peers aged 7–20 years, and they found 'alarming, disturbing and
worsening' problems with discrimination, lack of legal sites and accommodation, schooling and health care. Warrington (2006) researched
with 148 young travellers aged 4–15 years. At least ten were advisers to
the project, which examined their views on identity (having fun, love),
accommodation, racism, learning and school, 'when I grow up', and their
views on helpful and unhelpful services. The report is illustrated with their
art work. Their whole lives are coloured by the lack of enough legal
traveller sites.

In another beautifully illustrated practical report covering home and
school, Save the Children (2005a) worked with Salusbury WORLD Refugee
Centre, the only refugee centre to be based in a primary school, to promote the
welcome and inclusion of refugee children and families in school. Gidley
(2005) gives a powerful report of the severe restrictions and dangers for young
families living in violent inner London tower block estates.

As mentioned earlier, many children want a life–work divide between home and school (Alldred, David and Edwards 2002). They do not want teachers to know about some aspects of their lives and save up problems to share with parents when they get home. However, they are being ever more closely organised through extended schools (see Chapter 1). Play areas are disappearing from infant school classrooms, play times are being cut or cancelled (Blatchford 1998), and playgrounds and playing fields continue to be sold off. The Government's policy that parents can move their children into popular schools means that more classrooms are built on the shrinking playgrounds that are then used by more children. Teachers are advised to use formal instruction methods with narrow streamed ability groups, and activities that can be tested, rather than shared discovery and creative differentiated work in mixed ability groups.

From autumn 1999, parents were invited to sign home–school agreements promising regular and punctual attendance, good discipline and behaviour and homework (DfEE 1998b). These do not allow for children's reasonable reactions to things they are unhappy about at school, and are the opposite of real contracts which are specific agreements between fairly equal, informed and unpressured people or groups based on mutual consultation (Save the Children 1999). School governors do not have to consult pupils when each school designs its own contract. Governors are left to decide whether 'the pupils concerned are sufficiently mature to understand the contents of the agreement'. What is not clear is the point of parents making promises, such as those about their child's future behaviour, if the child is seen as unable to understand the promise.

At the local community level

Sara Bryson (2007, personal communication) described eight innovative children's participation projects, which include the following.

Babies' evaluations of a weekly Baby Social at a Sure Start Centre: the staff followed four babies for six weeks, using observation forms to note: when each child accepted or refused things offered, gazed intently, turned towards or reached out for objects or people, facial expressions, body movements, responses such as tears or laughter, indicated preferences through given options, and the length of time spent playing with a toy, object or person. Interviews were also conducted with parents and staff. Babies liked the treasure baskets and natural and household objects, the musical instruments and songs, and interaction with other children, and these aspects were promoted.

During a *Family Fun Day*, young children's views were gathered using disposable cameras, artwork, informal chat, observation sheets and parent and practitioner interviews. Toddlers enjoyed the events but babies became bored and irritable in their prams and buggies so that families had to leave. A baby tent was developed and became very popular.

During *sensory walks* around their local area, 113 two- to four-year-olds used disposable cameras to capture their likes (other people, green spaces) and dislikes (derelict housing, wound up swings, nettles). Some used dictaphones and others gave thumbs up and down signs. Their favourite photos were displayed to inform a meeting for local decision and policy makers. A report detailed their top ten likes and dislikes, and a poster summarised the project findings for the children. A repeat of the project after some years could assess responses to the children's views and any changes that had been made.

What Matters To Us consulted children aged from birth to 19 to inform the development of the Children and Young People's Plan for Newcastle. The children continue to be involved. Some centres are exploring how young children can identify areas for improvements, suggest ideas and allocate funds. Trained *Children's Champions* are working across Newcastle to promote young children's participation.

Children aged from eight years are involved in recruiting and selecting staff for Hull local authority (Barbara Ryan, 2007, personal communication).

Participation Education Group involved 187 of their members aged 5–25 in a survey for their report on how schools can seriously damage your health (Participation Education Group (PEG) 1997).

Working mainly with small groups, often of disadvantaged children, researchers have shown how skilful children can be when they are involved in giving evidence and in working as co-researchers. Researchers have written detailed reports of their research findings and their methods (Boyden and Ennew 1997; Willow 1997; Kirby 1999; Kirby *et al.* 2003; Willow *et al.* 2004): the funding, ethics and access; how children and adults together design research methods; topics and questions; numerous ways of collecting data; and their discussions about what the data mean and how they can be reported; and how to work with authorities to ensure that the findings are understood and used. The reports include work in the UK by, for example, children living on deprived housing estates, who are involved at various stages of the research (West 1995; Howarth and Hopscotch Asian Women's Centre 1997; Wellard, Tearse and West 1997). Most of those involved are young people; far less is known about the views of younger children, such as those being looked after by local authorities (Thomas 1998; Winter 2006) and the decisions they would like to share in making when their parents separate (O'Quigley 1999; Smart *et al.* 2001). Müller (2007, personal communication) asked nine children aged 4–12 years about their views on their role in the city and their use of social time and space. They each kept a camera for seven days. The response of each child is separately recorded and the complications of this kind of project are honestly recorded. All the children authorised the use of their real names and had editorial control over the report.

Willow (1997) includes assessments about what consultation methods do or do not work well, and the strong arguments for involving children – for example, the Langley Children's Forum, Rochdale, involves people aged 5–14; through Kids Count, the Newcastle Victoria Infirmary responds to children's views (Cunliffe and English 1997); and Derby Children's Hospital was designed with the help of 130 people aged 6–16 in workshops. The Derby architect said, 'It makes our job a lot easier…now we know what they want…this is their building', for example, lower reception desks enable the children to see over them when they check themselves in.

Hampshire Social Services asked foster carers' own children for their views about foster children. The views were quite positive, until the children were asked to complete the sentence 'When a foster child leaves I feel…' The children replied 'I feel relieved', which made social workers more concerned about their feelings, so that they now attend more to this group as well as to the fostered children.

In one project, over two years, health visitors in Tower Hamlets worked with four- to six-year-olds and found they disliked: cockroaches, dogs, dirty noisy streets, grassy areas because they had broken glass/dog dirt/rubbish, and the lack of trees, flowers and play areas. The adults reported: 'This project has clearly demonstrated that even children as young as four are able to communicate how they feel'.

In Greenwich, people aged 8–19 advised on the Borough's anti-poverty strategy and showed the value of consulting people of different age groups with different experiences of being excluded, with many valuable ideas coming to light. Over five years, several London boroughs consulted 4500 people aged 7–17 on regeneration. Careful planning, clear targets and outcomes with time scales are vital, and these the London project produced with the support of senior officials.

When children in Kirkholt, Rochdale, were consulted about improving their neighbourhood, using a 12-foot scaled model of the area, a seven-year-old asked: 'But how will we know when things have happened?'. So the Council kept in touch with the children, reported progress, and returned to consult them at each new stage. (All the examples are in Willow 1997.)

The Redbridge report, which included the book-corner survey mentioned on p.152 (National Early Years Network (NEYN)/Redbridge LA 1998), describes:

- the advantages and disadvantages of using outside consultants, and the value of using them to pass on their skills to the staff

- the principles of a successful consultation, such as being positive

- the need to agree on clear plans, timescales, and resource allocation, including cover for staff involved in the project

- plans for staff training, and for informing everyone affected by the project, before, during and afterwards; this may mean writing to some adults and children individually if messages are not passed on to them

- the necessary commitment of the adults concerned to listen respectfully and to act on the findings

- the flexible methods of varied meetings, interviews, surveys and observations used, and the detailed encounters and findings.

At the regional level

During 2000, the Office of Children's Rights Commissioner for London (OCRCL), a voluntary organisation allied to CRAE and set up to campaign for Children's Rights Commissioners) consulted nearly 3000 young Londoners aged 3–17 (1237 replies were from children aged 11 and under). The survey was conducted for and by children with the help of the Office staff, whom they had appointed. The young Londoners identified their eight main concerns as: poverty and economic wellbeing; health; enjoyment (play, arts, sports, leisure); education; transport and road safety; families and care; racism and violence; housing. They also valued children's participation. Their replies were summarised in *Sort It Out!*, an A3 size colourfully illustrated report, sent to all the participating individuals and groups.

The survey replies also went to inform the first report of *The State of London's Children* (Hood 2002), based on the eight themes, which extrapolated national and local borough records to show, for example, that inner London has the highest rates of child poverty in the country, in one of the richest cities in the world. Hard work by the young people and staff at OCRCL ensured that the Greater London Authority (GLA) took the reports very seriously. The GLA Act 1998 had set eight strategies for the Mayor, but did not mention children. By 2003, the GLA not only had a new Strategy for Children and Young People, but also young people from OCRCL attended meetings of GLA committees. (The adult members preferred the summaries for children to their own long papers.) And further, a new version of the OCRCL was installed inside the GLA building, as an intergal part of the Authority. The GLA published the second and third editions of *The State of London's Children* (Hood 2004; McNeish 2007).

The report *Effective Government Structures for Children* (Hodgkin and Newell 1996) called for national changes to enable central government to be more responsive to the needs and rights of children across the UK. These included: child impact and budget analyses of the effects directly on children (not just on families or schools) of all government policies; routine methods of consulting children and promoting their active participation; annual reports on the state of UK children; closer liaison between all government departments about how they affect children; a children's rights commissioner; and other changes which go right to the heart of government in the cabinet office. Few of these vital aims have yet been fully realised.

At the national level

Children's (Rights) Commissioners

Scotland, Wales and Northern Ireland do now have active Children's Rights Commissioners with busy offices and websites. NICCY (a popular media dog's name as well as the Northern Ireland Office's acronym), for example, has set up an ethics committee with young members to vet projects. The English Children's Commissioner was appointed more recently, in 2005. Unlike the other three Commissioners, the English one does not have 'rights' in the title, must consult the Secretary of State before holding an independent inquiry, can be directed by the Secretary of State to carry out an inquiry, cannot report directly to the national Parliament/Assembly, and is tied to government policy, so cannot be such an independent voice as the other three (CRAE 2006, s.16–7).

State of Children's Rights in England

CRAE is a coalition of more than 380 voluntary and statutory organisations committed to the full implementation of the UNCRC. CRAE's two recent reports give comprehensive overviews. The *Alternative Report to the Committee on the Rights of the Child* (CRAE 2007) coordinates the Children's non-governmental organisations' (NGOs') responses to the UK Government's Third Report to the UN Committee (DfES/DCFS 2007b). Over 100 dense pages, covering every aspect of children's lives and rights, are mainly critical of the Government's record. The UK Government submits reports to the UN for all four countries; laws about children apply to England and for non-devolved matters to Wales too, although Scotland and Northern Ireland tend to pass similar laws later on.

CRAE's (2006) *State of Children's Rights in England* reviews the UK Government's action up to 2006 to respond to the 2002 *Concluding Observations of the UN Committee* (UN 2002) to the UK Government's report in 2000. (The UNICEF website publishes the regular reports from every country, except from the USA and Somalia who have not ratified the UNCRC, with the UN Committee's responses.) CRAE reviews every statement from the UN Committee's 78 recommendations to make UK law, policy and practice compatible with the UNCRC and finds that significant progress has been made on only 12 of these. Each item shows an arrow, up for progress, down for deterioration, and level for no significant progress in the past year. Just one example will be reviewed here.

The Government claims that its policy *Every Child Matters* (ECM) and its five outcomes (being healthy, staying safe, enjoying and achieving, making a positive contribution and economic wellbeing) are in addition to, as if they are broader than, the UNCRC. The UNICEF UK website has a table linking the five outcomes to the UNCRC Articles. However, Article 16 on privacy rights is missing, even though, as discussed in Chapter 2, it is a central and original foundation right. CRAE (2006 s.12–15) has a table that includes the following:

What it gives children:

UNCRC   40 substantive rights on all aspects of childhood, a clear set of entitlements.

ECM   five outcome goals open to wide interpretation and discretion.

What it requires of Government:

UNCRC   a comprehensive set of legal obligations.

ECM   no legal obligations.

In comparison to UNCRC, ECM is weak in its legal status, lack of independent monitoring, likely transient and insecure status, guiding vague principles, and in its construction of childhood. In contrast, the UNCRC advances concepts of active child rights holders, enjoying civil rights and freedoms. Childhood is a precious time in its own right. CRAE shows further disadvantages to ECM, by comparing in detail the 'stay safe' and the 'make a positive contribution' outcomes with related UNCRC Articles. The Government claims that children were consulted when ECM was being planned. However, they were given a list of six outcomes to choose from, and one popular one on inclusion and non-discrimination was later dropped. This example of 'consultation' warns of the dangers of the present fashion for consulting children when their views are misrepresented. Scraton's report (2006) is among a range of thoughtful publications showing there is still a very long way to go if British children's rights are to be respected at national level.

At the international level

Children used to decorate international conferences, perhaps by singing or handing out the programmes. Now they hold parallel sessions and join the main body to present their own sessions. They want a world fit for children (UN 2002; and for a review see John 2003, pp.198–201). The UN Committee on the Rights of the Child hears regular reports from governments on their progress in implementing the Convention. More critical reports from NGOs are also submitted, through a growing body of evidence about children's lives, which includes some reports from children. The UNCRC works as a tool for consulting children about every aspect of their lives, in order to improve ways of implementing the UNCRC using their knowledge (Ennew 1997; European Commission Network on Childcare 1996).

One international organisation, initiated by street children, campaigns for better conditions (see the special issue of *Childhood* (3, 2), including Bemak 1996; Ennew and Connolly 1996). Since 1992, EcoCity has enabled young children to research and present their views about their city to councillors. Given enough time and resources, this can have 'valuable and significant outcomes…adults are always amazed and impressed at children's ability to understand complex issues such as city infrastructure and their realistic suggestions about how to improve their local and global environment, and to consider other needs, rights and responsibilities' (Willow 1997). As global communications and networks grow, international associations for children and young people are also likely to increase. One fast-growing method is through email and website contacts, which overcome many of the costs and other problems of travel and needing escorts for children.

General points

Most of the reports mentioned in this chapter discuss why it is important to consult children, the barriers to doing so, and ways around the barriers. There are limitations in over-individualising children's responses and not relating them to broader political contexts. One way to address this huge and neglected area of children speaking at national and international levels is through overviews and cooperation between many smaller projects. Overviews can show how the many views complement or contradict one another, and why, how gaps might be filled, and how research and practice reports could be coordinated to support more general recommendations based on children's views and experiences. For example, the Redbridge enquiry (NEYN/Redbridge LA 1998), mentioned earlier, involved over 70 children aged from two to eight years across the Borough. Among the outcomes of the enquiry, pre-school centres have listened through new methods, and schools are using the children's ideas on helping new children to settle into school, on dealing with bullying, improving a school map and resolving problems in dinner queues.

Another approach is to devise methods of large-scale enquiry among young children to complement smaller in-depth studies. The question-naire booklet mentioned on p.102 which divided children's participation rights into topics which concern children at school and asked them for their views, in simple sections, is one such example (Alderson 1999). Over 2500 young people replied, aged from 7–17 years. Younger children could take part more in such mass surveys developed with their help, and completed individually and in small groups, working with someone older to read and write for them. The first national government-funded programme of research about children's own views (1996–2000) concen-trated on the ages 5–16. Researchers became more convinced of how worthwhile it can be to consult children and to work with 'user' organisa-tions, as they were encouraged to do (Economic and Social Research Council (ESRC) 1996).

Levels of participation

Besides the levels of scale, there are also different degrees of participation when children and adults work together, as reviewed in this section. One of the first reports on participation to be published, about adults, takes an American model of democracy and liberty (Arnstein 1969).

At the lowest levels, people may be exploited against their will or inter-ests. The pretence of being involved can be worse than being excluded. At higher levels, people share power more equally, and at the highest level citizens or service users are free to develop their own concerns.

Roger Hart's (1992) ladder suits schools and nurseries more, though it is criticised as too cautious, to adult-centric, and too concerned with adults bestowing opportunities to participate on to children (Franklin 2002; John 2003).

Arnstein's ladder of participation

1. Manipulation – pretending to consult.

2. Therapy – talking which does not lead to any change.

3. Information – from those in authority.

4. Consultation – but not necessarily with any active results.

5. Placation – seeming to change and involve people more but with no real effects.

6. Partnership – sharing planning and decision-making.

7. Delegated power – citizens share control and bargain with officials.

8. Citizens' control – through routine programmes.

Hart's ladder of participation

1. Manipulation.

2. Decoration – like children singing at adult conferences.

3. Tokenism – such as children being used to seem to rubber-stamp adults' decisions.

4. Assigned but not informed.

5. Consulted and informed.

6. Adult-initiated, shared decisions with children.

7. Child-initiated and directed.

8. Child-initiated, shared decisions with adults.

There is some disagreement over whether children are most emancipated when they act independently or with adults. When young children have information and support from adults, they are more likely to be able to negotiate informed decisions, and to solve problems with practical effects. One example is the preschool group of children who planned a menu working to a budget, went shopping and cooked the meal together, with some adult help (Miller 2003). As with the dinosaur project in Chapter 2, this shows the benefits of children having time and space to share their own ways of creating and of solving problems, without needing adults to intervene. 'Working with young people is constantly changing and developing, and we must develop new models of good practice to...add to our power to influence' (Save the Children 1998). Here, the ladder is seen as:

E) child initiated and directed

D) child initiated, shared decisions

C) adult initiated, shared decisions

B) consulted and informed

A) assigned but informed

The ladders have been criticised as adult-centric (John 2003), and as over-general by Thomas (2002, 2007) who prefers a wall. Ladders are perhaps useful, not so much as markers to measure progress up the levels, but as ways of clarifying and checking how much children are involved in each part of a project, and how much more they might be involved depending on what is practical and effective. Children and adults may disagree about the assessments and need to discuss them. Groups often work at several different levels of the ladder at once.

Another way of clarifying degrees of participation is to divide them into two simple types. *Latent* participation is having a share or a stake in activities, taking part almost by default. *Active* participation means being actively involved at all levels of decision-making, having a real say. Children are quickly aware of tokenism and being 'played like fools'

(Morrow 1999b). As adults and young children gain experience, confidence and expertise in working together more actively, higher and wider (national and international) levels of participation are likely to be achieved.

CHAPTER SEVEN

Consulting Young Children and Taking Risks

One frequent theme in reports about consulting and researching with young children is about balancing play and work. Questions arise about who is working or playing, and the contribution of play. When it is fun and interesting for all concerned, this can encourage imaginative creativity and enjoyment in shared projects, as well as enthusiasm for the aims they might achieve. This chapter reviews how work and play mix, or are distinct from one another, and what play means. One main complication when consulting children is adults' concerns about risk, and potential loss of control, conflict and violence, and doubts about when adults should be in sole control or share responsibilities with young children. These are the topics for the second part of this chapter. Articles 12 and 13 are central to this chapter, expressing views, sharing information and decisions, resolving problems, but many other Articles are also relevant, on work and play and on the protections and provisions that are being negotiated. This chapter continues the theme of respect for young children's capacities and working out with them how competent they can be.

Playing and working

Adults sometimes give mixed messages to children. 'We're going to play some games and have fun doing this', a play worker might say, when she wants to find out their views on bullying. If the children respond by playing around and enjoying themselves, the adults worry that the balance between serious consulting and fun has gone wrong. This is partly because 'play' has conflicting meanings.

Play has been described as the child's work or language. Adults use 'play with a purpose' to educate children, to assess their physical, cognitive and emotional development, to help them to practise for their adult future, and to occupy and control them, usually gently but firmly. In contrast, to many children, this kind of play is too much mixed with duty. For them, play is freedom from adult control, spontaneously doing as they like and as they choose *because* they enjoy that, and for no other reason, an especially precious time, which many children rarely have. Adults often find this free play worrying and threatening, if it seems to border on danger or conflict, seems too noisy or chaotic or too much like time-wasting nonsense. However, other adults see this as real play, a complex 'unfolding narrative' (Mayles 1989; Strandell 2000), which children organise themselves if given the chance. In this second view, notions of 'poor quality' or 'inappropriate' play are contradictions in terms if play is valued for itself. Whereas adults tend to use play for other purposes, children see play as an end in itself. For adults, play is about developing the (future) self; for children, play is often about being in (present) relationships (Holdigan 2000).

Conflicts between adults' and children's meanings of play are increased when the adults begin a session on consulting children by emphasising the fun and play aspects. Adults may be vague about the consultation purposes, for fear of boring, confusing or deterring the children. If the children respond by playing at tasks they have been set, which are not very relevant to the consultation, the adults may then assume that children cannot be consulted – before they have tried asking them directly.

Other adult meanings of play include pretend play, and play as an escape from harsh reality and the pressures of real life. Play used as a diversion by consulters during breaks and energisers – games to renew children's enthusiasm – fits this view of play as fantasy, which children are used to adults assuming. However, if the consulting involves real serious work, to affect present realities, and not simply to practise for the future, then it is confusing to mix it too much with play.

In the majority world, almost all the work which children and young people do – housework, babysitting, washing a car, weekend work in a shop – is not seen as real work but as practising for adulthood (Morrow

1994), opportunities which adults provide for children. The play worker on the housing estate quoted in the Introduction, who said he was used to 'working' with young children but was amazed to find that he could consult them, expresses this assumed split between working adults and playful children. Consulting involves partly closing this split, and working on a serious equal level. When consulting is too playful, it is harder for adults and children to see their more equal status and shared serious purpose.

The same activity might be called play when children do it and work when adults do it, like making the dinosaur models (Chapter 2). In an art class, it is usually assumed that the teacher is working and the children are simply learning, whereas in reality, the children are doing the artwork and often the more the teacher holds back, the better the work will be, as Sibyl Marshall's (1963) beautiful book about a village school shows. The English language does not have a word for activity which is serious, challenging, may be difficult, enjoyable, amusing, fun, entertaining, and rewarding both in itself and for other reasons. When adults plan to consult young children seriously, they need to decide if they plan to use playful methods, and if so which kinds and why. Play can complement work and is useful in several ways for effective consultation. People of all ages can work more intensely and closely together when they also enjoy playful ice-breakers, and activities which mix fun with effort. By laughing together they may become more relaxed, open, trusting, and attentive.

Play and research

Play methods are integral to some methods of consulting children.

The naughty teddy. One of the most important scientific studies with young children was done with a 'naughty teddy'. As mentioned earlier, psychologists had been led to believe that young children's thinking is inconsistent and confused because, in tests devised by Piaget and replicated around the world, when they were asked the same question several times, they tended to vary their answers. It seems that the children assumed that researchers wanted a different answer each time the children were asked a question, but when the children tried to be helpful, researchers assumed that they could not think consistently. However, when asked the same questions by the teddy, the children laughed at his repetitions and firmly repeated their original answers. They did not feel they had to be polite to the teddy or pretend not to notice his curious repetitions (Donaldson 1978).

Similarly, researchers asking children about smacking enquired through Splodge, an ignorant visitor from another planet, so avoiding the problem of asking the children questions to which children would expect adults already to know the answers (Willow and Hyder 1998). Winter's (in progress) interviews with children aged four to seven years about abusive parents used creative artwork. The children could use the art to express their wishes and feelings and to control the timing, pace and topics of the interviews.

Researchers planning to interview children aged from eight years about how much they felt they were involved in decisions about their major surgery decided to use hospital play sets and art work. The aims were to help children to express themselves and to help them (and perhaps the researchers) to feel relaxed and comfortable when talking about stressful topics (Alderson 1993). However, the children were not interested in toys; rather, they wanted to be interviewed as they had seen people talking on television. Many seemed very pleased to have a chance to tell their story.

Children, including those with severe learning difficulties, often very much enjoy talking and singing into a tape recorder and hearing their voices (Alderson and Goodey 1998). Play methods can tap children's imagination. Talking about 'let's pretend' can involve young children in planning improvements in playgrounds and nurseries. One lively, well-illustrated pack produced with children shows how to promote genuine participation, negotiation and power sharing (Save the Children/Kirklees 1996). The play approaches help research teams to enjoy being together as well as working together. There are details on promoting equal opportunities and 'chat space methods'.

However, instead of assuming that play is the only language and method through which to work with young children, consulters could decide what kinds of play, if any, might be useful, and why, and with whom. Otherwise, children might feel used and not properly consulted, either over the methods they are expected to work with, or about the purpose of the consulting. They may want to opt out but feel that they can only refuse indirectly, by not cooperating. Then, the adults' methods of consulting will contradict their purposes of listening and respecting. Work and play often overlap, but there are times when one or other is most appropriate, and consulting young children involves 'working out' with them when this is so (Kefyalew 1996).

Making videos

Making videos enables children to express their experiences very directly. Yet the more elaborate and intriguing the equipment, the more the children may want to play and experiment with it, rather than using it as a tool to respond to adults' questions. Brazilian children acted to the video camera, which they were not allowed to hold, as if they were playing grand parts in a play. This frustrated the researchers who wanted the children to respond more 'naturally' (Faulkner 1998). When presented with a new gadget such as a video camera, some people read the handbook or ask an expert for help, and other people of all ages 'play around' with it, discovering and inventing imaginatively for themselves how to use it and how it works. This latter approach enables some children to use the camera more imaginatively.

Many young children handle cameras confidently, but if the equipment is new to them, it helps to allow enough time for them to play with it, and to see all their responses as useful parts of the consultation. If there is not time to play experimentally, then it may be better to use familiar or more simple tools. One project found that the children preferred not t ̕ write about their views, but to use video and Polaroid cameras as powerful tools to express their strong views (Smith, F. 1998). For example, one group disliked the term 'after-school club' and renamed their club as 'the crystal palace'.

Elaborate aids are not necessarily helpful. When young children were consulted about new playground plans, they tended to say 'yes' to everything which the attractive puppets asked them, and to run under the parachute because they liked doing that, rather than answer to the adults' questions. Later the questioners resorted to asking children simply to point to the pictures of equipment they preferred (Newson 1995b).

Focus groups

Children's (and adults') responses vary, depending on the setting, size of groups, methods and attitudes of the researchers. Focus groups generate new ideas through the interactions between all members of the group. The conversations are rather more like everyday talk, instead of stilted replies to set questions. Yet 'ordinary' talk can be rather chaotic and interrupted (as the next box shows).

Consulting in groups: between control and chaos. In focus groups about children's views of violence (Smith, M. 1998c), the girls cooperated with the researchers and tried to keep order and repair interruptions which the boys kept making. The boys tried to stay on the edges of the talk, and joined in rather disruptively as if they were interested but wanted to keep their independence and not fit in neatly with the adults' plans. The researchers were pleased with these revealing responses, and felt that the boys were joining in on their own terms, and that the aim to encourage everyday free talk worked well – despite problems with transcribing the audio-tapes.

Some of the main complications when consulting children are adults' concerns about risk, and potential loss of control, about conflict and violence, and doubts about when adults should be in sole control or share responsibilities with young children. These complications are now explored.

Risk and control

John, Susan, Roger and Titty, aged 7–12 years, asked their parents if they could go off sailing and camping on their own in the Lake District for three weeks. Their naval officer father sent a telegram giving permission by saying: 'Better drowned than duffers, if not duffers, won't drown' (Ransome 1930).

Although this is a fictional example, and exciting children's books have somehow to remove the parents in Chapter 1, it illustrates the great change in beliefs about reasonable risks over the past few decades in the UK. Matters on which children can be consulted and trusted are in many ways more limited today than they have ever been, because of fears about risk and control. There never was a golden age of respecting children, but in the past children tended to be left alone more by adults in their free time to play in the streets, the countryside and, for wealthier children, in large gardens.

Concern about risk reduces the scope for consulting children. The examples of William Blake, Albert, Margaret and Kevin in the Introduction show how beliefs about reasonable risk vary greatly. As reviewed earlier, fears of stranger danger and of increased traffic have cut down ways in which young children can express views, such as a wish to walk around the town alone. Adults do not offer choices; rather, they veto them. A young child out alone in an English street today tends to be seen with pity, and concern about parents' negligence, and even almost as fair game by molesters, not as an ordinary pedestrian like Albert or Margaret. It is as if the streets in the UK now belong to adults as well as the roads. Children are treated and seen, by adults and by themselves, as dependent and vulnerable when they do not have the chance to be independent. Through lack of opportunity they are less competent and confident. When children have to ask adults' permission about many aspects of their lives, this can reinforce beliefs that adults must decide all matters, such as when children eat or sleep, what they wear or read, when they go out or stay at home, without necessarily consulting children's views.

The mass media promote vulnerable child images. When this page was originally being written, in August 1999, every English national newspaper's front page reported two lost and then found ten-year-olds in Hastings. While this page was being revised for the second edition in 2007, for many months the daily headline news had been about a four-year-old English girl lost in Portugal. Intense publicity about dangers limits children's freedom to roam and to meet together in public spaces, far more in Britain than in many countries. If children stay in extended schools and do not learn to mix freely with friends and other age groups in solidarity in public spaces, they are left much more vulnerable. The questions arise: To whom does childhood belong when children's time and space are organised around adults' priorities about children's best inter-ests? And how much say can and should children have in daily choices? (Lorenzo 1992; Shamgar-Handleman 1994).

A decision, which seems cautious to one person, can look dangerously risky to another. Increasingly, risk is not simply the chance of slight harm to the child, but of all the possible dangers which might occur and should be prevented. In a risk-conscious society, accidents are believed not to exist; someone must always be found to blame (Green 1997). Risk man-agement transfers greater responsibility on to adults and more dependency on to children, as shown by the contrast between children's holidays in the 2000s and in the 1930s earlier sailing example (see page 176). These fears restrict children's rights and freedoms in Britain, just as fears about the risks of terrorism are restricting adults' freedoms.

The important gains in safety are seldom balanced, in public debates, with important losses of children's freedoms, independence, confidence and adventurousness that were once taken for granted.

School and college education for future parents and carers

While I was researching in a school, Helena showed me the first page of her GCSE childcare file, outlining the two-year curriculum. The course had three main themes: equipment, safety and food. The equipment section covered many items which babies and young children are supposed to need: clothes, cots and prams, baby chairs and travelling bags, trikes and slides. Pictures of these were cut from catalogues and neatly stuck into pages of notes. The play and activity sections emphasised, besides the required toys, the vital need to keep children safe from accidents, infection and any other dangers; they must be constantly cleaned and guarded. Chil-dren's slow cognitive development, set out in milestones, 'proved' their helpless irresponsibility and need for constant adult control.

The food sections were filled with leaflets from firms that provide refined and 'junk' food and drink which described the 'nutritional value' of their products. The leaflets mentioned children as fussy eaters who should be served very carefully prepared and presented food, for example, in the shape of a face or an animal to tempt them to eat. Science and tech-nology were emphasised, even in simple matters. Helena looked at her drawing of the milk ducts inside the breast, and when asked if she thought she might breast-feed she shuddered: 'Ugh no, it's dirty and you can't see how much the baby is getting'.

The main messages of the course appeared to be: children are very expensive and endlessly demanding; they are fussy and very hard to please; adults must never rest from guarding helpless children from all kinds of known or potential or invisible risks, like patients who need nursing. There seemed to be nothing about fun, adventure, rights, or children as agents who contribute to one another's enjoyment and learning. There was no questioning of the commercial interests and pressures in the leaflets. Instead of encouraging students to think about consulting children, the course included many ways of discouraging them from thinking of consulting children, or thinking independently and critically themselves. When we recently observed the under-3s room in a Children's Centre, we found that staff returned from courses enthusiastic to arrange more adventurous and messy play, but they seemed to be unable to change the routines and restrictions. The Government's aim to provide 'affordable' childcare, paid for by parents, with the huge bureaucratic and new build overheads, involves mainly very low paid and under-trained staff providing the care and the staff hierarchy, with more highly qualified staff being more remote from the children, and does not encourage reasonable risk-taking.

The Every Child Matters agenda is greatly expanding childcare training, but despite mention of the 'strong child' and the 'capable child' the emphasis is still on protecting and providing for children, rather than participating with them on more equal terms.

Risk and probability

Reasons for not consulting with young children include beliefs that they have very little idea about the future and therefore about dangers, risks and probabilities. Consulting often involves asking about past events in order to plan or alter future events. If children are too vague about past and future, they are barred from this process. Yet although the younger ones are often confused about terms like 'tomorrow', 'next week', 'in an hour' or 'soon' (perhaps because adults give this last word such an elastic vague meaning) they have some sense of past and future. Much depends on the way things are explained. Probability becomes clearer when children talk about how probable it might be that today it will rain, or a dragon will arrive, or they will have chips for lunch, or their parents might win the lottery. Risks and associated cautions can be discussed in terms of the risks of being knocked down by a car or an elephant. Surgeons describe children aged seven or eight years as understanding the risks of major high-risk surgery in terms of the risks of crossing the road. They described painful treatment now to prevent future problems maybe 10 or 20 years ahead as being like saving money in the bank to spend it in the future (Alderson 1993).

If adults are to overcome the complications of consulting children posed by worry about risks, they need to discuss exactly which risks they are worried about and why, what benefits are lost if they do not consult children, and if there are any real risks, why they could be worth taking and how they might be shared or reduced by involving the children.

Challenging conflict

Other complicated matters are conflict and violence. This section considers examples of adults' influences and of how aware young children can be in responding to violence, and in preventing or resolving it. Violence is usually talked of as a problem between children. Yet adults can very much increase or reduce levels of violence and stress in the extent to which they work respectfully with one another and with the children (Commission on Children and Violence 1995; John 2003; United Nations 2006).

An account of two lunch times on a course for early years staff, who strongly reacted to the ways they were treated, indicates how young children often feel. The adults enjoyed the leisurely well-planned first lunch. The second time, they became impatient, angry and uncooperative when their morning's work was suddenly interrupted, they were all hustled into the wash room together and told to hurry, but then they sat waiting for a long time at the table before the food arrived, and were told off for behaving badly (Goldschmeid and Jackson 2004)]. The example shows how, when adults are polite and respectful to the children, and value their time and work in greater partnership and equality with them, children of all ages feel happier and behave better. So at the level of planning, policy and daily practice in early years settings, intentionally or not, the staff can powerfully incite, defuse or prevent anger and aggression. In three Save the Children early years centres, which worked on anti-violence methods, it was found that the levels of violence differed in each centre. In the calmest one, with Asian staff, 'each child was treated as the centre of the universe – and with complete respect' (Finch 1998).

Research suggests that young children are highly aware of social skills and complex relationships, and like adults they use conflict skilfully to negotiate their relationships, as shown in the following two summaries of video recordings of Australian children (Danby and Barker 1998).

The jail. Amelia and Portia are four years old, and Elana is three. Amelia attends the preschool centre four times a week, Elena three times and Portia only twice a week. Portia tries to lock Elana into a 'jail', the home corner, while Amelia and John watch. Elana cries and a teacher comes to find out who has upset her and 'made her sad... You have to tell me so we can solve the problem'. The teacher tells Portia to 'make her feel better' and Portia hugs Elana. The teacher thanks Portia and walks away. The four children whisper and walk around, brushing against each other. Two girls end up in the home corner, and Portia stays on her own with a teacher.

'I'm bigger'. David and John are four years old and Connell is just three. Playing with wooden blocks, the older boys say they are bigger and they will 'just BASH YOU right off... THROW you through that television' and other threats to Connell until he starts to cry very loudly. The teacher arrives and says that 'he looks very sad... Can you make him feel better please? ...Give him a cuddle'. David gives a fleeting hug, but he argues with the teacher: 'We were just tricking him'. David turns his back on the teacher as she talks and, when she has gone, the boys continue to argue about who is the biggest.

The observing researchers commented that the teacher sees children's conflicts as a problem, a matter of upset feelings for teachers to resolve, rather as colonial administrators tried to do, without needing to find out the details of who really did what and why. When the teacher leaves, the girls seem to continue her approach, to console and care, as if they know that a brief hug is not enough and John takes some part in this. The older boys, however, argue against and contravene the teacher's instructions, using her as a foil to show their masculine independence in contrast to her feminine concern with care for feelings.

The researchers believe that the younger children use conflict to try to increase their power by crying and calling in the teacher on to their side to blame the others. The children try to involve the watching researcher, but she does not respond so they cry louder for the teacher to hear. The scenes show how, very early on, children in a weaker position learn to turn to teachers to resolve their differences.

The teacher is seen as more concerned with pity and blame, and soothing hurt feelings to restore calm and return to 'play'. Purposeful constructive play is supposed to be the children's main occupation. Yet they seem as preoccupied with their complex relationships, as when they brush past each other to repair friendship in subtle verbal and silent cues. The researchers add that boys and girls react very differently, but it is not a simple difference; John shares in the girls' brushing past movements.

The researchers do not question where the boys' pride and anxiety about being bigger come from, and do not consider the children's motives. It is likely that Portia, who attends only twice a week, is worried that she is losing her friend Amelia to the new younger girl. She began 'jailing' Elana as if to separate her from Amelia. When children attend sessions irregularly, or less frequently than their friends, disrupted relationships can leave them feeling lonely, unsupported and even disorientated, compared with those who can warmly greet their friends when they arrive (Penn 1997a).

Teaching children to rely on adults to sort out conflict does not help them to see how they can increase or reduce or resolve conflict themselves (Holdigan 2000). For this they need to be helped to see themselves as effective peace-makers, instead of aggressors and victims.

Bullying

Concerns about bullying in school are very common, and for thousands of children violence from other children is an extremely serious problem. Yet frequency is sometimes confused with severity. Bullying is often reported in many schools because, rightly, adults now often enquire about it and take it seriously. To put bullying in context, the survey mentioned in Chapter 3 of over 2250 school students aged from seven years in the UK about rights in schools found that many children reported that there was some bullying in their school. However, in open questions asking what they most and least liked about their school, only 47 people cited bullying as a main concern. Whereas peers were mentioned only in the top ten likes (friends, break times), teachers featured highly in both the most-liked features (named lessons) and most-disliked features (named lessons, teachers, rules) (Alderson and Arnold 1999). Contrary to most reports, the children said that their problems tended to be caused by adults rather than by other children in the school.

Some school codes go to extremes, so that 'not talking to someone', or mutually enjoyed rough play, can count as bullying. Children are punished and labelled as bullies for behaviour which is not intended to harm anyone and does not actually do so (Blatchford and Sharp 1994). This can undermine the important efforts in many schools and nurseries, mentioned earlier, to tackle bullying through involving and consulting with the children.

Working with children to prevent and resolve conflict

Like the Australian video, an example from an English school teacher describes children's intense reactions to one another. She described how a newly arrived refugee girl joined a pair of friends, and then became best friend to one of them, while the other girl became lonely, ill, very sad, and did not grow for months (Marlowe 1997). This story was told as if it was sad but inevitable. Yet there is much that adults can do from the earliest years to encourage mixed and group friendships, so that children need rely less on exclusive best friendships and rivalries. During many activities, children can work in groups rather than pairs, and the groups can form and reform so that everyone has the chance to work and play with everyone else and get to know them well. This helps all children to feel more at ease with their whole group (McNamara and Moreton 1995). For example, they can make cards which they pick from a bowl to see which group they will be in each time they do group work, instead of some children choosing the most popular ones and leaving the least popular ones obviously being left out.

A mainstream school with children aged 3–11 planned ways to protect and involve the 10 per cent of profoundly disabled children (Cleves School 1999). The school avoids queues and mass movements round the school – the times when conflict often occurs. They have little furniture, thereby reducing the chance of children knocking into things and each other and starting arguments. The children easily form and reform groups, sitting on the carpet, leaning against a work top, or quickly drawing up a few chairs. Staff try to ensure that the groups are always mixed in ability, ethnicity and gender. The inclusive equal opportunities policy on ability also works well for the many children who speak English as an additional language, and they are included and involved as soon as they arrive. Joint activities, like making a huge collage, include everyone at their own level, and help the children to enjoy each other's company. It is rare to see anyone playing alone at break times. The children are considerate almost without seeming to notice. Larger ones run around the playground and carefully miss knocking into other children.

When children are in conflict, listening to them about what is happening can provide better solutions than a quick hug. The following examples are given by Finch (1998), who reviews typical adult solutions like, 'say you are sorry', giving a reward or punishment, or using time out, and she notes their limitations. Observing and talking with children can work better through watching how, when and why violence begins, making preventive plans with children, and teaching them assertive non-aggressive ways to negotiate. Puppets and masks help children to express and respond to a whole range of feelings from anger to happiness, and to act out and resolve their conflicts.

When working and playing together, people have to find a balance between feeling they have some control but also sharing and letting go. Young children generally manage this very well, but there are ways of helping them to do so, if needed. In formal group discussions, children can roll a ball or pass an object from one speaker to the next to help them to listen and take turns (Mosley 1993). If one toy is very popular, a clock or an egg-timer can time the turns, and the children can check how the time is passing (Finch 1998). There are many practical ways of preventing conflict, from the way space, time, equipment and activities are organised, to the way disputes are resolved. Competitive games like snap or musical chairs, so common that their sometime negative effects often pass unrecognised, can be avoided if they might increase hostility, aggression or competitive anxiety. Children who have little free play space at home especially enjoy being energetic together on climbing toys and in large outdoor spaces. Early on, children enjoy cooperating in small groups, making pictures and collages, playing music, joining in cooperative games, cooking and painting together. Children aged three years practise negotiating skills. For example, when five children wanted to play a game for only four players, the staff asked them to solve the problem. After talking about how the left-out person would feel, and about other options, the children decided to play another game (Finch 1998).

Peer mediation

> **Turning arguments into questions.** Some teachers encourage children to use disagreements as questions to investigate. Five- and six-year-olds were preparing a booklet for the new children in an Italian pre-school centre. They talked about how the new children could not read and would like drawings. Someone then thought that as young children scribble they would prefer scribble drawings to more realistic ones of a map of the centre. The children prepared different drawings and then showed them to younger children to see which ones they liked best (Edwards et al. 1998).

Many schools now teach quite simple peer mediation techniques. Highfield School began by inviting in experts and having a long course for the oldest children, mixed with fun and games. Younger children also tried to use the methods, and later the head teacher decided to teach them the technique herself, in short sessions. She thought these worked better without being interrupted by the games (Highfield School 1997). While I was in the school, two large eight-year-old boys came up to their class teacher and said, 'We've had a row, we need mediation'. The teacher said

'All right', and they went into the corridor with one of the youngest girls in the school. 'I don't know what they do out there', said the teacher, 'but they always come back smiling', which, in a few moments, they did.

Longer-term problems in this school were tackled in class circle times, or by the school council, which had a boy and girl member from each class. They met in the head teacher's room, sitting on easy chairs round a coffee table, and she sat on the floor, at the same eye level. The council was a central part of the school and had its own budget. Classes might invite the parents of a child with behaviour difficulties to join their circle time, and to work out positive ways for everyone to help the child to change. The head teacher used to spend almost all her time sorting out behaviour problems, but she needed to spend much less time on them when the children took on much of the responsibility. All the staff welcomed the improvements, especially the meal-time supervisors (one per 70 children), who often called on the mediators.

For mediation, the children have to agree to listen, keep calm, and not interrupt. Usually two mediators ask each person in the conflict, in turn, to tell what they think happened and why, how they feel about it, and how they think the problem could be resolved. They ask them to agree on a resolution method, and to meet in a week's time to see how it worked. The head teacher believed that some of the younger children learned mediation skills most quickly as they had fewer negative habits to unlearn. Further research in early years groups on how children can use mediation to tackle conflict is urgently needed. The mediation involves restorative peace, looking to the future, rather than restorative justice, with its emphasis on admitting guilt and making amends for past actions.

Power, conflict and violence

Power as force or energy

In an international report on work with children, the authors wrote at length about the need to change power relations between children and adults. This is essential if children are to be consulted and to work with adults to make improvements, ranging from individual to international levels (Johnson *et al.* 1998). Sharing power involves adults in respecting children's views and networks, working with them as partners as far as possible, and as much as children want to. It involves changing routines and structures so that children can feel more comfortable, and included, and fairly treated. Here, power can be seen as positive energy, rather than negative force.

Dividing power as force

Power and rights are not generally popular words. Adults prefer to talk of their care or authority, or the need for their firm control, rather than their power over children. Child power is still less popular a term. This happens when power is seen as something zero–sum, to be divided rather than shared, like the slices of a cake when the more power one person has, the less everyone else has.

When adults believe they must set all the rules, which the children must then obey, adults may worry that if they let children have a little power they will want more and more – a process it is better not to start. This is especially so if it is believed that children should not have any power, with fearful visions of powerless but responsible adults and irresponsible but powerful children. This kind of open conflict and force has been called the least powerful kind of power (Lukes 2005). People are still aware of who is setting the rules and the choices, what these are, and whether they like them, and they may resist them.

A second level of power is to offer people misleading choices by not telling them all the options and information. For example, children might be told: 'There is only enough money to buy some small toys, not a slide you wanted'. They are not told that the staff decided how to spend the extra money. This could be reasonable (and the staff may be right that their choice is much better than a slide) unless they are pretending to share the full decision honestly with the children when they are not doing so.

The third and strongest kind of power as hidden force happens when people believe they have no choice and they must, and want to, behave in certain ways. Foucault (1980) has analysed how these dominant discourses and 'regimes of truth' are constructed and reconstructed. Many examples of this third kind are shown by the way today's Western parents believe 'in their souls' that they must supervise, protect and stimulate their children, keep them very clean and provided with many commodities, in ways that would surprise parents from other centuries and continents (Rose 1990). Another example is when boys believe they must be macho and violent, as the best and only way to be masculine and admired by their peers, however much anxiety and distress they also feel. Problems arise when people are unaware of options which they would choose if they knew about them.

If adults are to consult children honestly, it is vital for them to be aware of ways in which hidden power as force can limit the methods they use for sharing ideas, and the changes, which together they may want to make. Echoing Foucault, Rowe (1999, p.159) considers that 'power is the right to define how others should define'. Adults tend to believe that it is their right and duty to exert this power over children: if adults and children disagree then the children must be wrong and must be taught that they are wrong.

Sharing power as creative energy

Positive approaches to power see it as the essential energy which creates and channels ideas and achieves improvements. Sharing power and rights can bring greater freedom and fulfilment. One example is the young Scandinavian children mentioned in Chapter 3 who enjoy being independent at home on their own, and whose parents can also then enjoy more freedom. Many practical small examples are given in early years centres, such as providing mattresses instead of beds so children can easily lie down when they wish, and steps for children to climb up on to the changing table, so that they are consulted and deliberately cooperate in their care (Goldschmeid and Jackson 2004). There are also the many examples through this book. For an extended discussion about children's rights and power see John (2003).

Respecting children involves respecting and consulting all the staff, as this increases the chances for children also to be heard and their ideas to be taken seriously. The most senior person closely knows all the children in a centre, and takes account of all their views in planning and policy. This is done through talking with them, and with the staff who report the children's ideas as well as their own. However, the degrees to which junior staff are consulted and feel able to speak vary greatly.

Sharing power may involve waiting while everyone gradually works out solutions to problems and one solution perhaps leads to another, rather than a few senior people acting quickly. For example, the Highfield school staff and children worked for five years to improve relationships and be-haviour through methods like circle times, bully busters, guardian angels who flew to the rescue of children who bullied or were bullied, and peer mediation (Highfield School 1997). The goal of everyone to be positive and responsible was achieved through working with them; it could not be imposed on them. A poster about mediation shows two donkeys tied together and straining in opposite directions towards two piles of hay. They cannot eat until they share the same pile. Power as force means that much energy is wasted on conflict. Power as energy enables adults and children to work together toward agreed ends.

The crucial first step towards involving young children in solving problems of risk and control, conflict and violence is when adults take on positive views of children's competence and rights and of power, as creative energy, which can benefit everyone when it is shared to some extent.

CHAPTER EIGHT

Working Together: Sharing Decisions and Responsibility

This chapter considers how children take responsibility for themselves and for others, and how their powerful understanding, feelings and spiritual awareness help them to share activities and decision-making with other children and with adults. Some examples are drawn from ways that children are involved in their health care and in medical decisions because the ways children think, decide and act have been researched in some detail in this area. Much more detail needs to be known about how young children understand, and can or want to share in making decisions, about other aspects of their lives – at home, in day care centres, at school, during leisure times, and when they need extra help, such as from social and legal services.

Sharing decisions with other children

Can children understand democratic methods of consulting? Examples of young children listening and taking turns have already been given. Adults usually chair or facilitate the meetings, but young children could probably understand notions of the neutral chair in terms of the football referee who does not kick the ball but is there to make sure everyone else has a fair turn and keeps the rules.

The Participation Education Group (PEG) in Newcastle involved people aged from about eight years upwards from local schools and other centres. They ran Peer Induction, Education and Support (PIES) work-shops for young people and adults on 19 topics, such as advocacy, net-working, building confidence, fundraising, mediation, running events and evaluation.

Fourteen PEG members aged eight years upwards, with two adults, attended a planning meeting with researchers at London University. They wanted to work jointly on holding a two-day event in 1999 on democracy. On the train journey from Scotland and the north of England, they chose three eleven-year-old boys to chair the meeting and plan the agenda. The meeting began with everyone talking about 'Why are we having this meeting?'. At the end, they went round the circle, each saying what they had got out of the meeting. During the meeting, PEG members reminded the researchers of their terms, which everyone present seemed to under-stand clearly. These standards, like avoiding jargon, respecting everyone as an expert, making sure everyone knows and agrees with the broader agenda, are also being used with children and adults with learning difficul-ties (Ward 1997).

PEG's principles

1. We should have an equal share of everything.

2. We should have an equal say in everything.

3. We don't want adults to talk down to us.

4. Adults who work with us should respect us.

5. Adults should use language we can follow.

6. Adults shouldn't try to take over.

7. We should be able to disagree with adults.

8. We should be able to stand up to adults.

9. We want to be able to get our opinions and ideas across to adults.

10. Children and young people should be in charge (PEG 1998).

Taking responsibility for yourself and others making choices

The law and research about involving young children in major personal decisions are concerned mainly with health care (see Chapter 3). So far, the views of children aged under eight years about care and contact, such as where they want to live if the family separates, have been seldom researched (O'Quigley 1999; Thomas 2002; Winter 2006a, 2006b). For this reason, examples in this section of how young children can make personal decisions will be about health care. Children who are seriously consulted are less likely to misunderstand, or resist, or have to be forced to comply.

> **When Susan was aged four**, diabetes was diagnosed. She knew how ill she felt when her blood sugar level was too high or low. She quickly understood and was able to explain to other people that she needed injections of insulin, which her body no longer made. She knew that insulin is 'the key that turns sugar into energy'. She learned how to do frequent blood sugar level tests, and through her diet to try to avoid levels that were too high or low. She was expert at filling the syringe with insulin correctly, flicking for bubbles, and injecting herself twice a day. Her health was in her hands as she constantly needed to show her informed commitment to her treatment and to her low carbohydrate, low sugar diet. For example, she had to refuse sweets and biscuits, and watch other children enjoying these.

Whereas some people try too hard and too long at great personal cost, others give up too soon, and may feel unnecessary loss and failure. Young children are especially liable to be pushed too hard or stopped too soon unless adults consult them and trust their judgement. This can help children's confidence to try new things, persist through difficulties, and know when to stop or try an alternative, with less fear of failure. During a research interview, Linda aged eight, who uses crutches, and a wheelchair sometimes, raised the topic of whether people should be pressured to achieve as much as possible or be given extra protection and support.

When to carry on trying

Interviewer: Is there anything else important about your life I haven't asked you?

Linda: If you want to do recorder, you *try* it. Because my teacher says you can *do* recorder, you can *do* choir, you can *play* chess, you can *do* nature club.

Interviewer: Is she saying, if you want to do something, *do* it?

Linda: Yes.

Interviewer: Is that the way you want to live?

Linda: Yes, I'm going to learn it. Although it's quite hard I'm going to do it, to work hard.

Interviewer: Is that because your teachers say 'come on, come on', or because you've got lots of go in you?

Linda: I've got a lot of go. [When things are hard] I don't give up. I try, but if it's too much I give up.

Interviewer: That's interesting because lots of grown-ups find it hard to know when to try carrying on and when to give up.

Linda: Yes, my mummy's good about that (Alderson and Goodey 1998, pp.132–3).

Major decisions: the example of medical treatment

Can and should children be consulted about major complex decisions? Even if they can understand, do they want to take on responsibility for them? Some of the following examples involve life-threatening illness to show how young children can grasp ideas both intellectually and emotionally. They suggest that young children could be consulted far more about smaller everyday decisions. Children in a Bristol cancer ward, even two-year-olds, understood the names of drugs and their purpose, and cooperated with their treatment (Kendrick *et al.* 1986). In an American cancer unit, children talked together in the toilets in order to protect their parents from knowing how much they knew (Bluebond-Langner 1978). A three-year-old understood that his liver biopsy was not therapeutic but was a test and that they would 'put a little piece of the liver under a special glass to see if it was good' (Alderson 1993). When this example was mentioned to a four-year-old she said: 'Do you mean a microscope?'.

Children are not asked to make serious decisions, which involve remembering and balancing several risks and benefits, if it is assumed that they cannot think of several ideas at once. There was a brief period when pictures in children's books were expected to be very simple because 'children cannot cope with busy pictures'. Yet young children enjoy many different and complex television programmes without confusing the separate casts and story lines.

An example of very complex understanding is of a seven-year-old girl talking about the risks and benefits of having a heart–lung transplant. She knew it might not work, and it might not be done in time to save her life, but she still chose to go on the transplant list (Alderson 1993, pp.162–3). She illustrates how competent young children can be. Increasingly, doctors and nurses are consulting young children about making major decisions with their parents, because they believe it is better to care for informed co-operative children who want their treatment, than for ignorant, confused and resisting children.

The young children whose views are respected have often had disrupted schooling and have poor reading and maths skills. They are ordinary children, except in their unusually profound experiences of illness, disability, major treatments and being near to death. They show how ability is linked to experience far more than to age or scholastic ability. A senior nurse commented: 'Their understanding of life and death knocks spots off ours'. Fortunately, most young children are never faced with such serious and distressing decisions. Yet those who are suggest that many young children have these capacities and courage, including some children with learning difficulties. Six of the 120 young patients in the consent to surgery research project (Alderson 1993) had identified learning difficulties. Some children had very strong preferences. One was Amy who at eight years 'was only a metre high' and was determined to go through years of very painful leg-lengthening treatment. Her mother, a physiotherapist, said that only Amy could make this kind of decision; no-one could do it for her (Alderson 1993). Chapter 3 reviewed involvement in other surgery decisions.

Most children prefer others to decide with or for them. These examples are not given to suggest that young children should *have* to decide. Careful consultation can help staff and parents to find out how much children need and want to know, be involved in making decisions, and sort out misunderstandings and unnecessary fears.

Peace and justice

Another way in which people take responsibility for themselves and others is through political awareness and by challenging problems such as pollution and poverty. The annual *Blue Peter* television appeals show young children's active concern for the environment, and for helping disadvantaged people. Can young children understand general and partly abstract issues, such as the politics of racism, inequality and oppression? A teacher, Melissa Butler, describes how deeply conscious her class became of these issues when they discussed these intensely in class (Butler 1998):

> **In a class of seven-year-olds**, living on a black housing estate in Chicago, Gerald once pointed his finger like a gun to Christopher's head. Ebony asked: 'What do you mean by that? Are you trying to kill your beautiful Black Brother?' Gerald was taken aback and said 'No!' and then looked confused.

Butler believes that knowledge is about ways of thinking and understanding, less about items to remember. The children agreed, so that if someone wanted to talk about rocks or ants or something not obviously related to justice, they would say: 'That's nice, but what does that have to do with peace and power?' 'How you gonna help your Brothers and Sisters by talking about that?'. They talked about shootings, funerals, drugs, gangs and the police brutality they witnessed, to make sense of their experience and to challenge the clichés they had been taught. The school was in an area that had very high rates of black men in prison, and of poverty and drug-dealing. The children live with painful contradictions: gun men are cool heroes yet cruel murderers; the police are said, on television, to be good, yet they kill your friends and deal out drugs and guns. Drug-dealing is bad but may be the only way to earn money for the family to live on.

Butler helped the children to think critically and logically through these contradictions, to see the immense pressures on individuals, and to move on from blaming them to working for peace and justice. Ebony shows how they became critically conscious of the 'cool' macho gun sign, which they came to call the 'gun move'. They stopped copying the older boys who used it casually and unthinkingly, and came to see how this kind of 'cool' harms their community. Yet they also kept certain 'cools' in order to survive. Adults' instructions about what they should not do contradicted the examples they observed all around them. The easy rules seven-year-olds are expected to repeat – 'I'll be good and never touch a gun or join a gang' – cannot help them as they grow older. So they talked about social pressures and the limits of personal agency.

Awareness grew through taking everyone's stories very seriously, and appreciating layers of meaning and even inconsistencies. Consulting the children seriously involved interpreting their stories in several ways. For example, they often told stories of moving on ('Ah, uh, my mama say we be moving soon'), which were stories of longing for change and release, rather than factual. They told stories about Chuckie Cheese where they enjoyed pizzas, games, family celebrations and reunions – or were telling the story as if it happened because they longed for it to happen. Respecting their stories meant seeing when stories are told in order:

- to invent what the children wished was true (a way of coping)

- to show off and impress the others (being 'cool')

- to try to fit inconsistencies into a consistent understanding of the world (making sense)

- to live with the complexities of hyper reality

- to develop goals and practise ideas for empowerment.

They spent the year talking about social justice, power, unity and community change, and through this developed their Brotherhood and

Sisterhood, finding their place in a contradictory, unjust world, but one where they want to find hope, looking for aims to work towards instead of pressures to resist. One of the girls, Whitnesha, was expelled from her mainly-white dancing class, when the white children asked about her school: 'I just said that we learn peace and power and they just told on me. [The teacher] didn't want me telling those white kids about the projects and the other black kids. You know, Ms Butler, they is resisting me! Now what am I going to do? They need to know the truth!'

School education tends to turn practical matters into abstract ones which are harder for children to understand and become involved with, leading to assumptions that they cannot do so. But when abstract ideas about rights and justice are linked to the living reality of children's daily lives and their deep feelings, children show their knowledge and deep concern (Beane 1990; Griffiths and Davies 1995; Holden and Clough 1999; John 2003). Radical ideas about theatre, developed with South American peasants (Boal 1979), are used in a team visiting English schools (see next box). The original dramas involved both actors and audience in deep experiences. For example, a woman was asked to 'sculpt' a group of people into two scenes, one when an atrocity took place in her village, the second of how she would like the villagers to be in future. All the group were then asked how they would change people from the first to the second scene, by sculpting a third scene of change. So, for example, they took away the guns or pointed them at other people, and they changed the actors' pose from begging for mercy to challenging the soldiers.

Involvement through drama. The team of actors begin by finding out about pressing concerns in the school in England, such as bullying. Then they act a drama about it with an unhappy ending. They act the play again but stop halfway through and ask children to help them to create a happier ending. The actors will have warmed up the whole group by starting with fun and interactive sessions. They have a 'joker' as a go-between, who explains the rules, for example, everyone must use non-violent suggestions. Children as young as four years eagerly volunteer to join the drama, even in front of 200 people. They are asked to take on victim roles, not aggressor ones, and young children propose and act out imaginative ways of resolving the problems in the play, helping bullies to empathise and victims to be more confident. Young children can be 'amazingly assertive' when they talk and act from their personal experiences, as if they cannot bear to stand by and watch (Helen Gregory, personal communication).

This is another example, like those detailed in Chapter 1, of how the arts bring learning alive and show children's creative and moral awareness. These very different examples of taking responsibility for yourself and others, ranging from personal health-care choices to democratic responsibilities, indicate the wide range of views and decisions on which ordinary young children can be seriously consulted.

Respecting views and feelings

Consulting children involves respecting their views and feelings and their ability to respect other people's feelings. Peer mediation has worked well at Highfield School because of changes in the school at all levels: lots of personal work on feelings and expressing them creatively in words, art and drama; guessing and describing other people's feelings; learning a rich range of words, so that hitting out is no longer the easiest way to express anger or jealousy. Equally important have been structural changes in the school, the active, highly respected school council, other democratic approaches, an emphasis on practical citizenship and many enjoyable shared activities and rewards. For example, in this school, in a disadvantaged area, all classes sometimes have sleep-overs at school followed by breakfast, a way of having a kind of school trip which costs nothing and encourages friendly joint activities (Highfield School 1997).

The skilful way the Italian teachers described on p.127 listen to the children is also shown in the way the children listen to each other. It depends on assuming that the speaker is making sense, even if at first the listener does not realise what this sense is, as shown in the next example (Gardner 1998).

Stuart, aged four, and his speech therapist look at a picture of a spotty face, to start talking about 'sp'.

Therapist:	S:pots
Stuart:	Bots (looking at picture).
Therapist:	Pots?
Stuart:	Bots (looking at therapist then away).
Therapist:	Are they pots?
Stuart:	(Looks to therapist again and shakes head.)
Therapist:	Let's hear the Sammy snake sound at the beginning then. (Pause).h s:pot.
Stuart:	Bots.

The speech therapist wants Stuart to realise his pronunciation errors and learn to correct them spontaneously. To achieve this, she tends to suggest corrections implicitly and does not tell Stuart exactly what she wants him to do and why. It is as if she thinks that if Stuart becomes conscious of the problem and the correction he will not be able to do this spontaneously, and almost subconsciously. The main topic of her conversation is sounds, but Stuart assumes that, as in ordinary conversation, the main issue is the sense and meaning of the words not their sounds, and the aim is to check whether the things in the picture actually are spots. It is not that Stuart is too limited to understand the therapist's rules, but that she does not explain them. Stuart is skilful in the ordinary rules of conversation and keeps trying to apply them here but his efforts are not seen by the therapist as sense (trying to follow the usual rules), but as non-sense (not following any rules) and as a failure to understand sounds and 'repair errors'.

It could be helpful for the therapist to treat Stuart more as an informed partner. She could look at why Stuart's responses make sense to him, and explain to him her agenda. Before being able to correct himself spontaneously, Stuart has to understand her aim of teaching him a new skill (pronouncing 'sp'), and how and when to use it. This would involve moving from a rather behaviourist-training approach to an explicitly discussed and shared agenda, spending more time on consulting and appealing to his informed cooperation, and less on instruction.

Communicating beyond words

Another way of respecting the youngest children's views and feelings is to move beyond words. Valuable ways of consulting and learning from babies and children beyond words have been developed, for example, by psychotherapy. This gives insights into children's profound understanding of their difficulties and needs, as the account of Dib's play shows (Axline 1966). One young boy painted a flower with nine petals nine days before he died of cancer (Kübler-Ross 1983). When many such examples are given together they seem to have more than chance meanings. Even sceptics may still be puzzled by the striking differences between drawings like Figure 8.1 and the usual ones by six-year-olds and wonder what the child does understand and believe.

A child may be too young or too sick to share verbally in making health-care decisions, yet may influence decisions through expressed feelings and body language. Samantha, aged six, wanted to have her first two liver transplants, and showed she understood what was involved when she explained them to her class at school. When these failed she became very distressed and resisting, so much so that her parents sadly decided that they would refuse the third attempt, with its very small hope of success, for her sake not for their own real preference. After she died, her mother felt they had been right in respecting her wish (Irwin 1996). It is sometimes assumed that words are the only genuine way to communicate, and body language is mistrusted as vague and misleading. Yet words too can be misleading or confusing. Bodies can be the source of profound knowledge, when children learn through their illness and disability, and express themselves physically.

Consulting children by asking them to draw can provide illuminating evidence (Bach 1969), but many drawings are ambiguous or vague sketches. It is better to use them together with spoken or written comments from the child, explaining the picture. A smiling face to the viewer might have been a sad face to the artist.

Figure 8.1. The six suns and the slide.

A boy, aged six, with a life-threatening illness, who was not willing to talk about it, drew a slide which came to a dramatic stop in mid-air. The boy's therapist said that when they talked about the drawing:

I felt that he seemed to convey here the feeling that he was on a fast-moving downward course, which suddenly stops, possibly leading to a feeling of falling (if we notice that the bottom of the slide is well above ground level). Again, this confirms that the abrupt ending was ahead of him. The sun in a picture often denotes the parental presence or, in drawings of bereaved children, it is often placed over the dying or dead family member. The ordinary or usual depiction of the sun in a six-year-old's picture would be in a corner. This unusual display of suns here seems to carry a rich range of meanings: the six suns refer to his six years, which stop at the point where the slide stops; they hang over the picture oppressively, conveying both an over-attentive parent as well as, possibly, marking out the *whole* slide: he was leaving no doubt that this symbol of the person who is dying truly 'covers' the area. Interestingly, this child had never really thrived: he had experienced severe eating difficulties all his life. This background seems to tie in with the oppressive suns, which go back to the 'beginning', in the past – the left of the picture.

This drawing opened up the possibility of talking about his fears, and, indeed, his awareness that he was dying, but my comments on the picture are not meant to be prescriptions or recipes for interpreting other drawings: any understanding of a drawing is arrived at in conjunction with the child's comments, the situation in which the drawing is made, and possibly the overall knowledge of the child. Wide experience of the normal developmental stages through which children's drawings evolve is also important, as a yardstick for any unusual or striking features (Judd 1995, p.35).

Way (2007) described how 'James' was seven months old when his father died. His mother never talked about this with James, assuming that he could not understand. But when James was four years old he started shouting and laughing 'My dad died!' and his mother was very upset. However, James was trying to work out how he compared with the other children who had fathers at home. It helped James and his mother to attend a hospice candle project for children aged three to seven years, with music, talking and activities about understanding and accepting death and life. Before the next fathers day, James joined in with his friends to make his own fathers day card.

Arguments against consulting children refer to their lack of moral sense. Yet when talking with children, researchers have noted their empathy, sharing, turn-taking and reciprocation, and their ability from their second year to begin to talk about distributive justice, fairness based on merit, goodness, equality, and benefiting the disadvantaged, questions which still perplex philosophers (Damon 1988; Mayall 2002). There appears to be greater formal moral understanding in terms of right and wrong in three-year-olds than in two-year-olds, and a firmer sense of obligation to others though, as with adults, this competes with self-interest. Pritchard (1991, 1996) believes that children enter school with well-developed moral understanding and dispositions, which schools can expand through reasoned debate, rather than simply by trying to instruct children about differences between right and wrong. He describes his complex discussions with six to seven-year-olds about lying, fair punishment, or why the choice of three children to watch a television programme should count for more than one child's choice. Videos and detailed analysis of six-year-olds' discussions also show how skilfully they anticipate and prevent conflict when, for example, they work in pairs building a Lego model (Saunders and Freeman 1998).

Spirituality

Ways of consulting young children can include appealing to their spiritual wisdom. Spiritual awareness has been described as knowing there is: 'something more than meets the eye, something more than the material, something more than the obvious, something to wonder at, something to respond to' (Copley, quoted in Stone 1995). Young children tend to be very ready to wonder and admire, and to respond with fascination to simple things like snails inching along. All aspects of life can evoke wonder; maths, for example, concerns mysteries like space, time and infinity. Consulting and learning from children includes sharing their silences and absorbed attentiveness.

Spiritual awareness involves living intensely in the present, a capacity which people tend to lose as they get older. Being absorbed in the present can deepen feelings of delight or distress, and also make them seem to last much longer, which brings advantages and disadvantages. There are ways of helping children to be more conscious of their inner life and a little less vulnerable to distressing feelings. The methods involve learning consciously to be relaxed yet alert, and to enjoy experiences through the senses and imagination. Breathing slowly, people can experience a kind of mild hypnosis which taps 'the creative, therapeutic and spiritual potentialities of the imagination' (Raban 1987). Guided imagery can be used to deal positively with feelings, such as fear or dislike, anger, destructiveness or rejection. It can help to increase respect for oneself, other people, living things, and objects. A meditation might ask children to imagine being a leaf through from bud to leaf mould, or to imagine being someone who is rejected and then accepted as in the ugly duckling story.

Another value in guided imagery is the profound insights that can emerge from subconscious knowledge. Adults who attend a visualisation session followed by drawing, painting and talking about the images, are often surprised to gain new understanding of their memories and hopes, and links between them. Young children too may create poems or paintings, and talk in pairs or groups, after a visualisation. Like brainstorming, it can be a way of tapping highly imaginative ideas which might seem impractical at first until perhaps a way is found to use them, such as in planning a garden or playground, or solving a problem.

As with all contact with young children, there are the dangers of adults misusing their power in brain-washing or social engineering. Yet the power and depths of young children's imagination and spiritual awareness can lead to enriching and rewarding sessions for them and the adults who share experiences with them.

Children coping with distress, fear and pain

Young children who feel distress can become adept at controlling their feelings. Adults who teach them to do this are, in a sense, consulting and appealing to their inner resources of self-control. Methods like blowing bubbles or bird whistles help to distract and relax children through deeper breathing. Nurses consult very young children about their levels of pain. For instance, a girl might be asked to point at the position she feels she is at on a row of faces from laughing to crying. Or a boy is asked to point at a number from one to ten to show how bad his pain feels. Nurses also help children to use high technology equipment, such as personal analgesia control pumps to regulate their levels of pain relief medication between previously set upper and lower limits (Llewellyn 1993). Guided imagery is used in some hospitals to help children to create their own happy secret place in their imagination (Madders 1987), if they feel distressed. Five-year-olds can learn to use this by themselves after a few sessions. Each story has a beginning, middle and end. Before it begins, the child sits or lies as comfortably as possible and breathes slowly, eyes closed. The same kind of story can be used with groups of children. One way is to agree on the kind of place first, and perhaps to look at pictures of, for example, the seaside. Another is to tell a very general story, so that each child can imagine a different place: What colours can you see? What sounds can you hear? What can you feel with your hands? And your feet?

Guided imagery

Imagine you are going down ten steps very slowly, counting as you go down. At the bottom there is a door. What colour is it? Open the door slowly, and what do you see? (Some children see a wood, a room, a spaceship, a hot air balloon, or a beach.) Hear the sound of the waves gently breaking on the sand and the shingle stones rolling with the waves. Feel the warm sand between your toes. Walk over the wet sand to the edge of the waves and see the blue and green and white water. Feel it creeping over your feet and walk into the waves. As they come rushing up towards you, feel them gently lift you over the edge of the wave. Now you are safely swimming and floating in the warm water which gently lifts and carries you. Some fish swim round you in a dance. Some pink and green seaweed floats past spreading out its pattern in the water. Now the sea carries you back to the sand. You feel fresh and cool in the warm sunshine. You are so tired you lie down on the sand to rest and to listen to the waves and the other children playing. Now it is time to go back to the door, through the doorway, close the door behind you. Now walk up the steps, count them as you go and at the top you will back here again.

Young children's use of guided imagery shows the power of their imaginations and their courage when coping with serious illness and distress.

Personal and general pressures

This book has concentrated on individuals and small groups, in trying to convey how ordinary young children live every day in sophisticated and varied ways. Yet general pressures on children and adults greatly affect their daily living together, and it would be misleading to ignore these large-scale influences. Although many British families are prosperous, there are growing concerns about child poverty and economic inequality and rising mental health problems (see Chapter 1). With welfare states shrinking, parenting is being privatised with parents being held much more responsible for their children socially and economically (O'Neill 1994; Ferudi 2001; Hendrick 2003). This moves away from older ideas of extended families, close communities and friendly neighbours. To ignore these influences would imply that everyone has entirely free will to make moral choices, whereas some people are far more free to choose than others. The difference between having a garden or safe pleasant area where children can play together fairly independently, and living in bed and breakfast accommodation with stressed neighbours whose only communication is to complain about noise, radically affects family dynamics.

Liberals often argue that to plead that social pressures limit moral choice denigrates people who cope well, and wrongly excuses those who do not cope. Yet individuals and circumstances differ greatly. It would be more logical to appreciate children who manage to surmount serious difficulties, and to investigate how they do so, instead of regarding such survival as the norm, which everyone can and should equally easily achieve.

Another pressing question is how best adults can treat young children as trusted, responsible people when children lie, cheat, bully, disrupt and destroy. And people working with disadvantaged children, who are distressed through the effects of poverty, illness, war, neglect or abuse, may be thinking that the examples of trusted, responsible children must belong to privileged groups. This is why examples through the book have included disadvantaged and difficult children. Frequently, the children who are most energetically disruptive become leaders in, for example, helping to raise standards of behaviour in school (Highfield School 1997) or welcoming and supporting disabled children (Cleves School 1999). It is as if babies are not born as good or bad people, but as pre-moral people with more or less energy and independence. Their strengths are channelled into positive or negative ways, partly through their own choices and contexts, partly through their experiences and adults' powerful expectations.

CHAPTER NINE

The Key Messages from the Evidence and Experience

The main objections to children's rights are beliefs that children *cannot* be rights holders, or that they *should not* be rights holders, or that they *must not* be rights holders. Replies to the first objection, 'cannot', present evidence of young children's understanding and competencies to show that they can be rights holders. Examples through this book give a few examples from countless, mainly unrecorded, instances of young children's capacities to relate and understand as reasonable people.

Replies to the second objection, 'should not', depend on reasoned moral arguments, unravelling the history and meaning of specific human rights, which are not about being selfish and unruly. Arguments and struggles for women's and other minority groups' rights, the dangers when rights are denied to certain groups who are not seen or treated as real people, also apply to children. Adults' fears that respect for young children is somehow morally wrong need to be analysed. Earlier examples have shown how children are willing and able to be responsible, to share in caring for themselves and for others, and in making decisions with other children and with adults. The six-month-old baby who wants to share her soggy biscuit with her family shows these early impulses of concern for others. This is not to say that babies can make reasoned decisions, but that they are already on a continuum leading towards this moral and intellectual ability, which develops much earlier than used to be assumed.

The third objection, 'must not', is made by people who may accept that children can reason and exercise rights, but that to allow them to do so is too risky, disruptive and threatening to adults' rights and control. It is easier to respond to the first two objections with examples and arguments than to this third view, which is based more on feelings than reasons, on habit and prejudice. I suggest that at heart people tend to be providers (of services and information), or protectionists (anxious to be in control and protect children and also themselves from risks). Relatively few are participants (willing to risk sharing rights, power and responsibility).

Adults with great concern and compassion for children may be held back by unresolved contradictions between old and new thinking about childhood. While advocating greater care for children, seemingly unconsciously, they describe childhood only in negative derogatory terms and adulthood in solely favourable respectful terms (Palmer 2006; Williams 2006). Children and their rights are respected when young children are seen as real people having, like adults, both positive and negative human qualities.

People also tend to be functionalist, believing the present moral order is best, as long as minor problems are resolved. Fewer people are critical of present structures and inequalities, believing that real progress cannot be made until the present moral order is reformed (Alderson 1998). This book is about how the moral order could move towards the UNCRC Preamble's vision that 'recognition of the inherent dignity and of the equal and inalienable rights of all members of the human family is the foundation of freedom, justice and peace in the world' (UNCRC 1989).

Rights and obligations

The UNCRC is reviewed as a practical and principled framework for involving children. Their participation rights complement and overlap with their protection and provision rights. To sense and respond to babies' views and feelings, as parents and carers find, establishes habits of informed co-operation, which can be more beneficial and educational than adults simply instructing and organising – and potentially working against – children. The UNCRC transforms what were formerly defined as children's welfare, needs and interests, dependent on adults' definitions and goodwill, on whim or privilege, into equal entitlements for all children and shared obligations. Children's rights to express their views on all matters that affect them enable them to take a responsible share in defining their rights and obligations.

Children as people

Children have more similarities with adults than differences from them. Children actively learn through relationships with adults and other children, through their feelings and bodies, through sharing activities and ideas, especially in small groups and away from strong relationships of control and dependence. Education that is over-dominated by notions of active adults teaching relatively passive children under-uses children's powerful learning capacities. Policy, practice and research, which appreciate children as social beings in their daily context, and go beyond strong traditions of seeing them as isolated individuals, reveal children as much more competent than was formerly thought possible.

Changes in thinking and expression vary throughout life, especially in the early years, but these are perhaps better understood as changes of degree, rather then of kind. People come to think in more complicated ways, but not in entirely different ways. By five years, children have the kinds of intelligence – such as about self and others, language, science, technology and the arts – which last a life time.

Competence and intelligence

Children's strengths are often seen more clearly during adversity, when many cope well with deprivations and difficulties. These children, who are ordinary in all but their exceptional experiences, are often below average at school. They may be refugees or severely disabled, have been looked after by a local authority, or have endured racism. They challenge assumptions that children's competence relates to their measured intelligence, reading and maths ability, and placid compliance. Children who are fortunate to live sheltered and even privileged lives may be misperceived as inevitably very dependent when they do not have the chance to show their potential strengths. A further mistake is to assume that disadvantaged children are even less competent than sheltered ones. Competence grows through experience rather than with age or ability and very young children can have profound understanding.

Gender and age

Very early in life, children adopt gender roles, learning how to be a little boy or a little girl in numerous subtle ways endorsed by their society. They also adopt age roles and learn how to be 'little': helpless and weak or resisting in some societies, and helpful and strong in others. Many adults become concerned when masculinity is over-identified with, for example, being strong and femininity with being weak. Children obviously benefit from having strong, wise, stable adults to care for them but, as with gender, there are disadvantages in over-identifying strengths with one group and weaknesses with the opposite group. Adults can become over-confident in their own abilities and unaware of their weakness. Children, as women once were, can be forced into a false helplessness and vulnerability. Many are punished if they resist. Children are often trapped in a double bind, whether they comply and are seen as good but dependent and therefore not responsible, or whether they try to be more independent but are seen as naughty and therefore irresponsible. The growing awareness of sexism and racism in the early years needs also to be applied to ageist prejudices and the over-infantilising of children.

Theories of childhood

Adults' and children's beliefs about young children's competence shape behaviour and are self-fulfilling. People often confuse *inherent* biological dependence with *structural* social dependence, much of which is imposed by attitudes and ways of living (Lansdown 1995a, 1995b). To increase respect for children's views and feelings involves the shift of public and professional thinking towards more realistic appreciation of young children's abilities, so that adults engage with children's reasoning, rather than trying to control them through coercion and fear (Astington 1993).

One way forward is for adults to observe a baby in a group carefully for ten minutes. This is not a matter of getting rid of theories and seeing the 'real child'. Thinking always involves theories, in the sense of beliefs about what it means to be a child or an adult, and what kinds of behaviour are acceptable or not, and these shape how children live in different societies. But testing theories in real settings is the first step towards moving on from the theories about inexorable, slow, child development that have dominated the past century, towards more realistic theories that fit more nearly with how varied, versatile, competent and intensely aware children are. The play worker who was very surprised that young children could express clear views and do research (see Introduction) shows this rewarding process.

Time and space

Children's time and space are increasingly organised by adults in homes, nurseries and schools, public streets and leisure spaces. Over the past century, children have become more institutionalised away from the public places they once shared with adults, and they are the most closely surveyed, measured and regulated age group. They are safer and perhaps happier but many are much lonelier and there is less scope for children and the adults working with them to make spontaneous choices. 'Safety' arguments are used to constrict children's daily lives. To think about children's daily lives and welfare, starting from their viewpoints and rights, illuminates when their care is organised for adults' convenience, and against children's best interests.

Consulting young children

When adults routinely listen to children and consult and reflect with them, they help to increase children's competencies, and mutual trust and confidence. 'Giving children a voice' is a popular slogan, but children have voices, it is adults who need to listen. Anyone hoping to benefit people of any age tends to do so far more effectively by involving them as partners in planning as far as possible. Practical methods of working with babies and young children have been described through the book.

Barriers to working with children

Yet the major barrier to consulting is not children's (in)abilities, or adults' lack of skill, but prejudices that young children cannot or should not be consulted. For this reason, beliefs about childhood and about consulting children are main topics in this report, since examples of responsive children from observations or meticulous research are not going to convince people who deeply believe in older ideas about children's incapacities. The pros and cons of consulting children, set out in Chapter 5, according to what is right or beneficial or educational, are offered to encourage adults to discuss their beliefs and their deeper feelings about involving children. These beliefs and feelings can work as conduits or as barriers, like blocked pipes.

Concerns about risk and control, conflict and violence are important barriers which need to be addressed at many levels: from local communities giving more support to adults who take reasonable, often small, risks in respecting children's choices, such as going on outings, or playing outside more freely; to reforming school and college education for future carers and parents about young children; to the Government genuinely involving young children in forming policies, as it has promised to do in ratifying the UNCRC; and to the mass media being much more respectful towards children.

The ideas in this book are offered for adults to discuss and adapt because to consult children involves working flexibly with them, rather than applying pre-set plans. Consultations and research are more likely to work well, and be taken as evidence of young children's great capacities, if all the adults concerned are committed and expect the consultations to work well.

Arguments about research methods, including sometimes well-founded criticisms, may mask deeper disagreements and fears about betraying adults, and children, and morality generally, if research findings about competent children are taken seriously.

Practical interactions

Consultation tends to be seen in intellectual terms, as talking, thinking and choosing. Very young children might seem to have little part in this before they can talk confidently and fluently. Yet they can be involved, when consulting is also seen as sharing activities and feelings, and when each stage and method of researching or consulting with children is planned and designed as much as possible with their help. Als (1999) shows how this can be done with premature babies. Then adult expertise changes from knowing what is best for them to working skilfully with children instead of simply for them.

Research methods

Quantitative surveys provide valuable evidence, and so too do the intensive studies, which can only be done with a few children. It is important to use appropriate methods, rather than seeing certain methods as better or inferior. Whereas large numbers are necessary, for example, to measure levels of provision or poverty and to make generalisations, very few children need be involved to describe their daily life or to disprove a generalisation. A few three-year-olds, for instance, can show that *some* of them are able to do things which experts used to believe could only be achieved by older children. They may be exceptional children; it does not matter as long as researchers do not over-generalise from any type of research.

Most examples of published research are about children and adults working together individually or in small groups. The studies contain a wealth of information to inform parents and professionals, and local, national and international policies. Some examples are being drawn together into broader reports covering local, national and international studies to complement and reinforce one another. Such overviews help to clarify how the research is political as well as personal, with implications for many children on how they are consulted or excluded from sharing in decisions about resources.

Work and play

Earlier examples raised questions about how work and play overlap, when they differ, who works and who plays. There are advantages and disadvantages in combining play and playful methods when working with young children. It is important to be clear about what kinds of play are used, why, and how they might clarify or confuse communication.

Power

To work more equally with children involves sharing power with them. This involves rethinking negative beliefs in order to see 'power' and respect for 'children's rights' as positive energy. Rights are equal entitlements for all members of the human family, to respect their worth and dignity with peace and justice.

Mutual trust

It is easier for young children to show their maturity when adults are mature and confident. Shared trust partly depends on people of all ages searching for the meaning in each other's words and actions, even if these at first seem non-sense. The non-sense may occur when young children, far from not following any rules, are following complex rules which adults do not at first recognise, as shown in the example of speech therapy in Chapter 8. Young children's grasp of rules is shown, for example, by how they can soon grasp the idea that sounds have meanings; they learn not only thousands of words but also the grammar, which holds words together.

When interviewed during research about children's wisdom to make major decisions about surgery, a hospital chaplain and former headmaster spoke of adults being magnanimous and courageous, 'big enough to surrender power', and to trust children who wish to make the most serious of all decisions. He did not see this as abandoning children but as relating to them more closely. He asked:

> But are you going to lay on children the weight of their future? Perhaps let them make a decision that could lead to their death? These are impossible questions, but hospital staff have to find the answers. Am I big enough to say: 'Whatever you choose will be valued, even if you decide against the tide; okay, you've made that decision, I'll do all I can to support you, and we'll go forward together'? It's such a big step for the adult to surrender power to the child. (Alderson 1993, p.143)

Scientific modesty

Over three centuries, manuals about the care of young children show startling swings of fashion between indulgence and Spartan strictness. Judy Dunn (1977, p.115) advises caution.

> As parents, we have to hope that we know what we are doing with our children: to trust our eyes and feelings. As scientists, we have to recognise how little we can as yet know anything of the sort, and we have a duty not to pretend to know any more that we do in fact know. Scientific modesty is not a virtue, it is an obligation. And when what we are speaking of is what from the beginning makes for human joy and human pain, this is an obligation we should take seriously.

One safeguard against extremes is to try to listen to children and to work out with them ways of living together, which reward children and adults.

The twenty-first century

The twentieth century saw huge changes in relationships between men and women in many countries. Women are no longer routinely infantilised but are seen as adult equals to men. The changes have challenged men's power and convenience, and have brought many problems for men and women and for family life. Yet the advantages of greater justice, respect, care and equality between men and women, and more rewarding relationships, are usually believed to outweigh the disadvantages of the changed status of women.

Similarly, the twenty-first century may bring great changes for children, through more respect for their undoubted abilities, so that they are no longer misguidedly 'infantilised' – treated as far less able than they actually are. 'Infant' literally means without a voice, but as this book has shown, even babies have voices and sensible views. With greater respect for children, there will be greater justice, care that is more deeply informed by children's views and interests, and awareness of the major contributions children make.

Although this book has not attempted to cover global aspects of children's rights, it is set in an unjust world. In 2002, if the world were counted as a village of 100 people, there were 10 children aged under 5 years, 10 aged 5–9 years and 19 aged 10–19 years; 22 spoke Chinese, 9 English, 9 Hindi, 7 Spanish; 61 were in Asia and 13 in Africa. There was enough food for everyone, but 50 people were hungry some or all of the time and 20 were very undernourished. In 1800, 17 people lived in the village; by 1900, there were 32; in 2002, there were 100; and by 2100, there may be 250 people (Smith and Armstrong 2004). The concerns of children in Britian seem slight in comparison to the rest of the world, but my aim is to illustrate how the UNCRC and respect for the youngest children's rights can benefit all children – and adults. The hope for peace, justice and prosperity in the global village involves the massive transfer of power and resources from white to black and Asian peoples, from men to women, and from aging minority societies to the much younger majority world. This will happen when rich adults trust poor young people. Prejudices are too deeply entrenched for adults, from individual parents to world leaders, to change their attitudes to young people unaided. A crucial task for all societies in the twenty-first century is therefore to rethink traditions in order that adults can learn from and with children how to create a better future.

References

Action on Rights for Children, ARCH (2007) Available at www.arch-ed.org, accessed 12 December 2007.

Alanen, L. and Mayall, B. (2001) (eds) *Conceptualising Child–Adult Relations.* London: RoutledgeFalmer.

Alderson, P. (1993) *Children's Consent to Surgery.* Buckingham: Open University Press.

Alderson, P. (1998) 'Theories in health care and research.' *British Medical Journal 317,* 1007–10.

Alderson, P. (1999) 'Human rights and democracy in schools: do they mean more than "picking up litter and not killing whales?"' *International Journal of Children's Rights 7,* 185–205.

Alderson, P. (2003) *Institutional Rights and Rites: A Century of Childhood.* London: Institute of Education.

Alderson, P. (2008) 'Children as Researchers: The Effects of Participation Rights on Research Methodology.' In P. Christensen and A. James (eds) *Research with Children.* London: Falmer.

Alderson, P. and Arnold, S. (1999) *Civil Rights in School: Research Briefing.* Swindon: Economic and Social Research Council.

Alderson, P. and Goodey, C. (1998) *Enabling Education: Experiences in Special and Ordinary Schools.* London: Tufnell Press.

Alderson, P. and Montgomery, M. (1996) *Health Care Choices: Making Decisions with Children.* London: Institute for Public Policy Research.

Alderson, P. and Morrow, V. (2004) *Ethics, Social Research and Consulting with Children and Young People.* Barkingside: Barnardo's.

Alderson, P., Hawthorne, J. and Killen, M. (2005a) 'The participation rights of premature babies.' *International Journal of Children's Rights 13,* 31–50.

Alderson, P., Hawthorne, J. and Killen, M. (2005b) 'Are premature babies citizens with rights, provision rights and the edges of citizenship?' *Journal of Social Science 9,* 71–81.

Alderson, P., Hawthorne, J. and Killen, M. (2006) 'Parents' experiences of sharing neonatal information and decisions: Consent, risk and cost.' *Social Science & Medicine 62,* 1319–29.

Alderson, P., Sutcliffe, K. and Curtis, K. (2006a) 'Children's competence to consent to medical treatment.' *Hastings Center Report 36,* 6, 25–34.

Alderson, P., Sutcliffe, K. and Curtis, K. (2006b) 'Children as partners with adults in their medical care.' *Archives of Disease in Childhood 91,* 3000–3.

Aldred, J. and Becker, S. (2002) 'Children Who Care.' In B. Franklin (ed.) *The New Handbook of Children's Rights.* London: Routledge.

Alldred, P., David, M. and Edwards, R. (2002) 'Minding the Gap: Children and Young People Negotiating Relations between Home and School.' In R. Edwards (ed.) *Children, Home and School.* London: RoutledgeFalmer.

Als, H. (1999) 'Reading the Premature Infant.' In E. Goldson (ed.) *Developmental Interventions in the Neonatal Intensive Care Nursery.* New York: Oxford University Press.

Alston, P., Tobin, J. and Darrow, M. (2005) *Laying The Foundations For Children's Rights*. Florence: UNICEF Innocenti.

Archard, D. and MacLeod, C. (eds) (2002) *The Moral and Political Status of Children*. Oxford: Oxford University Press.

Arendt, H. (1986) *The Origins of Totalitarianism*. London: André Deutsch.

Aries, P. (1962) *Centuries of Childhood*. Harmondsworth: Penguin.

Arneil, B. (2002) 'Becoming Versus Being: A Critical Analysis of the Child in Liberal Theory.' In D. Archard and C. MacLeod (eds) (2002) *The Moral and Political Status of Children*. Oxford: Oxford University Press.

Arnstein, S. (1969) 'A ladder of citizen participation.' *Journal of the American Institute of Planners 35*, 4, 216–24.

Astington, J. (1993) *The Child's Discovery of the Mind*. Cambridge, MA: Harvard University Press.

Audit Commission/HMI (1992) *Getting in on the Act*. London: HMSO.

Axline, V. (1966) *Dibs in Search of Self*. London: Gollancz.

Bach, S. (1969) 'Spontaneous Paintings of Severely Ill Patients: A Contribution to Psychosomatic Medicine.' *Acta Psychosomatica 8*, 1–66.

Ball, S. (2007) *Education plc*. London: Routledge.

Barnes, P. (2003) 'Children's Friendships.' In M. J. Kehily and J. Swann (eds) *Children's Cultural Worlds*. Chichester: Wiley/Open University.

Barnes, P. and Maddocks, A. (2002) 'Standards in school toilets – a questionnaire survey.' *Journal of Public Health Medicine 24*, 2, 85–7.

Barrett, H. (1998) 'Protest–Despair–Detachment: Questioning the Myth.' In I. Hutchby and J. Moran Ellis (eds) *Children and Social Competence: Arenas of Action*. London: Falmer.

Batmanghelidjh, C. (ed.) (2006) *Shattered Lives*. London: Jessica Kingsley.

Beane, J. (1990) *Affect in the Curriculum: Towards Democracy, Dignity and Diversity*. New York: Teacher's College Press.

Bearison, D. (1991) *They Never Want to Tell You*. London: Harvard University Press.

Beck, U. (1997) 'Democratisation of the family.' *Childhood 4*, 2, 151–68.

Becker, S. and Aldridge, J. (1995) 'Children Who Care.' In B. Franklin (ed.) *The Handbook of Children's Rights*. London: Routledge.

Bemak, F. (1996) 'Street researchers: A new paradigm redefining future research with street children.' *Childhood 3*, 2, 147–56.

Berne, E. (1968) *Games People Play*. Harmondsworth: Penguin.

Birth to Three Matters, and Foundation Stage Framework Birth to 5. Available at www.everychildmatters.gov.uk; www.standards.dcfs.gov.uk, accessed 15 July 2007.

Blake, W. (1958) 'Songs of Innocence, and Songs of Experience.' In J. Bronowski (ed.) *William Blake*. First published 1789 and 1794. Harmondsworth: Penguin.

Blatchford, P. (1998) *Social Life in School: The Role of Break Time*. London: Institute of Education.

Blatchford, P. and Sharp, S. (1994) *Break-Time and the School: Understanding and Changing Playground Behaviour*. London: Kegan Paul.

Bluebond-Langner, M. (1978) *The Private Worlds of Dying Children*. Princeton, NJ: Princeton University Press.

Boal, A. (1979) *Theatre of the Oppressed*. London: Pluto.

Bourdieu, P. (1997) 'The Forms of Capital.' In A. Halsey, H. Lauder, P. Brown and A. Wells (eds) *Education, Culture, Economy, and Society*. Oxford: Oxford University Press.

Boyden, J. and Ennew, J. (1997) *Children in Focus: A Manual for Participatory Research with Children*. Stockholm: Rädda Barnen.

Bradley, B. (1989) *Visions of Infancy*. Cambridge: Polity Press.

Bradshaw, J. and Mayhew, E. (eds) (2005) *The Well-being of Children in the UK*, second edition. Plymouth: Save the Children/University of York.

Bråten, S. (1996) 'When toddlers provide care: Infants' companion space.' *Childhood 3*, 449–65.

Brazelton, T. B. and Nugent, J. K. (1995) *Neonatal Behavioral Assessment Scale*. London: MacKeith Press/Cambridge University Press.

Brett, R. and Specht, I. (2004) *Young Soldiers: Why They Choose To Fight*. London: Lynne Rienner.

Brighouse, H. (2002) 'What Rights (If Any) Do Children Have?' In D. Archard and C. MacLeod (eds) *The Moral and Political Status of Children*. Oxford: Oxford University Press.

Brooker, L. (2002) *Starting School: Young Children Learning Cultures*. Buckingham: Open University Press.

Brooker, L. (2006) 'The rights and wrongs of TV parenting programmes.' *Early Education 50*, 3–4.

Brooks, L. (2006) *The Story of Childhood: Growing Up in Modern Britain*. London: Bloomsbury.

Brown, B. (1989) 'Anti-racist Practice is Good Practice.' In V. Williams (ed.) (1989) *Babies in Daycare: An Examination of the Issues*. London: The Daycare Trust.

Brown, B. (1998) *Unlearning Discrimination in the Early Years*. Stoke-on-Trent: Trentham.

Bruner, J. (1966) *Towards a Theory of Instruction*. New York: W. W. Norton.

Bruner, J. (1980) *Under Five in Britain*. London: Grant McIntyre.

Buckingham, D. (2003) 'Multimedia Childhoods.' In M. J. Kehily and J. Swann (eds) *Children's Cultural Worlds*. Chichester: Wiley/Open University.

Burke, C. and Grosvenor, I. (2003) *The School I'd Like*. London: RoutledgeFalmer.

Burman, E. (2007) *Deconstructing Developmental Psychology*. London: Routledge.

Butler, M. (1998) 'Negotiating Place: The Importance of Children's Realities.' In S. Steinberg and J. Kincheloe (eds) *Students as Researchers: Creating Classrooms that Matter*. London: Falmer.

Cairns, L. (2006) 'Participation with Purpose in Children's Participation.' In K. Tisdall, J. Davis, M. Hill and A. Prout (eds) *Children, Young People and Social Inclusion: Participation for What?* Bristol: Policy Press.

Candappa, M. (2002) 'Human Rights and Refugee Children in the UK.' In B. Franklin (ed.) *The New Handbook of Children's Rights*. London: Routledge.

Cavet, J. (1998) *People Don't Understand: Children, Young People and their Families Living with a Hidden Disability*. London: National Children's Bureau.

Children's Play Council and The Children's Society (2003) *Grumpy Grownups Stop Children's Play*. London: The Children's Society.

Children's Rights Alliance for England (CRAE) (2006) *State of Children's Rights in England*, first draft. London: CRAE.

Children's Rights Alliance for England (CRAE) (2007) *UK Implementation of the Convention on the Rights of the Child; NGO (England) Alternative Report to the Committee on the Rights of the Child*, first draft. London: CRAE.

Children's Society (1998) *No Lessons Learnt*. London: The Children's Society.

Chinn, D. (2006) *Professionals Talk About Parents With Learning Difficulties*. PhD thesis, University of London.

Christensen, P. and James, A. (2008) (eds) *Research with Children*. London: Falmer.

Christensen, P. and O'Brien, M. (eds) (2003) *Children in the City*. London: RoutledgeFalmer.

Clark, A. and Moss, P. (2005) *Spaces to Play*. London: National Children's Bureau.

Clark, C. (2003) *In Sickness and In Play*. New Brunswick, NJ: Rutgers University Press.

Cleaver, F. (2001) 'Institutions, Agency and the Limitations of Participatory Approaches to Development.' In B. Cooke and U. Kothari (eds) *Participation: The New Tyranny?* London: Zed Books.

Cleves School (1999) P. Alderson (ed.) *Learning and Inclusion: The Cleves School Experience*. London: David Fulton.

Coates, E. (2004) '"I Forgot the Sky!" Children's Stories Contained within their Drawings.' In V. Lewis, M. Kellett, C. Robinson *et al.* (eds) *The Reality of Research with Children and Young People*. London: Sage.

Cockburn, T., Kenny, S. and Webb, M. (1997) *Moss Side Youth Audit*. Manchester: Manchester Metropolitan University.

Cohen, C. (2005) *Jurisprudence on the Rights of the Child*. Four volumes. New York: Transnational.

Commission for Racial Equality (CRE) (1996) *From Cradle to School: A Practical Guide to Race Equality and Child Care*, second edition. London: CRE.

Commission on Children and Violence (1995) *Children and Violence.* London: Calouste Gulbenkian Foundation.

Connolly, P., Smith, A. and Kelly, B. (2002) *Too Young To Notice? The Cultural and Political Awareness of 3–6 Year Olds In Northern Ireland.* Belfast: Community Relations Council.

Cooter, R. (ed.) (1992) *In the Name of the Child: Health and Welfare 1880–1940* London: Routledge.

Corston, Baroness (2007) *Report On Women Prisoners' Children.* London: House of Lords.

Cousens, P. and Stevens, M. (1997) 'The Rights of the Child in a Paediatric Oncology Unit.' In M. John (ed.) *A Charge Against Society: The Child's Right to Protection.* London: Jessica Kingsley.

Cousins, J. (2003) *Listening to Four Year Olds: How They Can Help Us Plan Their Education And Care.* London: National Children's Bureau.

Cox, M. (1997) *Children and the Arts: Creative Action for the Next Millennium.* Birmingham: Playtrain.

Cunliffe, E. and English, C. (1997) *The First Report of Kids Count: A Children's Rights Project.* Newcastle: Royal Victoria Infirmary.

Dahlberg, G., Moss, P. and Pence, P. (1999) *Beyond Quality in Early Childhood Services.* London: Falmer.

Damon, W. (1988) *The Moral Child.* New York: Free Press.

Danby, S. and Barker, C. (1998) 'What's the Problem? Restoring Order in the Preschool Classroom.' In I. Hutchby and J. Moran Ellis (eds) *Children and Social Competence: Arenas of Action.* London: Falmer.

Davies, Z. and McMahon, W. (2007) *Debating Youth Justice.* London: Crime and Society Foundation.

De Bernier, L. (2005) *Birds Without Wings.* London: Vintage.

Declaration of Helsinki (1964, latest revision 2000) Fernay-Voltaire: World Medical Association.

Denning, LJ. *Hewer v. Bryant* [1970] 1 Q 357 said that parents have a 'dwindling right which the courts will hesitate to enforce against the wishes of the child. It starts with a right of control and ends with little more than advice'.

Department for Education and Employment, DfEE (1998a) *Early Years Development and Child Care: Partnership, Planning, Guidance, 1999–2000.* London: Stationery Office.

Department for Education and Employment, DfEE (1998b) *School Standards and Framework Act.* London: Stationery Office.

Department for Education and Skills, DfES (2004) *Children Act.* London: Stationery Office.

Department for Education and Skills, DfES/Department for Children, Schools and Families, DCFS (2007a) *Every Parent Matters.* London: DfES.

Department for Education and Skills, DfES/Department for Children, Schools and Families, DCSF (2007b) *UK Government Report to the UN Committee on the Rights of the Child.* London: DCSF.

Department of Health, DoH (1989) *Children Act.* London: Stationery Office.

Dickens, M., Emerson, S. and Gordon-Smith, P. (2004) *Starting With Choice; Inclusive Strategies For Consulting Young Children.* London: Save the Children.

Doise, W. and Myng, L. (1981) *La Construction Sociale de l'Intelligence.* Paris: InterEditions.

Donaldson, M. (1978) *Children's Minds.* Glasgow: Fontana.

Douthwaite, R. (1999) 'The Need to End Economic Growth.' In M. Scott Cato and M. Kennett (eds) *Green Economics.* Aberystwyth: Green Audit Books.

Dowty, T. (2007) *Draft Children Act 2004 Information Database (England) regulations 2007: Report to House of Lords Select Committee on the Merits of Statutory Instruments.* London: Action on Rights for Children. Available at www.arch-ed.org, accessed 20 December 2007.

Dreger, A. (2004) *One Of Us: Conjoined Twins and The Future of Normal.* Cambridge MA: Harvard University Press.

Dunn, J. (1977) *Distress and Comfort.* Glasgow: Fontana.

Dunn, J. (1987) 'The Beginnings of Moral Understanding: Development in the Second Year.' In J. Kagan and S. Lamb (eds) *The Emergence of Morality in Young Children.* Chicago, IL: University of Chicago Press.

Dunn, J. (1993) *Young Children's Close Relationships: Beyond Attachment.* London: Sage.

Dunn, J. (ed.) (1995) Connections between emotion and understanding in development. *Cognition and Emotion 9,* 2–3, 113–285.

Dunn, J. (2004) *Children's Friendships: The Beginnings of Intimacy.* Oxford: Blackwell.

Durendt, J. (2007) 'Drugs mules in UK jails need help too'. *Guardian* Letters, 17 July.

Dworkin, R. (1997) *Taking Rights Seriously.* London: Duckworth.

Early Childhood Education Forum (1998) *Quality and Diversity in Early Learning.* London: National Children's Bureau.

Economic and Social Research Council, ESRC (1996) *Brochure of the Research Programme, Children 5–16, 1996–1999.* London: ESRC.

Edwards, C., Gandini, I. and Forman, G. (1998) *The Hundred Languages of Children.* London: Ablex.

Effective Provision of Pre-School Education Project, EPPE. Available at www.ioe.ac.uk/schools/ecpe/eppe, accessed 22 February 2008.

Eisenberg, N. (1992) *The Caring Child.* Hove: Erlbaum Associates.

11 Million (2007) *Five Year Plan of the Children's Commissioner For England.* London: 11 Million.

Elfer, P., Goldschmied, E. and Selleck, D. (2003) *Key Persons in the Nursery.* London: David Fulton.

End Child Poverty, ECP, and Association of London Government, ALG (2005) *Not One of London's Children Lives in Poverty, 700,000 Do.* London: ECP, ALG.

Ennew, J. (1997) *Monitoring Children's Rights: Indicators for Children's Rights Project.* Newmarket: Global Gutter Press.

Ennew, J. (2002) 'Outside Childhood: Street Children's Rights.' In B. Franklin (ed.) *The New Handbook of Children's Rights.* London: Routledge.

Ennew, J. and Connolly, M. (1996) 'Introduction: Children out of place.' *Childhood 3,* 2, 131–46.

Ennew, J. and Morrow, V. (1994) 'Out of the Mouths of Babes.' In E. Verhellen and F. Spiesschaert (eds) *Children's Rights: Monitoring Issues.* Gent: Mys and Breesch.

European Commission Network on Childcare, ECNC (1996) *Quality Targets in Services for Young Children.* Brussels: EC Network on Children.

Faulkner, J. (1998) 'Participatory video-making in Brazil.' In V. Johnson, E. Ivan-Smith, G. Gordon, P. Pridmore and P. Scott (eds) *Stepping Forward: Children and Young People's Participation in the Development Process.* London: Intermediate Technology.

Feinstein, L. (2003) 'Very early cognitive evidence.' *CentrePiece,* Summer, 24–30.

Ferudi, F. (2001) *Paranoid Parenting.* London: Allen Lane.

Finch, S. (1998) *'An Eye for an Eye Leaves Everyone Blind': Teaching Young Children to Settle Conflicts without Violence.* London: National Early Years Network; Save the Children.

Foucault, M. (1980) *Power/Knowledge; Selected Interviews and Other Writings, 1972–1977.* Brighton: Harvester.

Fox, N., Leavitt, L. and Warhol, J. (1999) *The Role of Early Experience in Infant Development.* New York, NY: Johnson and Johnson Pediatric Institute.

Franklin, B. (ed.) (2002) *The New Handbook of Children's Rights.* London: Routledge.

Freeman, M. (1983) *The Rights and Wrongs of Children.* London: Frances Pinter.

Freeman, M. (2004) *Children's Rights.* Vols 1 and 2 of the International Library of Essays on Children's Rights. Aldershot: Ashgate.

Freeman, M. (2007) 'Why it remains important to take children's rights seriously.' *International Journal of Children's Rights 15,*1, 5–23.

Frönes, I. (1994) 'Dimensions of Childhood.' In J. Qvortrup, M. Bardy, G. Sgritta and H. Wintersberger (eds) (1994) *Childhood Matters: Social Theory, Practice and Politics.* Aldershot: Avebury.

Gardner, R. (1989) *Who Says? Choice and Control in Care.* London: National Children's Bureau.

Gardner, H. (1993) *The Unschooled Mind: How Children Think and How Schools Should Teach.* London: Fontana.

Gardner, H. (1998) 'Social and Cognitive Competencies in Learning: Which is Which?' In I. Hutchby and J. Moran-Ellis (eds) (1998) *Children and Social Competence: Arenas of Action.* London: Falmer.

Gerhardt, S. (2004) *Why Love Matters: How Affection Shapes a Baby's Brain.* Hove: Routledge.

Giddens, A. (1991) *Modernity and Self-Identity.* Cambridge: Polity.

Gidley, B. (2005) *No Ball Games Here; Geographies of Risk, Play and Social Exclusion.* London: Goldsmiths College, Centre for Urban and Community Research.

Gillick v. *Wisbech & W. Norfolk AHA* [1985], 3All ER. For a review of complications following this Law Lord's ruling see P. Alderson and J. Montgomery (1996) *Health Care Choices: Making Decisions with Children.* London: Institute for Public Policy Research.

Goldschmeid, E. and Jackson, S. (2004) *People Under Three: Young Children in Day Care.* London: Routledge.

Goldschmeid, S. and Selleck, D. (1996) *Communication between Babies in their First Year,* Video and Pack. London: National Children's Bureau.

Goldson, B. and Peters, E. (2000) *Tough Justice – Responding to Children in Trouble.* London: Children's Society.

Goldson, E. (ed.) (1999) *Developmental Interventions in the Neonatal Intensive Care Nursery.* New York: Oxford University Press.

Goldstein, J., Freud, J. and Solnit, A. (1996) *The Best Interests Of The Child.* New York: Free Press.

Gordon-Smith, P. (2007) *The Morality of Young Children in Their Early Years Setting.* MA dissertation. London: Institute of Education.

Green, J. (1997) *Risk and Misfortune: The Social Construction of Accidents.* London: University College London Press.

Griffin, J. (2002) 'Do Children Have Rights?' In D. Archard and C. MacLeod (eds) *The Moral and Political Status of Children.* Oxford: Oxford University Press.

Griffith, R. (1998) *Educational Citizenship and Independent Learning.* London: Jessica Kingsley.

Griffiths, M. and Davies, L. (1995) *In Fairness to Children: Working for Social Justice in the Primary School.* London: David Fulton.

Grisso, T. and Vierling, L. (1978) 'Minors' consent to treatment: A developmental perspective.' *Professional Psychology 9,* 412–27.

Grover, S. (2005) 'Advocacy by children as a causal factor in promoting resilience.' *Childhood 12*: 527–38.

Guggenheim, M. (2005) *What's Wrong With Children's Rights?* Cambridge, MA: Harvard University Press.

Gupta, P. (2005) 'India.' In H. Penn (ed.) *Unequal Childhoods.* London: RoutledgeFalmer.

Hall, J. (2001) 'Children and crime reduction – victims not villains.' *Howard League Magazine 19,* 4, 8.

Hallam, S. (2004) *Homework: The Evidence.* London: Institute of Education.

Hanson, K. and Vandaele, A. (2003) 'Working children and international labour law: a critical analysis.' *International Journal of Children's Rights 11,* 1, 73–146.

Hardyment, C. (1984) *Dream Babies: Child Care from Locke to Spock.* Oxford: Oxford University Press.

Harris, J. (1985) *The Value of Life.* London: Routledge.

Harris, M. and Butterworth, G. (2002) *Developmental Psychology: A Student's Handbook.* Hove: Psychology Press.

Hart, R. (1992) *Children's Participation from Tokenism to Citizenship.* Paris: UNICEF.

Hart, R. (1997) *Children's Participation: The Theory and Practice of Involving Young Children in Community Development and Environmental Care.* London: Earthscan/UNESCO.

Hendrick, H. (1997) 'Constructions and Reconstructions of British Childhood: An Interpretive Survey 1800 to the Present.' In A. James and A. Prout (eds) *Constructing and Reconstructing Childhood: Contemporary Issues of the Sociology of Childhood.* London: Falmer.

Hendrick, H. (2003) *Child Welfare: Historical Dimensions, Contemporary Debate.* Bristol: Policy Press.

Herbert, E. and Moir, J. (1996) 'Children and Special Educational Needs.' In C. Nutbrown (ed.) *Respectful Educators – Capable Learners: Children's Rights in Early Education.* London: Paul Chapman.

Highfield School (1997) *Changing our School: Promoting Positive Behaviour.* P. Alderson (ed.). Plymouth: Highfield School/London: Institute of Education.

Hillman, M. (2003) 'The Relevance of Climate Change to Future Policy on Walking and Cycling.' In R. Tolley (ed.) *Sustainable Transport.* Abingdon: Woodhead Publishing.

Hillman, M., Adams, J. and Whiteleg, J. (1990) *One False Move: A Study of Children's Independent Mobility.* London: Policy Studies Institute.

Hillman, M. and Fawcett, T. (2004) *How We Can Save the Planet?* Harmondsworth: Penguin.

HM Treasury, Department for Education and Skills, Department for Work and Pensions and Department for Trade and Industry (2003) *Every Child Matters.* London: Stationery Office.

HM Treasury, Department for Education and Skills, Department for Work and Pensions and Department for Trade and Industry (2006) *Childcare Act.* London: Stationery Office.

Hodgkin, R. and Newell, P. (1996) *Effective Government Structures for Children.* London: Calouste Gulbenkian Foundation.

Hodgson, D. (1995) *Promoting Children's Rights in Practice.* London: NCVO.

Holden, C. and Clough, N. (1999) *Children as Citizens: Education for Participation.* London: Jessica Kingsley.

Holdigan, C. (2000) 'Discipline and Normalisation in the Nursery, the Foucauldian Gaze. In H. Penn (ed.) *Early Childhood Services: Theory, Policy and Practice.* Buckingham: Open University Press.

Holt, J. (1975) *Escape from Childhood.* Harmondsworth: Penguin.

Hood, S. (2002) *The State of London's Children Report, number 1.* London: Greater London Authority.

Hood, S. (2004) *The State of London's Children Report, number 2.* London: Greater London Authority.

House, R. (2003) 'Beyond "paranoid parenting": Raising children in a fear-filled age.' *The Mother Magazine 8,* 6–9.

Howarth, R. and Hopscotch Asian Women's Centre (1997) *If We Don't Play Now, When Can We?* London: Hopscotch Asian Women's Centre.

Hoxter, S. (1977) 'Play and Communication.' In A. Boston and D. Daws (eds) *The Child Psychotherapist and Problems of Young People.* London: Wildwood House.

Hurley, N. (1998) *Straight Talk: Working with Children and Young People in Groups.* York: Joseph Rowntree Foundation.

Ingenhorst, H. (2001) 'Child Labour in the Federal Republic of Germany.' In P. Mizen, C. Pole and A. Bolton (2001) (eds) *Hidden Hands: International Perspectives On Children's Work And Labour.* London: RoutledgeFalmer.

International Save the Children Alliance (1995) *UN Convention on the Rights of the Child Training Kit.* London: Save the Children.

Invernizzi, A. and Milne, B. (2002) 'Are children entitled to contribute to international policy making?' *International Journal of Children's Rights 10,* 4, 403–31.

Irwin, C. (1996) 'Samantha's wish.' *Nursing Times 92,* 36, 30–31.

James, A. and James, A. (2004) *Constructing Childhood.* Basingstoke: Palgrave.

James, A. and Jenks, C. (1996) 'Public perceptions of childhood criminality.' *British Journal of Sociology 47,* 2, 315–31.

James, A. and Prout, A. (eds) (1997) *Constructing and Reconstructing Childhood: Contemporary Issues of the Sociology of Childhood.* London: Falmer.

Jebb, E. (1906) *Cambridge: A Study in Social Questions.* Cambridge: Macmillan and Bowes.

Jeffs, T. (2002) 'Schooling, Education and Children's Rights.' In B. Franklin (ed.) *The New Handbook of Children's Rights.* London: Routledge.

Jenkins, R. (2004) *Social Identity.* London: Routledge.

John, M. (2003) *Children's Rights and Power: Charging up for a New Century.* London: Jessica Kingsley.

Johnson, V., Hill, J. and Ivan-Smith, E. (1995) *Listening to Smaller Voices: Children in an Environment of Change.* Chard: ACTIONAID.

Johnson, V., Ivan-Smith, E., Gordon, G., Pridmore, P. and Scott, P. (1998) *Stepping Forward: Children and Young People's Participation in the Development Process.* London: Intermediate Technology.

Joseph Rowntree Foundation (JRF) (2006) *What Will It Take To End Child Poverty?* York: Joseph Rowntree Foundation.

Joseph, S. (ed.) (1999) *A Voice for the Child – the Inspirational Work of Janusz Korczak.* London: Thorsons/NSPCC.

Judd, D. (1995) *Give Sorrow Words: Working with a Dying Child,* second edition. London: Whurr.

Katz, A. (ed.) (2002) *Parenting Under Pressure: Prison.* London: Young Voice.

Katz, C. (2004) *Growing Up Global.* Minneapolis, MN: University of Minnesota Press.

Katz, C. (2005) 'The Terrors of Hyper-vigilance.' In J. Qvortrup (ed.) *Studies in Modern Childhood.* Basingstoke: Palgrave.

Kefyalew, F. (1996) 'The reality of child participation in research: Experience from a capacity-building programme.' *Childhood 3,* 2, 203–14.

Kehily, M. J. (2003) 'Consumption and Creativity.' In M. J. Kehily and J. Swann (eds) *Children's Cultural Worlds.* Chichester: Wiley/Open University.

Kendrick, C., Culling, J., Oakhill, T. and Molt, M. (1986) 'Children's understanding of their illness and treatment within a paediatric oncology unit.' *ACP Newsletter 8,* 2, 16–20.

Kennedy, I. (1988) *Treat Me Right.* Oxford: Clarendon Press.

Kennet, M. and Heinemann, V. (2005) 'Green economics: Setting the scene. Aims, context, and philosophical underpinning of the distinctive new solutions offered by green economics.' *International Journal of Green Economics 1,* 1–2, 68–102.

Khan, S. (1997) *A Street Children's Research.* London: Save the Children/Dhaka: Chinnamul Shishu Kishore Sangstha.

Kiddle, C. (1999) *Traveller Children: A Voice for Themselves.* London: Jessica Kingsley.

Kirby, P. (1999) *Involving Young Researchers.* York: Joseph Rowntree Foundation.

Kirby, P., Lanyon, C., Cronin, K. and Sinclair, R. (2003) *Building a Culture of Participation.* London: DfES.

Knight, A. (1998) *Valued or Forgotten? Independent Visitors and Disabled Young People.* London: National Children's Bureau.

Komesaroff, L. (2002) *Surgical Consent: Bioethics and Cochlear Implantation.* Washington, DC: Gallaudet University.

Kübler-Ross, E. (1983) *On Children and Death.* London: Macmillan.

Laing, C. (1993) Statement at the launch of the National Playing Fields Association Report, 6 July, quoted in G. Lansdown and P. Newell (eds) *UK Agenda for Children.* London: Children's Rights Office.

Lancaster, P. (2004) *Listening to Young Children Resource Pack.* Buckingham: Open University Press.

Lane, J. (1999) *Action for Racial Equality in the Early Years: Understanding the Past, Thinking about the Present, Planning for the Future.* London: National Early Years Network.

Lansdown, G. (1995a) *Taking Part, Children's Participation in Decision Making.* London: Institute for Public Policy Research.

Lansdown, G. (1995b) *Building Small Democracies, the Implications of the UN Convention on the Rights of the Child for Respecting Children's Civil Rights within the Family.* London: Children's Rights Office.

Lansdown, G. (2001) *It's Our World Too! A Report on the Lives of Disabled Children for the UN General Assembly Special Session on Children.* London: Disability Awareness in Action.

Lansdown, G. (2002) Children's Rights Commissioners for the UK. In B. Franklin (ed.) *The New Handbook of Children's Rights.* London: Routledge.

Lansdown, G. (2005a) *The Evolving Capacities of the Child.* Florence: UNICEF Innocenti/Rädda Barnen.

Lansdown, G. (2005b) *Can You Hear Me? The Rights of Young Children to Participate in Decisions Affecting Them.* The Hague: Bernard van Leer.

Lansdown, G. (2006) 'International Developments in Children's Participation.' In K. Tisdall, J. Davis, M. Hill and A. Prout (eds) *Children, Young People and Social Inclusion: Participation for What?* Bristol: Policy Press.

Lansdown, G. and Newell, P. (eds) (1994) *UK Agenda for Children.* London: Children's Rights Office.

Leach, P. (1999) *The Physical Punishment of Children: Some Input from Recent Research.* London: NSPCC.

Lee, L. (1959) *Cider with Rosie.* London: Hogarth.

Leidloff, J. (1976) *The Continuum Concept.* London: Futura.

Levine, H. (1993) 'Context and Scaffolding in Developmental Studies of Mother–Child Problem-Solving Dyads.' In S. Chaiklin and J. Lave (eds) *Understanding Practice.* Cambridge: Cambridge University Press.

Lewis, A. (1994) *Children's Understanding of Disability.* London: Routledge.

Liebel, M. (2004) *A Will of Their Own: Cross-cultural Perspectives on Working Children.* London: Zed Books.

Lindon, J. (2003) *Too Safe For their Own Good? Helping Children Learn About Risk And Lifeskills.* London: National Children's Bureau.

Lindon, J. (2006) *Care and Caring Matter.* London: British Association for Early Childhood Education.

Llewellyn, N. (1993) 'The use of PCA for paediatric post-operative pain management.' *Paediatric Nursing 5,* 12–15.

Lorenzo, R. (1992) *Too Little Time and Space for Childhood.* Florence: UNICEF.

Lukes, S. (2005) *Power.* Basingstoke: Macmillan.

Lynas, M. (2007) *Six Degrees: Our Future on a Hotter Planet.* London: Fourth Estate.

Lyon, C. (2007) 'Interrogating the concentration on the UNCRC instead of the ECHR in the development of children's rights in England?' *Children & Society 21,* 147–53.

MacCarthy, D. (1979) *The Under-Fives in Hospital.* London: National Association for the Welfare of Children in Hospital.

Madders, J. (1987) *Relax and Be Happy: Techniques for 5–18 Year Olds.* London: Unwin.

Maidment, P. (2006) London's billionaires. Available at www.forbes.com, accessed 1 July 2007.

Mansurov, V. (2001) 'Child labour in Russia.' In P. Mizen, C. Pole and A. Bolton (eds) *Hidden Hands: International Perspectives On Children's Work And Labour.* London: RoutledgeFalmer.

Marlowe, J. (1997) 'Cries and whispers: Children are eager to show you their bleeding knees but not their broken hearts.' *Guardian,* 11 February.

Marshall, S. (1963) *An Experiment in Education.* Cambridge: Cambridge University Press.

Masson, J. and Winn, M. (1999) *Out of Hearing: Representing Children in Care Proceedings.* Chichester: Wiley.

Masson, J., Harrison, C. and Pavlovic, A. (1997) *Working with Children and 'Lost' Parents.* York: Joseph Rowntree Foundation.

Matthews, H. (2003) 'Children and regeneration.' *Children & Society 17,* 4, 264–76.

Mayall, B. (1993) Keeping children healthy. *Social Science and Medicine 36,* 77–84.

Mayall, B. (1994a) *Negotiating Health: Primary School Children at Home and School.* London: Cassell.

Mayall, B. (1994b) *Children's Childhoods: Observed and Experienced.* London: Falmer.

Mayall, B. (2002) *Towards a Sociology for Childhood.* Buckingham: Open University Press.

Mayall, B. (2006) 'Child–Adult Relations in Social Space.' In K. Tisdall, J. Davis, M. Hill and A. Prout (eds) *Children, Young People and Social Inclusion: Participation for What?* Bristol: Policy Press.

Mayall, B., Bendelow, G., Barker, S., Storey, P. and Veltman, S. (1996) *Children's Health in Primary Schools.* London: Falmer.

Mayall, B. and Foster, M-C. (1989) *Child Health Care: Living with Children, Working for Children.* Oxford: Heinemann.

Mayhew, E., Uprichard, E., Beresford, B., Ridge T. and Bradshaw, J. (2005) *Children and Childhood in the United Kingdom?* European Childhood Economics Survey, COST A19. pp.403–56.

Mayles, J. (1989) *Just Playing?* Buckingham: Open University Press.

McNamara, S. and Moreton, G. (1993) *Teaching Special Needs in Mainstream Classes.* London: David Fulton.

McNamara, S. and Moreton, G. (1995) *Changing Behaviour.* London: David Fulton.

McNamara, S. and Moreton, G. (1997) *Understanding Differentiation.* London: David Fulton.

McNeish, D. (2007) *The State of London's Children Report, number 3.* London: Greater London Authority.

Mellor, M. (2006) 'Ecofeminist political economy.' *International Journal of Green Economics 1,* 1–2, 139–50.

Mendus, S. (1987) 'Kant: An Honest but Narrow-minded Bourgeois?' In E. Kennedy and S. Mendus (eds) *Women in Western Political Philosophy.* Brighton: Wheatsheaf.

Menzies Lyth, I. (1988) *Containing Anxiety in Institutions.* London: Free Association Books.

Mepani, B. and Emerson, S. (1998) *Report for the Steering Committee on Consulting with Children in East London.* London: Children's Discovery Centre; Save the Children.

Midgley, M. (1996) *Utopias, Dolphins and Computer: Problems of Philosophical Plumbing.* London: Routledge.

Mies, M. (2007) 'Patriarchy and accumulation on a world scale.' *International Journal of Green Economics 1,* 3–4, 268–75.

Millar, J. and Gardiner, K. (2004) *Low Pay, Household Resources and Poverty.* York: Joseph Rowntree Foundation.

Miller, A. (1983) *Thou Shalt Not Be Aware: Society's Betrayal of the Child.* London: Pluto.

Miller, J. (2003) *Never Too Young: How Young Children Can Take Responsibility and Make Decisions.* London: National Early Years Network; Save the Children.

Mizen, P., Pole, C. and Bolton, A. (eds) (2001) *Hidden Hands: International Perspectives on Children's Work and Labour.* London: RoutledgeFalmer.

Monbiot, G. (2007) *Heat: How to Stop The Planet Burning.* Harmondsworth: Penguin.

Morris, J. (1998) *Don't Leave Us Out: Involving Disabled Children and Young People With Communication Impairments.* York: Joseph Rowntree Foundation.

Morris, S. (1999) 'Want a baby? Read this first.' *The Times,* 12 March, p.21.

Morrow, V. (1994) 'Responsible Children?' In B. Mayall (ed.) *Children's Childhoods Observed and Experienced.* London: Falmer.

Morrow, V. (1998) *Understanding Families; Children's Perspectives.* London: National Children's Bureau.

Morrow, V. (1999a) '"We are people too." Children's perspectives on rights and decision-making in England.' *International Journal of Children's Rights 7,* 149–70.

Morrow, V. (1999b) '"We Get Played Like Fools": Young people's accounts of community and institutional participation.' *Health Education Authority Conference: Changing Families, Changing Communities.* London.

Morrow, V. (2002) 'Children's Rights to Public Space.' In B. Franklin (ed.) *The New Handbook of Children's Rights.* London: Routledge.

Morrow, V. (2003) 'Improving the Neighbourhood for Children: Possibilities and Limitations of "Social Capital" Discourses.' In P. Christensen and M. O'Brien (eds) *Children in the City.* London: RoutledgeFalmer.

Morss, J. (1990) *The Biologising of Childhood.* Hillsdale, NJ: Lawrence Erlbaum.

Morss, J. (1996) *Growing Critical: Alternatives to Developmental Psychology.* London: Routledge.

Mosley, J. (1993) *Turn Your School Around.* Wisbech: Learning Development Aids.

Murray, L. and Andrews, H. (2000) *The Social Baby: Understanding Babies' Communication from Birth.* Richmond: The Children's Project.

National Children's Bureau, NCB (1993) *Guidelines for Research.* London: NCB.

National Early Years Network/Redbridge Local Authority, NEYN (1998) *Developing Effective Consultation with Children and their Parents.* London: NEYN.

National Voluntary Council for Children's Play (1992) *A Charter for Children's Play.* London: National Children's Bureau.

Neale, B. (2002) 'Dialogues with children: Children, divorce and citizenship.' *Childhood 9,* 4, 455–76.

Neustatter, A. (1998) 'Kids – what the papers say.' *Guardian,* 8 April.

Newell, P. (1989) *Children Are People Too: The Case Against Physical Punishment.* London: Bedford Square Press.

Newson, J. (1977) 'An Inter-subjective Approach to the Systematic Description of Mother–Infant Interaction.' In H. Schaffer (ed.) *Studies in Mother–Infant Interaction.* London: Academic Press.

Newson, C. (1995a) 'The patio projects.' *Co-ordinate 45,* 10–11.

Newson, C. (1995b) 'Too much fun?' *Co-ordinate 45,* 11.

Newson, J. and Newson, E. (1963) *Infant Care in an Urban Community.* London: George Allan and Unwin.

Newson, J. and Newson, E. (1990) *The Extent of Parental Physical Punishment in the UK.* London: APPROACH.

Noyes, J. (1999) *The Voices and Choices of Children on Long-Term Ventilation.* London: Stationery Office.

Nuremberg Code (1947) Available at http://ohsr.od.nih.gov/guidelines/nuremberg.html, accessed 12 December 2007.

Nutbrown, C. (ed.) (1996a) *Respectful Educators – Capable Learners: Children's Rights in Early Education.* London: Paul Chapman.

Nutbrown, C. (1996b) 'Wide Eyes and Open Minds.' In C. Nutbrown (ed.) *Respectful Educators – Capable Learners: Children's Rights in Early Education.* London: Paul Chapman.

O'Kane, C. (2003) 'Street and working children's participation in programming for their rights.' *Children, Youth and Environments 13,* 153–79.

O'Neill, J. (1994) *The Missing Child in Liberal Theory: Towards a Covenant Theory of Family, Community, Welfare and the Civic State.* Toronto: University of Toronto Press.

O'Neill, O. (1988) 'Children's rights and children's lives.' *Ethics 98,* 445–63.

Opie, I. (1993) *The People in the Playground.* Oxford: Oxford University Press.

O'Quigley, A. (1999) *Listening to Children and Representing their Best Interests.* York: Joseph Rowntree Foundation.

Organisation of African Unity, OAU (1990) *The African Charter on the Rights and Welfare of the Child.* Addis Ababa: OAU.

Osler, A. and Starkey, H. (2005) *Changing Citizenship: Democracy and Inclusion in Education.* Maidenhead: Open University Press.

Osler, A. and Vincent, K. (2003) *Girls and Exclusion.* London: Routledge Falmer.

Paley, V. (1999) *The Kindness of Children.* Cambridge, MA: University of Harvard Press.

Palmer, S. (2006) *Toxic Childhood.* London: Orion.

Pantazis, C., Gordon, D. and Levitas, R. (2006) *Poverty and Social Exclusion in Britain: The Millennium Survey.* Bristol: Policy Press.

Parens, E. (ed.) (2006) *Surgically Shaping Children.* Baltimore, MD: Johns Hopkins University Press.

Parr, A., quoted in Ward, C. (1994) 'Opportunities for Childhood in late Twentieth Century Britain.' In B. Mayall (ed.) *Children's Childhoods Observed and Experienced.* London: Falmer.

Participation Education Group, PEG (1997) *School Can Seriously Damage Your Health: How Children Think School Affects and Deals with their Health.* Newcastle-upon-Tyne: Participation Education Group (PEG).

Participation Education Group, PEG (1998) *Newsletter, Celebration Edition,* May.

Penn, H. (1997a) *Comparing Nurseries: The Experiences of Children and Staff in Day Nurseries in Spain, Italy and the UK.* London: Paul Chapman.

Penn, H. (1997b) *Childcare As a Gendered Organisation. Research Report RR23.* London: DfEE.

Penn, H. (1998a) *A Review of Kindergarten Provision in Mongolia.* Report for the Ministry of Education and Culture, Mongolia.

Penn, H. (1998b) Children and childhood in the majority world. *Conference on Childhood: Relating Research to Policy.* London.

Penn, H. (2001) 'Culture and Childhood in Pastoralist Communities: The Example of Outer Mongolia.' In L. Alanen and B. Mayall (eds) *Conceptualising Child–Adult Relations.* London: RoutledgeFalmer.

Penn, H. (2002) 'The World Bank's views of early childhood.' *Childhood 9,* 118–32.

Penn, H. (2005) *Unequal Childhoods: Young Children's Lives in Poorer Countries.* London: RoutledgeFalmer.

Penn, H., Lloyd, E,, Potter, S. *et al.* (2006) *Early Years: What is Known about the Long-term Economic Impact of Centre-Based Early Childhood Interventions?* London: EPPI-Centre (Social Science Research Unit, Institute of Education, University of London).

Phillips, B. and Alderson, P. (2003) 'Beyond "Anti-smacking": Challenging violence and coercion in parent–child relations.' *International Journal of Children's Rights 115,* 175–97.

Piaget, J. (1924) *The Language and Thought of the Child.* London: Routledge.

Piaget, J. (1932) *The Moral Judgement of the Child.* London: Routledge.

Piaget, J. and Inhelder, B. (1956) *The Child's Conception of Space.* London: Routledge.

Pilger, J. (1998) *Hidden Agendas.* London: Vintage.

Pratt, B. and Loizos, P. (1992) *Choosing Research Methods: Data Collection for Development Workers.* Oxford: Oxfam.

Pritchard, M. (1991) *On Becoming Responsible.* Lawrence, KS: University of Kansas Press.

Pritchard, M. (1996) *Reasonable Children: Moral Education and Moral Learning.* Lawrence, KS: University of Kansas Press.

Prout, A., Davis, J., Hill, M. *et al.* (eds) (2006) *Children, Young People and Social Inclusion: Participation for What?* Bristol: Policy Press.

Punch, S. (2001) 'Negotiating Autonomy: Childhoods in Rural Bolivia.' In L. Alanen and B. Mayall (eds) *Conceptualising Child–Adult Relations.* London: RoutledgeFalmer.

Purves, L. and Selleck, D. (1999) *Tuning Into Children.* (The handbook for the *Radio 4* series.) London: BBC Educational Publsihing.

Qualifications and Curriculum Authority (QCA) (1998) *Education for Citizenship and Democracy* (The Crick Report). London: QCA.

Qualification and Curriculum Authority (QCA) (2000) *Foundation Stage.* London: QCA.

Qvortrup, J. (1997) 'A Voice for Children in Statistical and Social Accounting: A Plea for Children's Right to be Heard.' In A. James and A. Prout (eds) *Constructing and Reconstructing Childhood.* London: RoutledgeFalmer.

Qvortrup, J. (2001) 'School-work, Paid Work and the Changing Obligations of Childhood.' In P. Mizen, C. Pole and A. Bolton (eds) *Hidden Hands: International Perspectives on Children's Work and Labour.* London: RoutledgeFalmer.

Qvortrup, J. (ed.) (2005) *Studies in Modern Childhood.* Basingstoke: Palgrave.

Raban, K. (1987) 'Young children, guided imagery and religious education.' *British Journal of Religious Education 10,* 1.

Ramsden, S. (1998) *Working with Children of Prisoners: A Resource for Teachers.* London: Save the Children.

Rankin, B. (1998) 'Curriculum Development in Reggio Emilia.' In C. Edwards, I. Gandini and G. Forman (eds) *The Hundred Languages of Children.* London: Ablex.

Ransome, A. (1930) *Swallows and Amazons.* London: Jonathan Cape.

Richards, M. (1974) *The Integration of a Child into a Social World.* Cambridge: Cambridge University Press.

Richman, N. (1993) *Communicating with Children: Helping Children in Distress.* London: Save the Children.

Riihelda, M. (1996) *How Do We Deal with Children's Questions?* Published PhD Thesis. Helsinki: STAKES.

Robb, S. (2007) 'It's not only what we eat, but *how* we eat.' *Early Education 51,* 5–6.

Robertson, J. and Robertson, J. (1989) *Separation and the Very Young.* London: Free Association Books.

Robinson, J. (2004) 'Health visitors or health police?' *Association for the Improvement of Maternity Services Journal 16,* 3. Available at www.aims.org.uk, accessed 12 December 2007.

Rose, N. (1990) *Governing the Soul: The Shaping of the Private Self.* London: Routledge.

Rosen, M. (1998) *The Penguin Book of Childhood.* Harmondsworth: Penguin.

Ross, L. E. (1998) *Families and Health Care Decision Making.* New York: Oxford University Press.

Rowe, D. (1999) *The Business of School Councils.* London: Citizenship Foundation.

Rutter, J. and Hyder, T. (1998) *Refugee Children in the Early Years: Issues for Policy-Makers and Providers.* London: Refugee Council and Save the Children.

Saunders, R. and Freeman, K. (1998) 'Children's Neo-rhetorical Participation in Peer Interactions.' In I. Hutchby and J. Moran-Ellis (eds) *Children and Social Competence: Arenas of Action.* London: Falmer.

Save the Children (n.d.) *Focus on Images.* London: Save the Children.

Save the Children (1995) *Towards a Children's Agenda: New Challenges for Social Development.* London: Save the Children.

Save the Children (1997) *Learning From Experience: Participatory Approaches in SCF*. London: Save the Children.

Save the Children (1998) *Staying Power*. London: Save the Children.

Save the Children (1999) *We Have Rights Okay!* London: Save the Children.

Save the Children (2000) *Anti-Bias Approaches in the Early Years*. London: Save the Children.

Save the Children (2003) *Stepping Together for Education*. Kathmandu: Save the Children.

Save the Children (2005a) *Home From Home: A Guidance and Resource Pack for the Welcome and Inclusion of Refugee Children and Families in Schools*. London: Salusbury Road WORLD Refugee Centre/Save the Children.

Save the Children (2005b) *Having Our Say. A Peer Review Project with Young Gypsy/Travellers in Scotland*. Edinburgh: Save the Children.

Save the Children (2005c) *Local Authority Support to Unaccompanied Asylum-Seeking Young People. Changes since the Hillingdon Judgement*. London: Save the Children.

Save the Children (2007) *Severe Child Poverty*. Available at www.savethechildren.org.uk/childpov.pdf, accessed 22 February 2008.

Save the Children/Kirklees Metropolitan Council (1996) *Children's Participation Pack: A Practical Guide for Playworkers*. London: Save the Children.

Schweinhart, L. and Weikart, D. (1997) 'The high/scope preschool curriculum comparison study through age 23.' *Early Childhood Research Quarterly 12*, 117–43.

Scraton, P. (2006) *The Denial of Children's Rights and Liberties in the UK and the North of Ireland*. European Civil Liberties Network. Available at www.ecln.org, accessed 18 February 2008.

Seaman, P., Turner, K., Hill, M., Stafford, A. and Walker, M. (2006) *Parenting and Children's Resilience in Disadvantaged Communities*. London: National Children's Bureau.

Selleck, D. and Griffin, S. (1996) 'Quality for the Under-3s.' In G. Pugh (ed.) *Contemporary Issues in the Early Years: Working Collaboratively for Children*. London: National Children's Bureau.

Shamgar-Handelman, L. (1994) 'To Whom Does Childhood Belong?' In J. Qvortop, M. Bardy, G. Sgritta, and H. Wintersberger (eds) *Childhood Matters: Social Theory, Practice and Politics*. Aldershot: Avebury.

Sharman, C., Cross, W. and Vennis, D. (1995) *Observing Children: A Practical Guide, Case Studies*. London: Cassell.

Sherman, A. (1996) *Rules, Routines and Regimentation: Young Children Reporting on their Schooling*. Nottingham: Education Heretics Press.

Shier, H. (1995) *Article 31 Action Pack: Children's Rights and Children's Play*. Birmingham, England: PLAY-TRAIN.

Siegal, M. (1997) *Knowing Children: Experiments in Conversation and Cognition*. Hove: Lawrence Erlbaum Associates.

Sinclair, R. (2004) 'Participation in practice: Making it meaningful, effective and sustainable.' *Children & Society 18*, 2, 106–18.

Siraj-Blatchford, I. (1996) 'Language, Cultures and Difference: Challenging Inequalities and Promoting Respect.' In C. Nutbrown (ed.) *Respectful Educators – Capable Learners: Children's Rights in Early Education*. London: Paul Chapman.

Skeat, W. (1983) *Concise Etymological Dictionary of the English Language*. Oxford: Oxford University Press.

Smart, C., Neale, B. and Wade, A. (2001) *The Changing Experience of Childhood: Families and Divorce*. Cambridge: Polity.

Smith, C. (1998) 'Children with "Special Rights".' In C. Edwards, I. Gandini and G. Forman (eds) *The Hundred Languages of Children*. London: Ablex.

Smith, F. (1998) 'Child-centred after school and holiday child care.' *Report to ESRC Children 5–16 Programme Meeting*. Manchester.

Smith, M. (1995) 'A community study of physical violence to children in the home and associated variables.' *Fifth European Conference, International Society for the Prevention of Child Abuse and Neglect*. Oslo.

Smith, M. (1998) 'Paper on Children's views about violence.' *Report to ESRC Children 5–16 Programme Meeting.* Manchester.

Smith, D. and Armstrong, S. (2004) *If the World were a Village.* London: A & C Black.

Solberg, A. (1993) 'The Social Construction of Childhood.' In B. Mayall (ed.) *Family Life and Social Control: Report of Child Study Group Seminar.* London: Social Science Research Unit.

Solberg, A. (1997) 'Negotiating Childhood.' In A. James and A. Prout (eds) *Constructing and Reconstructing Childhood: Contemporary Issues of the Sociology of Childhood.* London: Falmer.

Stainton-Rogers, R. and Stainton-Rogers, W. (1992) *Stories of Childhood: Shifting Agendas in Child Concern.* Hemel Hempstead: Harvester.

Stern, D. (1977) *The First Relationship: Infant and Mother.* Glasgow: Fontana.

Stern, D. (1990) *Diary of a Baby.* New York: Basic Books.

Stiglitz, J. (2002) *Globalization and Its Discontents.* London: Penguin.

Stone, M. (1995) *Don't Just Do Something, Sit There: Developing Children's Spiritual Awareness.* Norwich: Religious and Moral Education Press.

Stoppard, M. (1998) *The New Parent.* London: Dorling Kindersley.

Strandell, H. (2000) 'What is the Use of Children's Play: Preparation or Social Participation?' In H. Penn (ed.) *Early Childhood Services: Theory, Policy and Practice.* Buckingham: Open University Press.

Sure Start (2002) *Birth to Three Matters: A Framework to Support Children in Their Earliest Years.* London: DfES, Sure Start.

Sutcliffe, K., Sutcliffe, R. and Alderson, P. (2004) 'Can very young children share in their diabetes care? Ruby's story.' *Paediatric Nursing 16*, 10, 24–26.

Thomas, N. (1998) 'Finding a voice for a "muted group": Children's involvement in decision-making when they are "looked after" in middle childhood.' Paper to *Children and Social Exclusion Conference.* Hull.

Thomas, N. (2002) *Children, Family and The State: Decision-Making and Child Participation.* London: Macmillan/Bristol: Policy Press.

Thomas, N. (2007) 'Towards a theory of children's participation.' *International Journal of Children's Rights 15*, 2, 199–218.

Thornborrow, J. (1998) 'Children's Participation in the Discourse of Children's Television.' In I. Hutchby and J. Moran-Ellis (eds) *Children and Social Competence: Arenas of Action.* London: Falmer.

Tisdall, K., Davis, J., Hill, M. and Prout, A. (eds) (2006) *Children, Young People and Social Inclusion: Participation for What?* Bristol: Policy Press.

Tizard, B. (1990) 'Educational research and educational policy – is there a link? (The ninth Vernon-Wall lecture reprinted in *The Psychologist* as 'Research and policy: Is there a link?')' *The Psychologist*, October 1984, 435.

Tizard, B. and Hughes, M. (1984) *Young Children Learning.* London: Faber.

Treseder, P. (1997) *Empowering Children and Young People: A Training Manual for Promoting Involvement in Decision-Making.* London: Save the Children/Children's Rights Office.

Trevarthen, C. (1999) Quoted in L. Purves and D. Selleck. *Tuning into Children.* London: BBC Educational Publishing.

UNICEF (2007a) *State of the World's Children, 2006.* New York: UNICEF.

UNICEF (2007b) *An Overview of Child Well-Being in Rich Countries.* New York: UNICEF.

United Nations (1989) *Convention on the Rights of the Child (UNCRC).* Geneva: UNICEF.

United Nations (2002) *Children's Statement to the 2002 UN Session on the Rights of the Child.* Available at http://www.unicef.org/specialsession/documentation/childrens-statement.htm, accessed 3 July 2005.

United Nations (2006) *The United Nations Secretary General's Study on Violence against Children.* New York: United Nations.

United Nations Committee on the Rights of the Child (1995) (2002) *Concluding Observation of the Committee on the Rights of the Child: UK of Great Britain and Northern Ireland. Consideration of Reports Submitted by States Parties under Article 44 of the Convention.* Geneva: United Nations.

Vaughan, M. (2006) *Summerhill and A. S. Neil.* Buckingham: Open University Press.

Vygotsky, L. (1978) *Mind In Society.* Cambridge, MA: Harvard University Press.

Ward, L. (1997) *Seen and Heard: Involving Disabled Children and Young People in Research and Development Projects.* York: Joseph Rowntree Foundation.

Ward, L. (2007) '3,300 sales and rising – ultrasound answer to teenage gangs sets alarm bells ringing.' *The Guardian,* 17 March.

Warrington, C. (2006) *Children's Voices: Changing Futures.* Ipswich: Ormiston Children and Families Trust.

Way, P. (2007) 'What do we tell the children…about death?' *Early Education 51,* 11–13.

Wellard, S., Tearse, M. and West, A. (1997) *All Together Now: Community Participation for Children and Young People.* London: Save the Children.

West, A. (1995) *'You are on Your Own': Young People's Research on Leaving Care.* London: Save the Children.

Wheeler, R. (2006) 'Gillick or Fraser? A plea for consistency over competence in children.' *British Medical Journal 332,* 807.

White, B. (1996) 'Globalisation and the child labour problem.' *Journal of International Development 8,* 6, 829–39.

Williams, Archbishop R. (2006) 'Who is bringing up our children?' *Soundings 31,* 35–42.

Williams, S. (2002) 'Children's Express.' In B. Franklin (ed.) *The New Handbook of Children's Rights.* London: Routledge.

Williams, Z. (2006) *The Commercialisation of Childhood.* London: Compass.

Willow, C. (1996) *Children's Rights and Participation in Residential Care.* London: NCB.

Willow, C. (1997) *Hear! Hear! Promoting Children and Young People's Democratic Participation in Local Government.* London: Local Government Information Unit.

Willow, C. and Hyder, T. (1998) *It Hurts You Inside: Children Talk About Smacking.* London: National Children's Bureau/Save the Children.

Willow, C., Marchant, R., Kirby, P. and Neale, B. (2004) *Young Children's Citizenship: Ideas Into Practice.* York: Joseph Rowntree Foundation.

Winter, K. (2006a) 'The participation rights of looked after children in their health care: A critical review of the research.' *International Journal of Children's Rights 14,* 1, 77–95.

Winter, K. (2006b) 'Widening our knowledge concerning young "looked-after" children: The case for research using sociological models of childhood.' *Child and Family Social Work 11,* 55–64.

Winter, K. (PhD thesis in progress) *The Participation of Young Looked After Children in Decision Making Processes.* University of London.

Woodhead, M. (1997) 'Psychology and the Cultural Construction of Children's Needs.' In A. James and A. Prout (eds) *Constructing and Reconstructing Childhood: Contemporary Issues of the Sociology of Childhood.* London: Falmer.

Woodhead, M. (1998) 'Understanding Child Development in the Context of Children's Rights.' In C. Cunninghame (ed.) *Realising Children's Rights.* London: Save the Children.

Woodhead, M. (1999) 'Reconstructing developmental psychology – some first steps.' *Children & Society 13,* 3–19.

Woodhead, M. (2005) *Implementing Child Rights in Early Childhood, United Nations Committee on the Rights of the Child, General Comment 7.* Florence: UNICEF Innocenti Research Centre.

Woodiwiss, A. (2005) *Human Rights.* London: Routledge.

Wyatt, J. and Alderson, P. (2005) *Submission to the Nuffield Council on Bioethics Working Party on the Ethics of Prolonging Life in Fetuses and the Newborn.* London: University College and Institute of Education.

Zeiher, H. (2001) 'Dependent, Independent and Interdependent Relations: Children as Members of the Family Household in West Berlin.' In L. Alanen and B. Mayall (2001) *Conceptualizing Child–Adult Relations.* London: RoutledgeFalmer.

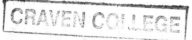

Subject Index

Author Index